Speaking in a Second Language

# AILA Applied Linguistics Series (AALS)

ISSN 1875-1113

The AILA Applied Linguistics Series (AALS) provides a forum for established scholars in any area of Applied Linguistics. The series aims at representing the field in its diversity. It covers different topics in applied linguistics from a multidisciplinary approach and it aims at including different theoretical and methodological perspectives. As an official publication of AILA the series will include contributors from different geographical and linguistic backgrounds. The volumes in the series should be of high quality; they should break new ground and stimulate further research in Applied Linguistics.

For an overview of all books published in this series, please see
*http://benjamins.com/catalog/aals*

## Editor

Antje Wilton
University of Siegen

## Editorial Board

Hannele Dufva
University of Jyväskylä

Susan M. Gass
Michigan State University

Folkert Kuiken
University of Amsterdam

Rosa M. Manchón
University of Murcia

Susanne Niemeier
University of Koblenz-Landau

**Volume 17**

Speaking in a Second Language
Edited by Rosa Alonso Alonso

# Speaking in a Second Language

*Edited by*

Rosa Alonso Alonso
University of Vigo

John Benjamins Publishing Company
Amsterdam / Philadelphia

∞™ The paper used in this publication meets the minimum requirements of the American National Standard for Information Sciences – Permanence of Paper for Printed Library Materials, ANSI z39.48-1984.

DOI 10.1075/aals.17

Cataloging-in-Publication Data available from Library of Congress:
LCCN 2017059006 (PRINT) / 2018000635 (E-BOOK)

ISBN 978 90 272 0044 0 (HB)
ISBN 978 90 272 6432 9 (E-BOOK)

John Benjamins Publishing Company · https://benjamins.com

# Table of contents

# Preface

When I first started learning a foreign language (French), speaking practice largely consisted in reading aloud from the text book or providing carefully calculated answers to the teacher's drills. Exams were focused on grammatical accuracy, and the written word dominated. We all knew that you couldn't actually learn to speak French in class, and so, for the most part, we did not. But, fortunately, a lot has changed since then. In addition to increasing interest in study abroad, there has also been a rethinking of why it is we learn languages, and, with this, great changes in how we go about teaching them. While my school-girl French, like my school-girl Latin, was approached more as an intellectual exercise than a mode of communication, there has been a revolution in the way we think about language learning, and with it a reassessment of the role of speaking. With the foregrounding of language as a means of communication has come recognition of the crucial role of developing learners' speaking skills. After all, when we enquire after someone's competence in a language, we ask whether they can 'speak' a language, not whether they can be 'grammatically accurate'. This said, however, the communicative revolution has been patchy, and research has not always kept up with the need to provide teachers with evidence-based insights to improve classroom practice.

It is therefore with great pleasure that I write the preface to this collected volume that brings together a diversity of approaches to speaking, each capable of illuminating a different aspect of this rewarding but most challenging of skills. Although the studies reported here were conducted in different paradigms on different aspects of speaking, the researchers share a view of language learning as a human endeavor. Unlike the authors of my first French textbook, they focus on language as a multi-faceted, dynamic and embodied, and speaking as a socially-situated, context-sensitive means of communication. The resulting collection highlights both the challenges and the excitements of learning how to speak in a second language, offering at the same time important insights for teachers on how they can better support this process.

In the first chapter, a state-of-the-art review of current research in the socio-linguistic aspects of second language competence sets the scene for those that follow. Each of these draws on empirical research into some of the challenges of learning how to speak in a second language and considers the implications for teachers. From their different areas of expertise Kimberly Geeslin, Aarnes Gudmestad, Matthew Kanwit, Bret Linford, Avizia Yim Long, Lauren Schmidt and Megan Solon provide a comprehensive overview of the many different areas of sociolinguistic knowledge and skill that learners need to use in their efforts to speak appropriately in context. Speakers not only have to pay due attention to matters of register, formality, and politeness, but at the same time they must, consciously or otherwise, index their own identities and group memberships. All this while striving for accuracy and intelligibility, and ensuring that they are making a coherent contribution that makes sense, hits the right note and achieves their purposes. A tall order in our native language, let alone one learned in a classroom.

The second chapter focuses on the importance of helping learners develop a sensitivity to context when they are speaking and offers examples of classroom activities that address this need to make appropriate sociolinguistic adjustments. In contrast to traditional cognitivist-psycholinguistic views which allow for the separation of knowledge from context, Rémi van Compernolle takes a Vygotskian perspective, arguing that interactional competence, and therefore its development, is very much a situated activity, and that speakers manage aspects of the talk such as topic, participant frameworks, the taking of turn turns and register by drawing on a range of communicative resources to construct a shared mental context. As each interaction is different, he argues that appropriate planning is an important focus for instruction, underpinning as it does, both execution and formal control. Drawing on his framework of concept-based pragmatics instruction or CPBI, he reports on how learners can be oriented to the kinds of meanings they want to create before tackling the forms themselves through tasks specifically tailored to their level of ability. These involve a sequence of reflection, problem-solving and opportunities to use the language that enable learners to build up the knowledge, skills and control that they need to use their second language appropriately in context.

In Chapter 3, Gale Stam focusses on the importance of gesture for speaking, arguing that their appropriate use is a vital part of communicative competence. She outlines three kinds of gesture: co-speech, speech-linked and emblems. The first of these, co-speech gestures, are synchronous, largely unconscious and integrated into spoken language to complement what is actually said. They tend to occur with new, contrastive or focused information, and they are both communicative and cognitive in function in that they may complement what a speaker has to say and also, at times, relieve the speaker's cognitive load. The other two types of gestures, speech-linked gestures and emblems, may be produced more or less consciously. The first are used asynchronously with speech to fill a speech gap or a grammatical slot as speakers search for the language they need to communicate their meaning. This makes them an important resource for speakers. Emblems are conventionalized gestures, such as the traditional 'thumbs up' sign for 'ok', and may occur with or without speech. Since they convey meaning and therefore carry important cultural information, they form an important part of a speaker's repertoire. Stam not only suggests fruitful areas for future research into various aspects of gesture use by both native speakers and learners, but also offers some useful implications for practice and suggestions for second language pedagogy.

Søren Wind Eskildsen and Numa Markee explore the nature of second language talk as an embodied and socially distributed social accomplishment in Chapter 4. Using CA methodology to analyse data from inside and outside the classroom, they make visible the ways in which speakers collaborate in meaning-making, and thus demonstrate how an emic perspective can give insight into speech as integrated with action. They provide illustrations of how speakers together address communicative difficulties and make repairs though word search and completion sequences in ways that give rise to learning opportunities. Their analysis showcases the complex ecology of situated language learning, and how, through this kind of extended cognition, speakers can achieve more than they can on their own. On the basis of this, they argue that problem-solving can be distributed across speakers and that learning how to speak is fundamentally dependent on other people. This makes social interaction the natural point of departure for understanding SLA and the acquisition of speaking skills, making obsolete unproductive historical divisions between the social and the cognitive in second language learning.

In the following chapter, Wander Lowie, Marjolijn Verspoor and Marijn van Dijk also address the embodied and embedded nature of language development as a socially-situated process. Using a Dynamic Systems Theory approach, they illustrate the iterative, nonlinear and therefore highly variable nature of language learning by following the performance over time of identical twins learning English in similar circumstances. Their analysis highlights the dynamism, complexity and individual nature of the way speaking skills develop in a second language as myriad factors interact to influence the process in unique ways for every individual. They argue that this 'unruly' behavior of the emerging linguistic system is not random, but an indication of a system that is self-organising. Thus, variability can be seen as experimentation and a precursor to an increase in language development. Their findings therefore reinforce the need for caution in the use of one-time assessments, and the need for teachers to take a long-term perspective on the development of speaking skills. They argue that classes should cater for, or at least take into account, the individual learning trajectories of individual students, and that teaching should be seen as coaching in which the focus is on providing opportunities to learn, rather than on delivering instruction.

In Chapter 6, Gaëtanelle Gilquin contributes a broad overview of the constructions that may commonly be found in learner speech on the basis of her corpus study. Working within an Applied Construction Grammar framework with the Louvain International Database of Spoken English Interlanguage, a large corpus of EFL speech, she uses part-of-speech tagging to identify recurrent sequences. The findings of this innovative study suggest that both learners and native speakers tend to use basic noun phrase or subject-verb constructions. In comparison with native speakers, however, learners rely more heavily on coordinated constructions and position their adverbs differently. As she argues, this approach has the capacity to provide detailed and quantitative information about constructions common in learner spoken English. Future studies therefore have the potential to offer teachers rich insights into the nature of learner language and thus into how their developing spoken skills may best be supported.

Martin Bygate, in Chapter 7, focusses specifically on how tasks can best be designed to ensure than speaking skills receive the attention they deserve. They need to be developed in their own right because spoken language reflects the way in which it is produced, on-line and in interaction, and is therefore different from written language. It is often more fragmented and less formal than written discourse, and characterised by pauses, interruptions and more frequent use of vague language, mitigation and lexical repetition. So that learners can acquire the skills and knowledge they need to speak, they therefore need opportunities to handle different discourse patterns dynamically and collaboratively in their second language, and to receive appropriate feedback. To ensure the practice of both speaking processes and the language itself, and to counter the challenges posed by the dynamic and ephemeral nature of speech, Bygate proposes some basic principles for the teaching of speaking. Tasks, he argues, need to tackle the range of purposes to which speaking is put, and they must allow for repetition and rehearsal. He goes on to outline an approach to task design in which students recycle the language they have used in pairs to an extended audience in the whole class. By carefully planning the link between group work and whole class talk, students can get the rehearsal time and feedback that they need. He also suggests that tasks be designed to have specific outcomes and so that students feel that their talk is meaningful, and so that one task can lead more naturally to another in cycles.

A setting that has received rather less attention, the Spanish heritage classroom, is the context for Ana Fernández Dobao's analysis of speaking practices in Chapter 8. For her study of code-switching, Dobao recorded peer to peer interactions among students studying in an academic communication skills classroom for heritage speakers of Spanish who were fluent speakers, but who lacked more formal academic skills in the language. Although code-switching is discouraged as potentially interfering in language acquisition, Dobao found that switches were common in group work and typically quite brief and stylistic in nature. The longest served a variety of both on task and off task functions. Switches to English were sometimes used to talk about how to accomplish the task, often to solve language-related problems of vocabulary spelling and grammar. In this way, they helped students to focus their attention on what was new and to build their knowledge. Rather than simply the result of 'laziness', therefore, codeswitching was used to gain knowledge and help to complete the task, in addition to being a marker of intergroup solidarity and bilingual identity. On the basis of her findings, Dobao concludes that codeswitching served important communicative and social functions and was a useful cognitive tool to help their learning. She therefore proposes that, even for speakers with advanced spoken proficiency, it can play a useful role in the heritage language classroom.

Continuing the focus on advanced language learners, in Chapter 9 Elaine Tarone and Colleen Meyers offer a case study of Mary as she uses the mirroring technique in order to improve her intelligibility, a much-neglected area in the teaching of speaking. In line with other chapters in this volume, and unlike traditional approaches which tend to treat it as a technical, disembodied skill, pronunciation is approached in this chapter in a holistic way as part of embodied linguistic performance. Their nine-step pedagogical approach to improving intelligibility embraces the multimodal nature of learning to communicate in another language, treating social context and audience as central. Drawing on recent work on the role of suprasegmentals in clarifying information structure, the trans-disciplinary framework of the Douglas Fir Group and Bakhtin's constructs of double voicing and semantic language play, it addresses the central roles played by identity agency and emotion in the development of intelligible pronunciation in a second language. Following this approach, the learner studies a speech by a native speaker or expert non-native speaker that they have chosen. They closely study multiple aspects of the original delivery, including gestures, eye contact and suprasegmental patterns, and mirror them, focusing not only on accuracy, but also on how passion and conviction are conveyed. Acoustic and perceptual analysis of Mary's performances over time showed improvement in her use of intonation, stress and body language as a result of following the nine steps. Her final performance was not only more intelligible, but also more engaging. This is very encouraging, as teachers often struggle to find motivating ways to address issues of pronunciation and intelligibility with learners who are otherwise quite advanced in their second language development.

Finally, Chapter 10 reflects on the implications for the teaching of speaking of the perspectives articulated in the volume. Rosa Alonso Alonso first presents a brief historical outline of the place of speaking skills in language learning pedagogy, starting from the grammar translation pedagogies that formed my own first experiences, to more contemporary, task-based approaches. She then goes on to consider the impact of recognizing the centrality of meaning in language and language learning on the teaching of speaking and the abandonment of artificial divisions between the social and the cognitive.

It is an exciting time in our understanding of how languages can be learned and in the contributions that research can now make to improving classroom practice. This volume is innovative in bringing together insights from a range of perspectives that nevertheless converge on a view speaking as a socially-situated, dynamic and meaningful mode of communication. More than this, it is a collection that offers teachers evidence-based insights that will help them to bring this productive and motivating view of language and language learning into the classroom. My only regret is that it has arrived rather too late for those early French teachers of mine!

CHAPTER 1

# Sociolinguistic competence and the acquisition of speaking

Kimberly L. Geeslin[1], Aarnes Gudmestad[2],
Matthew Kanwit[3], Bret Linford[4], Avizia Yim Long[5],
Lauren Schmidt[6] & Megan Solon[7]

[1] Indiana University | [2] Virginia Polytechnic Institute and State University | [3] University of Pittsburgh | [4] Grand Valley State University | [5] Texas Tech University | [6] San Diego State University | [7] University at Albany, SUNY

In face-to-face spoken interactions, language learners must construct a meaningful message consistent with the L2 grammar, articulate it comprehensibly, and manage the aspects of oral communication that reflect speaker identity, interlocutor identities, and the characteristics of the interactional context. A lack of sociolinguistic competence can lead to a failure to convey formality, politeness, solidarity, friendship, and group membership, and this will negatively affect the communicative outcome. The current chapter examines the social and situational information one conveys through linguistic variants in speech, offering a state-of-the-art account of empirical research, including a discussion of pressing issues in the field, such as the roles of lexical frequency, geographic variation, and language attitudes, as well as the pedagogical implications of this research.

## Introduction and overview

Research on second language (L2) sociolinguistic competence stands at the crossroads of the fields of second language acquisition and sociolinguistics and, consequently, must respect the assumptions and methodological standards demanded by each field of inquiry. In the context of second (and additional) language learning, sociolinguistic competence entails the ability to vary one's speech according to a host of factors and to perceive these details in the speech of others (see Regan, 2010; Regan, Howard, & Lemée, 2009 for overviews). Native speakers (NSs) are able to convey information about their own identities through the use of variable structures that denote membership to particular social groups or speech

https://doi.org/10.1075/aals.17.01gee

communities, defined by factors such as age, gender, social class, level of education, ethnicity, and geographic location, to name only a few (Tagliamonte, 2012).[1] Additionally, NSs are able to adjust their own production in response to characteristics of their interlocutors and the setting in which an interaction takes place (e.g., Eckert & Rickford, 2001). These subtle indicators of social and contextual information are perceived by native-speaking hearers and, thus, the social dimension of an interaction can be co-constructed and may evolve during the course of an interaction. Making this ability all the more complex is the fact that much of this social information is conveyed below the level of consciousness such that perceptions may not be explicit to the speakers, despite evidence that they do, in fact, shape speaker and hearer expectations (e.g., Hay & Drager, 2010). Research on sociolinguistic variation among NSs forms the basis of our understanding of the many context-dependent facts a language learner must come to manage in order to achieve sociolinguistic competence.

Within the field of L2 acquisition and teaching, sociolinguistic competence is contextualized within the larger construct of communicative competence. This view of competence recognizes the multi-faceted nature of effective communication as one that involves abilities that extend beyond the formal grammatical properties of a language (e.g., Canale & Swain, 1980; Hymes, 1971). This definition is not unlike what would be found in the first language (L1) context but departs from more traditional approaches to L2s that focus exclusively on acquisition of formal properties of a grammar. Bachman (1990), building on work by Canale and Swain (1980), distinguishes between organizational competence, comprised of grammatical and discourse competence, and pragmatic competence. This final category includes illocutionary and sociolinguistic competence. Under this approach, sociolinguistic competence refers to the ability to style shift and use various registers appropriately. As with sociolinguistic approaches to native patterns of use, this view of L2 learning recognizes the importance of the social and situational information conveyed along with the propositional content during spoken interactions (see also Tsai, 2013).

For both native and non-native speakers, the variationist paradigm, which focuses on the details of speech patterns (Regan, 2010), provides researchers with the tools to describe how language is used in a particular interaction, by a particular speech community or by a given individual. What is more, these same tools allow us to explore the differences between highly advanced non-native speakers

---

1. To be sure, NS speech communities have a range of expected patterns and, when considered pan-dialectally or across various levels of education, ethnicity, and gender, for example, this range expands considerably. The key point is that learners must acquire the ability to fall within this range.

and NSs, to describe development over time, and to identify particular challenges for language learners. The variationist approach provides several metrics for comparison and measurement, including an analysis of the frequency of use of a given form (i.e., a variant) in a particular functional context, the linguistic and extralinguistic factors that constrain that use, the direction of the effect of these factors, and their relative importance to one another.[2] With this in mind, we can see the limits of advanced levels of attainment through differing frequencies of use from NSs, differing constraints or a combination of these (e.g., even advanced learners of Spanish differ from NSs in frequency of use of present progressive forms vs. present indicative forms, [Fafulas, 2015], and in constraints on copula selection [Geeslin, 2003]). Additionally, we might chart development as a change in the frequency of use of a given form (e.g., increases in the rates of use of the Spanish copula *estar* generally indicate development at lower levels [Geeslin, 2000]), or as a shift in the constraints on those patterns of use over time (e.g., Geeslin, Linford & Fafulas, 2015, show that the linguistic constraint *person and number of the verb* loses importance over time in the development of subject expression in L2 Spanish, whereas the constraint *change in reference* becomes important at intermediate levels and this continues over time). The present chapter provides an overview of our current knowledge of the acquisition of sociolinguistic variation in L2 speech and identifies areas with potential for future contributions.

## Linguistic variation and speaking in learner grammars

L2 speaking is often the cornerstone of sociolinguistic competence to the extent that through speaking learners are able to convey a wealth of social and situational information along with the intended propositional content of an utterance. Speakers convey this meaning through multiple linguistic recourses, including patterns of use of variable linguistic structures. These patterns affect all areas of grammar, including the sound system, morphology and syntactic structures, as well as pragmatic and word choices. To demonstrate how linguistic variation is acquired and exhibited through learners' spoken interactions, we provide an account of the current state of research on speaking and sociolinguistic competence and we identify directions for future research.

---

2.  The variationist paradigm can be used to study the variable use of non-native-like variants (i.e., Type I variation) but the domain of sociolinguistic competence is the native-like variability that reflects the interactional context (i.e., Type II variation; e.g., Adamson & Regan, 1991).

## L2 speaking and the acquisition of sociolinguistically-variable sounds

Sounds are, in many ways, the building blocks of speaking and oral communication. Most obviously, we form our words and utterances via the combination of sounds. However, we also communicate information about ourselves and our context via the use of particular sounds in certain contexts (and possibly not in others). In more formal situations, for example, we may utilize specific sounds that seem inappropriate or unnatural in less formal situations. A classic example from English is variation in the pronunciation of "-ing" – standardly as [ɪŋ] (e.g., "working") but often as [ɪn] (e.g., "workin'"; especially in informal situations or among speakers of lower socioeconomic status; e.g., Labov, 2001). The L2 acquisition of speaking in relation to sounds, thus, involves not just learning to use targetlike sounds (i.e., the particular sounds that pertain to the L2) but also learning to vary the use of one phonetic form versus another with targetlike frequency and in the appropriate contexts. Central questions pertaining to speaking and the acquisition of sociolinguistically variable L2 sounds include whether L2 learners employ variable forms, and, if they do, whether they do so with the same frequency and in the same contexts (or in patterns constrained by the same social and contextual factors) as NSs. Also important is whether the variants produced by learners have similar phonetic features to and/or vary along the same acoustic dimensions as those of native speakers (and, if not, how they are different). A final aspect of research in this area is the exploration of how such patterns and relationships change over time and/or with additional (or specific) experience in the L2.

To date, the majority of work on speaking and the acquisition of sociolinguistically variable L2 sounds has explored the acquisition and use of phonetic features particular to a language variety spoken in a region in which learners study abroad. For example, George (2014), Knouse (2012), and Ringer-Hilfinger (2012) all examined the acquisition and use of the peninsular Spanish interdental fricative /θ/ (i.e., *zapatos* "shoes" [θa.pá.tos]) by learners studying abroad in various parts of north-central Spain, and George (2014) additionally explored use of the post-velar/uvular fricative [χ], another salient phonetic feature of Castilian Spanish. Similarly, Raish (2015) examined use of the voiced velar occlusive by L2 learners of Egyptian Arabic before and after a semester and/or year studying abroad in Cairo. Although, in general, these studies documented greater use of region-specific variants after time abroad, Ringer-Hilfinger's (2012) results present an exception: Her learners exhibited greater awareness of Spanish /θ/ after 4 months abroad but very little use of the variant at all. In fact, even in studies that document gains in the use of dialect-specific variants during or after study abroad, relatively low rates of use of the variants by learners (as compared, for example, to NS rates of use) are observed (cf., Raish, 2015, as a notable exception to this general pattern). Following and expanding upon these recent empirical endeavors, research should continue to examine whether learners employ sound features particular to a dialect with which they have contact and to further explore what individual learner, contextual, and language- or sound-specific factors influence adoption versus non-adoption of particular phonetic variants.

Also focusing largely on learners studying abroad, other studies have explored the acquisition and use of segments and processes whose realization and use are variable in the speech of native speakers (though such variation is not necessarily specific to a particular region). Most studies in this vein have examined the acquisition of /l/-deletion in L2 French (e.g., Howard, Lemée, & Regan, 2006; Kennedy Terry, 2016; Regan, Howard, & Lemée, 2009) and have presented evidence of gains –and of the role of time abroad in encouraging such gains – in the use of variable sounds in targetlike ways in L2 speech. Howard et al. (2006) and Regan et al. (2009), for example, point to an increase in /l/-deletion in L2 French (a move in a targetlike direction) for learners spending time abroad as compared to learners at home. Kennedy Terry (2016) expands upon such findings, presenting evidence for an implicational scale for /l/-deletion – with such elision occurring first in predictable and constrained token types (i.e., *il* 3s.impersonal "it") before spreading to other contexts – and demonstrating that /l/-elision among her learner sample was significantly predicted by the social network ties and levels of interaction that learners had with native French speakers. Thus, as with research on the acquisition of dialect-specific features, work in this area should continue to explore the factors that influence learners' use of variable L2 sound features in their own speech.

A few studies have explored similar features and phenomena in the speech of learners in at-home university environments as well, examining whether L2 learners exhibit particular variable features in their speech, whether variation in the use of such features differs according to the same factors as for NSs of the target language, and how such frequency of use and/or patterns and constraints develop or change as proficiency level increases. Geeslin and Gudmestad (2008a), for instance, explored use of Spanish /θ/ (a dialect-specific phoneme) and /s/-weakening (a socially and linguistically constrained process common to many dialects of Spanish) in the speech of 130 university-level L2 learners of Spanish. They found that only nine learners utilized [θ] in their speech, and even fewer (five) showed any evidence of /s/-weakening. An important finding of their study was that the majority of the learners who exhibited use of these variable sound features were higher-proficiency learners – specifically, learners at the graduate level of study – and that this pattern was especially true for /s/-weakening. They suggest that this finding (considered in conjunction with the individual characteristics of these learners) points to the need for significant exposure to the language and to NSs for the use of variable sound features to develop. Focusing only on high-level learners, Solon, Linford, and Geeslin (accepted) examined intervocalic /d/ reduction and deletion in Spanish – a phenomena constrained by numerous social and linguistic factors in a wide variety of Spanish dialects – by advanced L2 learners as compared to bilingual Spanish native speakers. The authors coded the spoken data in two ways: (a) categorically (i.e., with each /d/ token exhibiting a stop, approximant, deleted, or other realization) and continuously (i.e., measuring degree of reduction in all nondeleted tokens using an intensity difference measure). Results revealed that these advanced learners of Spanish did delete intervocalic /d/ but at much lower rates than do NSs (i.e., 18% as compared to 46%); their patterns of deletion were also influenced differently by linguistic factors than were the NSs' patterns. Also important were the findings regarding degree of reduction: The learners' reduced (but not deleted) forms exhibited less reduction (measured continuously) than the NSs' reduced /d/ realizations. Taking a similar approach, Dalola and Bullock (2016) explored phrase-final vowel devoicing in L1 and L2 French as a function of several style-based factors in the communicative context including task type (i.e., role play vs. read speech), register (i.e., formal vs. informal speech), and speech rate (i.e., slow vs. conversational). The authors showed that rates of phrase-final devoicing were similar for the L1 and L2 groups but did exhibit differences according to task type. Additionally, the degree of devoicing varied between the L1 and L2 groups on the basis of linguistic and stylistic factors. As the results of these last two studies (Solon et al., accepted, and Dalola & Bullock, 2016) suggest, the phonetic-acoustic properties of variable sounds produced by learners may also warrant further examination as the specific realizations of such variants certainly impact speaking and communication.

Lastly, although most research on the acquisition of sociolinguistically-variable sounds has explored L2 production, perception of variable sound features and processes is also important to the acquisition of speaking. Research is needed both on how the production of variable forms by L2 learners is perceived and received in communication and on how the acquisition of perceptual aspects of phonetic/phonological variation in a L2 may influence interaction, communication, and production. Work by Schmidt (2011), for example, lays an important foundation for understanding how learners categorize a particular phonetic variant. Schmidt tested whether L2 learners of Spanish categorize aspirated /s/ in coda position in nonce Spanish words as /s/ or as some other sound. Although not directly testing speaking, establishing whether learners acquire the ability to perceive this variable sound feature is an important first step for understanding how it may develop and be used in communication both on receptive and productive levels. Likewise, Schmidt (2009) showed that different phonetic/phonological dialectal features influence learners' comprehension of L1 speech differently. Specifically, Schmidt analyzed L2 Spanish learners' comprehension of Dominican Spanish speech prior to and after a 3-week study abroad program in Santo Domingo. She found that certain dialectal variants and phonetic phenomena (i.e., deletion of syllable-final /s/ and lateralization of syllable-final /ɾ/) impeded learners' comprehension to a greater extent than other features such as deletion of word-final /d/ or velarization of word-final nasals. Such research points to the role of specific sound features in L2 comprehension and may provide important clues about subsequent speech patterns. Finally, preliminary work is currently being conducted on the acceptance of and preference for particular L2 sociophonetic variants by learners. Building upon the production study previously described (Solon et al., accepted), Solon (2017) examined whether learners demonstrate sensitivity to certain social and linguistic factors in accepting and/or preferring forms exhibiting deleted /d/ (over forms exhibiting a realized [ð]). Stemming from the idea that production may only reveal a portion of learners' sociophonetic competence, this study aimed to establish whether L2 learners are sensitive to patterns of sound variation in listening, regardless of whether they produce such variation in their own speech. This line of research is important in establishing how sociolinguistic knowledge is developed, when it appears, and how it changes as proficiency develops in a L2 as well as in establishing the nature of the relationship between perception and production in such acquisition. Ultimately, collecting data on the perception *and* production of sociolinguistically variable sounds in L2s will illuminate how the many characteristics and factors involved influence speech and communication in social contexts.

## L2 speaking and the acquisition of sociolinguistically variable morphosyntactic structures

As with the L2 sound system, the acquisition of variable morphosyntactic structures in speech consists of producing and comprehending the full range of variants of a given structure, using these variants with appropriate frequency, and varying their occurrence according to the relevant linguistic and extralinguistic factors. We examine each of these issues in turn, focusing exclusively on studies that have analyzed speech, which consists of data elicited using a host of tasks, such as interviews, conversations, and oral-elicitation tasks. The focus on production in the current section is consistent with research to date but indicates a need for future expansion to investigate comprehension.

Beginning with the repertoire of variants and the frequency of occurrence of these forms, four main observations have emerged from research on speaking and oral-production tasks. First, research has demonstrated that at some point along the developmental trajectory, learners use many if not all of the same variants that NSs use. For instance, Fafulas (2015) examined the inventory of present-tense verb forms produced in an oral, simultaneous film narration. Two groups of NSs of Spanish, one from Mexico and one from Spain, used simple present (*ella come* 'she eats'), *estar* 'to be' + present participle constructions (*ella está comiendo* 'she is eating'), and other canonical and non-canonical bases + present participle constructions (canonical: *ella sigue comiendo* 'she continues eating' and non-canonical: "*los chicos pasan comiendo peras* 'the boys pass by eating pears'" (p. 106)) to narrate the film in Spanish. The L2 participants spanned four instructional levels (fourth-semester undergraduate, third-year undergraduate, fourth-year undergraduate, and graduate level). While each group used simple present and *estar* + present participle forms in this oral production task, the other canonical and non-canonical bases + present participle constructions did not emerge until the fourth year of undergraduate study.

Additionally, frequency of use of variable forms changes during the developmental process. For example, Long (2016) identified changes in rates of use of subject forms among undergraduate learners who were NSs of either Korean (a pro-drop language) or English (a non-pro-drop language). The data come from two oral tasks – a sociolinguistic interview and a picture-book description instrument – and four proficiency levels for each L2 group. Concerning the three most frequent subject forms – null subjects, lexical noun phrases, and personal pronouns – the NSs of English gradually increased their use of null subjects and decreased their use of lexical nouns phrases as proficiency level increased. For personal pronouns, rates of use increased from Level 1 to 2, decreased from Levels 2 to 3 and again between Levels 3 and 4. Different patterns emerged for the L1 Korean learners. Their use of null subjects decreased between Levels 1 and 2 and then gradually increased from Levels 2 to 4. The opposite occurred for lexical noun phrases: use increased between Levels 1 and 2 and then decreased steadily between Levels 2 and 4. Production rates of personal pronouns were similar at each proficiency level. These results are in line with other investigations that have shown evidence of fluctuations in frequency of use, including non-linear changes in development (e.g., Gudmestad, 2012).

A third observation concerns instructed learners and the formality of the variants. Research on L2 learners of French in an immersion context in Canada has demonstrated that classroom learners, in contrast to NSs, typically use formal variants at higher rates than vernacular ones in interviews (Mougeon, Nadasdi, & Rehner, 2010). Their examination of interview data and several variable structures revealed that classroom learners of French in an immersion setting tended to overuse formal and hyper-formal variants (e.g., the past auxiliary *être* 'to be' and the negative particle *ne* 'not', respectively), while they underused marked and mildly marked informal variants (e.g., the auxilaries *m'as* and *je vas*, respectively, in the periphrastic future). Regan et al., (2009) found similar results for Irish, university-level learners of French before they spent an academic year abroad. At the end of their residence abroad and after having increased contact with NSs, the learners increased their use of vernacular variants. Thus, similar to what has been found for the acquisition of reduced sounds, we see a tendency on the part of learners to lag in the acquisition of informal variants, even when their use is appropriate in the context of interaction.

Finally, multiple studies have indicated that adult learners can acquire target-like rates of use for certain morphosyntactic structures. For instance, graduate-level participants in Gudmestad (2012) used the subjunctive mood in Spanish at the same rate as a NS comparison group in three oral-elicitation tasks. Geeslin and Gudmestad (2008b) also found that a graduate-level group of non-native speakers used the copular verbs *ser* and *estar* in Spanish at the same rate as NSs in a semi-guided interview. Thus, in general learners appear to move in the direction of the target in terms of the repertoire of variants and their frequency of use when speaking an additional language.

Turning to contexts of use, the use of morphosyntactic variants is influenced simultaneously by multiple linguistic and extra-linguistic factors, and research shows that learners are able to incorporate these factors into their interlanguage when they speak. For example, Gudmestad (2012), conducted a cross-sectional examination of variable mood use in Spanish and demonstrated that, as learners gained experience with the language, they were sensitive to more of the linguistic factors that influenced NS use. Verb semantic category was significant beginning at Level 2 (learners enrolled in fifth semester culture course); time reference and hypotheticality were significant predictors starting at Level 3 (learners enrolled in upper level content courses); and verb form regularity became influential at Level 4 (also learners enrolled in upper level content courses). Additionally, learners must respond to these factors in the same way as NSs. The time reference factor illustrates this observation. The NSs in Gudmestad (2012) used the subjunctive most often in future-time, followed by present-time, and lastly past-time contexts. While Level 4 and Level 5 learners showed the same direction of effect in their use of verbal moods with this factor, Levels 2 and 3 differed from the targetlike norm. Although this linguistic factor conditioned their use of the subjunctive, Levels 2 and 3 did not exhibit the same hierarchy of use as the NSs. Evidence of the subtle developmental changes that occur in the constraints on the use of variable morphosyntactic structures in L2 Spanish continues to grow (e.g., Fafulas, 2015; Kanwit, 2017; Long, 2016).

Variationist research has also shed light on near-native abilities. In general, evidence has emerged revealing that highly advanced and near-native speakers exhibit some targetlike patterns in their use of variable morphosyntactic structures but they do not converge entirely on the target. One example is Donaldson

(2016), who investigated verbal negation in French by near-native speakers who had been living in France for at least four years. This well-studied linguistic variable consists of the absence or deletion of the pre-verbal negative particle *ne*. The deletion of this particle is frequent in informal, spoken French but it is typically retained in writing. The data came from informal, spontaneous conversations between near-native and NSs of French in France. The near-native speakers had been living in France for at least four years. The NS conversation partners were their spouses or close acquaintances. Donaldson investigated eight linguistic and three sociostylistic factors and found that the near-native speakers' deletion of *ne* was conditioned by the same sociostylistic factors and most of the same linguistic factors as the NSs'. However, unlike the NSs, they were not sensitive to the factor called lexicalized expression and they were more likely to retain *ne* in subordinate clauses. Thus, near-native speakers who have had extensive experience with the target language can acquire sensitivity to many of the same linguistic factors that condition NS use and still exhibit some non-targetlike behavior.

The acquisition of variable morphosyntactic structures also entails developing sensitivity to the social and situational factors that condition use among NSs. Although this area of L2 variationist research has received comparatively less attention than research on linguistic factors, extralinguistic variables such as socioeconomic status (e.g., Mougeon et al., 2010), task (e.g., Gudmestad, 2012; Long, 2016), and geographic region (see Section 3.2) have been investigated. Perhaps the social factor that has received the most attention is gender. For instance, Li (2010) examined instructed learners of Chinese living in China and their use of DE, a particle that serves a range of grammatical functions (e.g., genitive and nominalization markers) and exhibits Type I and Type II variation. The non-native speakers exhibited a targetlike pattern with regard to gender in interview data. Absence of the particle is characteristic of informal speech and overall men were more likely than women to omit the particle. Several other studies have shown that L2 learners of French in immersion contexts in Canada or following an academic year abroad in France exhibited linguistic differences based on gender, some of which were also characteristic of NSs. Female learners have been found to be more likely than males to use formal variants such as the first-person plural pronoun *nous*, the inflectional future, and retention of the preverbal negative particle *ne* (cf. Mougeon et al., 2010; Regan et al., 2009). Thus, the observation that instructed learners tend to overuse formal and underuse informal variants appears to be even stronger among women. This brief review highlights findings on L2 morphosyntactic variation that contribute to our understanding of how learners come to use spoken language in socially appropriate ways over time.

## Current issues in sociolinguistic competence and speaking

The preceding sections provide examples of research that connects the acquisition of sociolinguistic variation and L2 speech. This disciplinary intersection also provides a good avenue for exploring some of the most pressing issues in L2 acquisition more broadly. In the sections that follow we explore three such issues: the role of lexical frequency, the role of geographic varieties, and the role of learner language attitudes in L2 acquisition. We maintain our focus on speaking and sociolinguistic competence, showing the contributions made by connecting these (and additional) fields of study.

### L2 speaking and the role of lexical frequency

Research on L2 oral production has examined the influence that the frequency of linguistic forms in the input has on their acquisition and use. L2 learners tend to associate frequent forms with a particular usage and as they gain greater proficiency in the L2, they begin to apply theses associations to less-frequent forms (Ellis & Collins, 2009). Hence, similar to L1 acquisition and use, L2 learners acquire a probabilistically constructed grammar (Ellis, 1996). For instance, in Spanish, L2 learners tend to produce more preterit forms with verbs that are found most frequently in the preterit in the input (e.g., achievement verbs) and employ more imperfect verb forms with verbs that are more commonly found in the imperfect in the input (e.g., stative verbs) (e.g., Shirai & Andersen, 1995). Indeed, despite the fact that the preterit verb forms are more complex morphologically than the imperfect verb forms, students tend to employ the preterit – which is more frequent than the imperfect – as the default past-tense form (Salaberry, 2000).

More recent research has sought to determine whether L2 learners are affected by frequency in a similar manner to NSs. For instance, usage-based accounts of language propose that linguistic forms and/or collocations[3] that are more frequent are more susceptible to phonetic reduction, such as the reduction of /d/ in Spanish (e.g., Díaz-Campos & Gradoville, 2011). Research on NSs shows that frequent forms are associated with reduced /d/ more often than infrequent forms. As mentioned earlier, the same has been shown for highly advanced L2 speakers of Spanish: Solon et al. (accepted) found that 13 highly - advanced L2 speakers of Spanish deleted /d/ in intervocalic position more often

---

3.  A collocation refers to a group of words that appears together frequently and may function as a single lexicalized unit or "chunk."

among tokens categorized as frequent, than among those categorized as infrequent based on a corpus-based count of frequency.

Research on frequency has also shown that the frequency of linguistic structures may mediate the effect of other linguistic factors known to influence a given variable structure. For instance, Erker and Guy (2012), who studied native Spanish speakers residing in New York, found that the factors that constrain subject pronoun variation in native Spanish are either activated or amplified by lexical frequency. That is, the effect is only present or is stronger among those verbs that are frequent. Regarding L2 speakers, Linford and Shin (2013) found a similar mediating effect of frequency within the production of subject pronouns among fourth-year university L2 learners of Spanish: factors that were found to constrain subject pronoun variation were either activated or amplified among the frequent verbs for those learners as well. However, lexical frequency did not appear to have an activating or amplifying effect for L2 learners at the lower levels of proficiency included in the study. In contrast, variation was constrained by lexical frequency in a direct manner, that is, these lower level learners produced significantly more overt subject pronouns with words that were frequent than those that were infrequent.

There is further evidence of the complexity of the role of lexical frequency. For example, Linford, Long, Solon, Whatley, and Geeslin (2016) examined the production of third-person subject forms by 13 NSs of Spanish and 12 highly proficient non-native speakers of Spanish in sociolinguistic interviews. The analysis showed that in only one case did the measure of lexical frequency appear to activate sensitivity to another independent linguistic factor. Specifically, high lexical frequency appeared to activate the influence of the specificity of the referent such that this factor was only a significant predictor of subject forms among the frequent verbs.

In a related follow-up study, Linford, Long, Solon, and Geeslin (2016) examined the oral production of first-person singular subject pronouns by the same groups of speakers. In this study, four different measures of lexical frequency were compared to explore the way in which methods for measuring lexical frequency could influence findings. Their analysis showed that the most frequent verb tokens were generally the same regardless of the measure of frequency. However, the amount of the data that the frequent verbs represented greatly differed according to the measure. In addition, they found that high lexical frequency did not appear to activate/amplify the effect of other factors. In fact, the factor switch reference was found to significantly constrain subject form use for verbs categorized as infrequent, but not for those that were categorized as frequent. The authors hypothesized that certain highly frequent verb tokens (e.g., *sé* 'I know') are less susceptible to discourse-level factors such as switch reference.

A similar explanation was suggested in Solon et al. (accepted) for the reduction of /d/ through a hypothesis that certain frequent lexical items may actually be stored as deleted exemplars. The implication then is that learners' patterns of deletion are more constrained by other linguistic factors because they are not stored in the same way. In connecting these findings with the broader field of research on lexical frequency, we see that these analyses provide new insights into how lexical frequency affects language production uniquely for L2 learners and that its effects depend crucially on the grammatical structure under investigation as well as the level of proficiency of the learners.

## L2 speaking and the role of geographic variation

Researchers interested in L2 sociolinguistic competence have turned their attention to the development that occurs when learners participate in study abroad (SA) because SA participants have experience using language in meaningful contexts. Additionally, since a number of languages are spoken on multiple continents (e.g., English, Spanish, French), researchers may decide to compare groups of learners studying in different regions where the language is spoken in order to see whether learners approximate divergent local norms. Early research on acquisition in immersion contexts often centered on a single location (e.g., Rehner, Mougeon, & Nadasdi, 2003), but later work has more frequently compared learner groups in multiple regions (e.g., Kanwit & Solon, 2013; Salgado-Robles, 2014). Some of this work has investigated L2 speaking (i.e., oral production, such as in sociolinguistic interviews), although much work has targeted learner preference, since certain structures can be difficult to elicit, particularly if a range of linguistic contexts must be produced in order to examine the relative influence of multiple factors. Early work generally employed assessments that did not target regionally variable input, but recently authors have called for more fine-grained methods to assess gains in L2 sociolinguistic competence (e.g., Lafford & Uscinski, 2013).

Research on the acquisition of variable norms in the target environment has included a range of structures and evidence has generally pointed to the ability of learners to approximate local NS norms. Although a full description of the structures examined is beyond the scope of the current section, variationists have studied the role of SA in the L2 acquisition of many variable structures, notably in English, French, and Spanish. In English, variationist researchers have considered variable *t/d* deletion, variable *-ing* reduction (Adamson & Regan, 1991), variable production of syllable codas (Hansen, 2001), variation in the article system (Young, 1996), and variable past-time expression marking (Bayley & Langman, 2004), among other structures and segments. For L2 French, this work has included variable deletion of word-final /l/ (Regan et al., 2009), variation between *on* and *nous* as first-person plural subject pronouns (Dewaele, 2002; Regan et al., 2009), *tu* and *vous* as second-person (informal and formal, respectively) singular subject pronouns (Kinginger & Farrell, 2004), variable *ne* deletion (Regan, 2004), variable subject doubling (Nagy, Blondeau, & Auger, 2002), variable past-time expression (Howard, 2004) and variable future-time expression (Lemée, 2002; Regan et al., 2009). In Spanish, recent work has included /s/-weakening and the interdental fricative (Geeslin & Gudmestad, 2008a; Knouse, 2012; Ringer-Hilfinger, 2012), the perfective past distinction (Kanwit, Geeslin, & Fafulas, 2015), object pronouns (Salgado-Robles, 2014), the copulas *ser* and *estar* (Kanwit et al., 2015), and forms of future-time expression (Kanwit & Solon, 2013). Across languages, these studies indicate that following a stay abroad learners demonstrate movement toward local NS norms in terms of rates of use/selection and independent predictors of such use, but that such development may vary across grammatical structures. Although differential development is indicated across studies, it is perhaps best seen within studies, in work that considers the acquisition of more than one structure by the same group of learners.

For example, Kanwit, Geeslin, and Fafulas (2015) analyzed three variable structures in L2 Spanish in a written contextualized preference task and found that some norms may be acquired earlier than others (including prior to a stay abroad), some are acquired in terms of frequency of selection before predictors of such selection, and others follow the opposite path. For example, for the well-documented change in progress in perfective past-time reference, learners in Spain favored the present perfect in same-day contexts after their stay abroad, whereas learners in Mexico disfavored the form in this context, with both groups approximating respective local NS norms. In contrast, the researchers found that for present-time expression of events in progress, for which there is less certainty about the status of change in Spanish, the learner groups moved slightly away from the local NS rates of selection of the present progressive. The authors hypothesize that the status of the change and the degree to which it is socially stigmatized may mediate the degree to which the input to which learners have access actually differs from one region to another.

Differential development is also indicated in the analysis of the multiple phonetic variables studied in Díaz-Campos (2006). The researcher found that a stay abroad was beneficial for learners for two phonetic variables (i.e., the word-initial voiceless plosives /p t k/ and syllable-final lateral /l/), but that at-home learners outperformed abroad learners on a third variable (i.e., the voiced intervocalic approximants /b d g/). A key insight of the study is that study abroad is not necessarily more beneficial than classroom learning for accurate speech production because social contacts also play a role. Coupled with the results of Kanwit et al. (2015), we see again that different morphosyntactic structures and phonetic segments may respond differently during a stay abroad, and that such differences may be seen both in speech (i.e., oral production) and written preference.

Finally, a pair of recent studies consider learners studying abroad in multiple regions and utilize oral data. Salgado-Robles (2014) considered the variable expression of object pronouns in oral speech in L2 Spanish and reported that learners in Valladolid, Spain moved toward the local norm by increasing use of *le* (which can be used as both a dative and accusative pronoun locally), whereas learners in Seville, Spain advanced toward the regional, case-system norm by decreasing use of *le* during their stay abroad, as they instead increased use of the masculine and feminine pronouns *lo* and *la,* respectively, as accusative pronouns. Likewise, Linford (2016) compared learners studying in the Dominican Republic with those studying in Spain and analyzed a range of structures in oral speech, including perfective past-time expression, subject pronoun expression, and object pronouns. Linford's analysis also showed evidence that learners move toward regional norms, although this is mediated by individual learner factors as well as the linguistic factors related to a particular variable structure. Although task-related differences are well documented in SLA research (e.g., Geeslin & Gudmestad, 2008b), these two studies provide compelling evidence for the acquisition of regional distinctions in oral speech following a stay abroad and, thus, indicate that the attested development on written preference tasks may well extend beyond the written modality. Nevertheless, future empirical work on acquisition abroad should consider differences of modality and to what extent the SA gains compare to longitudinal development in the at-home context.

## L2 speaking and the role of language attitudes

The construction of language attitudes by L2 learners toward different regional and social varieties of the target language is also an important component in the development of sociolinguistic competence. Listeners perceive different linguistic forms that carry social and stylistic meaning and evaluate speakers based on how they speak. L2 acquisition research has primarily focused on connections between language attitudes toward the target language in general and L2 linguistic achievement, and has found that positive attitudes toward the new language and its cultural group(s) are related to success in acquiring the target language (e.g., Dörnyei, Csizer, & Nemeth, 2006). L2 learner attitudes toward specific varieties of the target language, however, have been less studied, but nonetheless also play an important role in language development: for example, these variety-specific attitudes may influence access to input, as well as dictate the target language model the learner desires to emulate, ultimately shaping the language the learner produces.

Overall, studies on L2 language attitudes toward specific target language varieties have found that learners can distinguish between different accents of the target language and that they do hold different attitudes toward specific varieties. These studies have predominantly examined learner attitudes toward varieties of English (Alford & Strother, 1990; Chiba, Matsuura & Yamamoto, 1995; Clark & Schleef, 2010; Dalton-Puffer, Kaltenboeck & Smit, 1997; Jarvella et al., 2001; Ladegaard, 1998; Scales et al., 2006), with some work also on Spanish (Geeslin & Schmidt, 2016; Ortiz Jiménez, 2013; Ramírez, 1983); and have primarily employed the methodological tool of the matched guise technique (Lambert et al., 1960). Under this technique, listeners hear guises (short recordings) of different languages or language varieties and rate the speakers of the guises on various personal characteristics, such as status or likeability. In this way, listeners' stereotypes and attitudes held toward different linguistic varieties are accessed. For example, in Ladegaard (1998), 96 Danish learners of L2 English rated speakers of five different English regional accents (Scottish, Received Pronunciation, Cockney, Australian, and Standard American English) on five-point scales for status, competence, personal integrity, and social attractiveness. Ladegaard found that the L2 learners evaluated RP English most positively for status, competence, and correctness, Scottish English most positively for friendliness and helpfulness, Australian English most reliable, and American English most humorous, revealing underlying attitudes of the Danish learners toward the different English-speaking groups.

Language attitudes are an important component in L2 development as they may influence access to target language input. Language attitudes and beliefs (as construed by the learner, but also as perpetuated by language instructors and educational programs, see Ortiz Jiménez, 2013) may influence student choices, such as which target dialect to model, where to study abroad, or which target language community's media to partake in, which, in turn, lead to increased or decreased opportunities for exposure to certain varieties of the target language. Moreover, language attitudes may dictate how learners respond to incoming target language input: linguistic forms from positively evaluated target language varieties may be processed and stored differently than incoming forms from negatively perceived varieties. Furthermore, language attitudes held by the L2 learner may dictate the target language variety that the learner desires to use as a model, and ultimately, the linguistic forms that the learner aims to use in his or her own speech. Unfortunately, few studies to date have tested direct links between language attitudes held by L2 learners and the actual language that the learners produce (George, 2014; Ringer-Hilfinger, 2012). One such study is Ringer-Hilfinger (2012), who tested English-speaking intermediate level learners of Spanish participating in a semester-long study abroad program in Madrid, Spain, on language attitudes toward and use of the dialectal variant /θ/. Learners completed a matched guise test and questionnaire coupled with production tasks (a reading task and an informal interview). Ringer-Hilfinger found no overall differences in learner evaluations in the matched guises whether the /θ/ variant was present or absent, and use of the dialectal variant was very low in the learner speech (used intermittently by only two of the 15 participants). Future study is needed to further clarify how developing language attitudes relate to use (or non-use) of sociolinguistic variants in learner speech.

Lastly, it is not clear how L2 learners construct language attitudes toward different varieties of the target language, nor how these fluid constructions may be reshaped over time and interact with a host of other factors that influence human behavior. Consequently, there is a need for studies that examine how various factors are interrelated in the construction of language attitudes by an individual, such as through a dynamic systems approach (see Dörnyei, MacIntyre, & Henry, 2015). Results from studies to date have suggested multiple factors that may contribute to the development of learner language attitudes, some of which vary from those involved in the construction of language attitudes in a L1 context, and which can serve as a point of departure for future work that takes a more holistic approach. These include: the speech variety used by instructors in the language classroom (George, 2014; Ladegaard, 1998); familiarity and intelligibility of the varieties (Dalton-Puffer, Kaltenboeck, & Smit, 1997; Scales et al., 2006); peers and other types of social interactions with speakers of different varieties (Dalton-Puffer et al., 1997; George, 2014); portrayal of the speech varieties in the media and in popular culture (Ladegaard, 1998); as well as transfer of sociolinguistic interpretations from the L1 (Clopper & Bradlow, 2009). Future research is needed to clarify how these factors work together in the construction of learner language attitudes toward specific varieties of the target language, how these constructs may be reshaped throughout development and language experience, and, importantly, how these attitudes, in turn, shape L2 speaking.

## Pedagogical implications

Throughout this chapter, we have emphasized the importance of sociolinguistic competence in spoken interactions. Speakers of any language convey a variety of social and situational information using a variety of linguistic resources, all of which learners must acquire to communicate efficiently and appropriately. Given the current state of knowledge on L2 sociolinguistic competence, and the importance attributed to speaking in the L2 classroom, the pedagogical implications of these research findings have become increasingly more explicit: Learners must have access to language across multiple speakers and varied interactional contexts.

Nevertheless, we must continue to explore how we might best facilitate classroom learners' acquisition of sociolinguistic competence in spoken interactions. In this final section, we explore the current best practices for L2 instruction that might prove most effective in achieving this goal.

One approach that holds promise for the instruction of variable structures involves explicit attention to and practice with variable aspects of the second language. For instance, Lyster (1994) examined the impact of functional-analytic teaching (i.e., a method of form-focused instruction whereby emphasis is placed on accuracy with specific components of the L2) on French immersion students' use of *tu* and *vous*. Instructional techniques employed in his study included role plays, exercises that highlighted differences in the verbal form used with *tu* as opposed to *vous*, and various reading and writing activities. Students in the experimental group demonstrated significant improvement in the use of formal *vous* while speaking, suggesting that these techniques facilitated learners' acquisition of sociolinguistic competence as it relates to use of the pronouns under study. It should be noted that some of the aforementioned techniques may be more appropriate for highlighting a particular variable structure over another. Nevertheless, Lyster's study offers a variety of instructional techniques that may increase learners' exposure to variable language, thereby facilitating potential opportunities to notice variable linguistic input (R. Schmidt, 1990).

Task-based language teaching, which encompasses methods of instruction that use *tasks* to facilitate or promote L2 learning during meaningful interaction (e.g., M. H. Long, 2015), is also promising. A task, broadly speaking, provides a communicative context for meaningful interaction and negotiation in the L2.[4] Given the importance of *meaningful* interaction in the L2, tasks may be particularly suited for the incorporation of variable structures in the classroom. Just as SA settings have the potential for exposure to and use of the L2 in meaningful contexts, tasks, by definition, can provide such contexts thus increasing opportunities for learners' exposure to and production of variable structures in the classroom. Take the case of intervocalic /d/-weakening in Spanish. A hypothetical task featuring this variable structure might require a learner to listen to a voicemail message left by a NS peer who employs this feature in his or her speech, and then communicate the gist of the message to a mutual friend. Immediately before or after the task (i.e., the pre-task or post-task phases, respectively), the instructor could draw learners' attention to the variable structure being featured implicitly or explicitly to encourage awareness of it. This is but one example of a task that could be designed and incorporated in the classroom to encourage awareness of a

---

4. Note that several definitions of task exist (see R. Ellis, 2009). The description of tasks provided here highlights those characteristics found across existing definitions.

particular variable structure. This task, and any other, could also feature naturally occurring language in its design, thereby increasing learners' exposure to authentic variable input. The use of tasks is sorely needed not only to facilitate awareness and (potentially) development of variable structures in L2 classrooms but also to contribute to research on the acquisition of variation in task-based approaches to language teaching.

Instructors must also consider factors such as how often the structure occurs in speech. There are likely more opportunities and fewer challenges in incorporating frequent structures, such as pronouns of address (e.g., *tu* and *vous* in French), than relatively infrequent structures, such as contexts with variable use of the subjunctive in Spanish. Certainly, explicit instruction should target structures that are likely to be encountered most often by the L2 learner (e.g., Gutiérrez & Fairclough, 2006; Valdman, 1988). A second factor to consider is regional or geographically-linked variation, such as /s/-weakening and use of /θ/ in some varieties of Spanish (see also Geeslin & Long, 2014). Instructors should be encouraged to foster exposure to and awareness of geographically-linked language variation, particularly in cases where a variety is relevant for the learning goals of that population. One way this might be achieved is by accessing online samples of speech that reflect regional variation and incorporating these samples into role-play activities. These activities in turn facilitate comprehension across varieties of the language and perhaps even provide opportunities for learners to produce the sounds that correspond to a given variety. Additionally, with web-based conferencing tools such as Skype, learners may be paired with NSs in different regions, making exposure to and awareness of regional variation a ripe area for collaboration. Thus, instructors can make conscious decisions to expose learners to a range of voices and varieties of the L2 and then use current technologies and best pedagogical practices to incorporate these voices into classroom activities and materials.

A final factor to consider is the nature of variable linguistic structures themselves. As the preceding sections made clear, the factors (internal and external) involved in linguistic variation are complex and, thus, it follows that learners require extensive and adequate exposure to the target language to (eventually) acquire the appropriate constraints on variable use. Nevertheless, the very properties that condition the use of certain variants, most especially those that indicate group membership, informality and the like, make them less likely to occur in the language classroom (see Regan et al., 2009). Gurzynski-Weiss et al. (2018) showed that the frequency of use and the constraints on the use of subject forms inside the L2 Spanish classroom were not identical to those for the same speakers (instructors) outside the classroom. In the context of sociolinguistic research, this is not at all surprising. Nevertheless, it presents a challenge for instructors who wish to expose learners to these less informal variants. Community-based or experiential learning (McIlrath, Lyons, & Munck, 2012) could address this challenge: Interaction with users of the target language in the community offers opportunities for learners to experience a wider range of linguistic variants, and to engage more broadly with the people(s) and culture(s) of the target language. The example we provide of the use of current technologies to develop a role-play activity is yet another suggestion through which instructors may overcome this challenge, but the greatest success likely stems initially from an awareness of these challenges at the planning stages of any activity.

## Conclusions

The present chapter has demonstrated an increasingly detailed and robust body of research examining the L2 acquisition of sociolinguistic competence in spoken language. We see both depth in the detailed accounts of single phenomena and breadth in the growing number of language pairs and learning contexts that have now been investigated. Furthermore, there is clear evidence that this intersection of fields of study provides important test cases for theoretical issues such as the role of lexical frequency, or geographic variety of a L2, or the attitudes a learner holds toward a given language or language variety. Finally, we have seen that these findings must come to inform our approach to teaching additional languages and to the selection of language samples to which we expose classroom learners. With these insights in mind, we also see that there is a wealth of research yet to be conducted, including but not limited to the expansion of the repertoire of language structures and language pairs,[5] a closer look at non-classroom instructed learners, an exploration of the interplay between perception and production, and, more generally, an increased number of comparative studies that hold more than one learning context and/or more than one linguistic structure in focus so that more careful generalizations may be made.

## References

Adamson, H. D., & Regan, V. (1991). The acquisition of community speech norms by Asian immigrants learning English as a second language. *Studies in Second Language Acquisition*, 13, 1–22.

---

5. This particular direction may be especially important in gaining an understanding of whether the L2 acquisition of sociolinguistic competence is related to cultural and/or typological distance between languages.

Alford, R. L., & Strother, J. B. (1990). Attitudes of native and nonnative speakers toward selected regional accents of U.S. English. *TESOL Quarterly*, 24, 479–495.

Bachman, L. F. (1990). *Fundamental considerations in language testing*. Oxford: Oxford University Press.

Bayley, R., & Langman, J. (2004). Variation in the group and the individual: Evidence from second language acquisition. *International Review of Applied Linguistics in Language* Teaching, 42, 303–318.

Canale, M., & Swain, M. (1980). Theoretical bases of communicative approaches to second language teaching and testing. *Applied Linguistics*, 1, 1–47.

Chiba, R., Matsuura, H., & Yamamoto, A. (1995). Japanese attitudes toward English accents. *World Englishes*, 14, 77–86.

Clark, L., & Schleef, E. (2010). The acquisition of sociolinguistic evaluations among Polish-born adolescents learning English: Evidence from perception. *Language Awareness*, 19, 299–322.

Clopper, C., & Bradlow, A. (2009). Free classification of American English dialects by native and nonnative listeners. *Journal of Phonetics*, 37, 436–451.

Dalola, A., & Bullock, B. E. (2016). On sociophonetic competence: Phrase-final vowel devoicing in native and advanced L2 speakers of French. *Studies in Second Language Acquisition*. Advance online publication. https://doi.org/10.1017/S0272263116000309

Dalton-Puffer, C., Kaltenboeck, G., & Smit, U. (1997). Learner attitudes and L2 pronunciation in Austria. *World Englishes*, 16, 115–128.

Dewaele, J.-M. (2002). Using sociostylistic variants in advanced French IL: The case of nous/on. *Eurosla Yearbook*, 3, 205–226.

Díaz-Campos, M. (2006). The effect of style in second language phonology: An analysis of segmental acquisition in study abroad and regular-classroom students. In C. A. Klee & T. L. Face (Eds.), *Selected Proceedings of the 7th Conference on the Acquisition of Spanish and Portuguese as First and Second Languages* (pp. 26–39). Somerville, MA: Cascadilla Proceedings Project.

Díaz-Campos, M., & Gradoville, M. (2011). An analysis of frequency as a factor contributing to the diffusion of variable phenomena: Evidence from Spanish data. In L. A. Ortiz López (Ed.), *Selected Proceedings of the 13th Hispanic Linguistics Symposium* (pp. 224–238). Somerville, MA: Cascadilla Proceedings Project.

Donaldson, B. (2016). Negation in near-native French: Variation and sociolinguistic competence. *Language Learning*, 67, 141–170.

Dörnyei, Z., Csizer, K., & Nemeth, N. (2006). *Motivation, language attitudes and globalisation: A Hungarian perspective*. Clevedon, UK: Multilingual Matters.

Dörnyei, Z., MacIntyre, P., & Henry, A. (Eds.). (2015). *Motivational dynamics in language learning*. Bristol: Multilingual Matters.

Eckert, P., & Rickford, J. R. (2001). *Style and sociolinguistic variation*. Cambridge: Cambridge University Press.

Ellis, N. C. (1996). Analyzing language sequence in the sequence of language acquisition: Some comments on Major and Ioup. *Studies in Second Language Acquisition*, 18, 361–368.

Ellis, N. C., & Collins, L. (2009). Input and second language acquisition: The roles of frequency, form, and function introduction to the special issue. *The Modern Language Journal*, 93, 329–335.

Ellis, R. (2009). Task-based language teaching: Sorting out the misunderstandings. *International Journal of Applied Linguistics*, 19, 221–246.

Erker, D., & Guy, G. R. (2012). The role of lexical frequency in syntactic variability: Variable subject personal pronoun expression in Spanish. *Language*, 88, 526–557.

Fafulas, S. (2015). Progressive constructions in native-speaker and adult-acquired Spanish. *Studies in Hispanic and Lusophone Linguistics*, 8, 85–133.

Geeslin, K. (2000). A new approach to the second language acquisition of copula choice in Spanish. In R. P. Leow & C. Sanz (Eds.), *Spanish Applied Linguistics at the Turn of the Millennium: Papers from the 1999 Conference on the L1 & L2 Acquisition of Spanish and Portuguese*, (pp. 50–66). Philadelphia, PA: University of Pennsylvania Press.

Geeslin, K. L. (2003). A comparison of copula choice: Native Spanish speakers and advanced learners. *Language Learning*, 53, 703–764.

Geeslin, K. L., & Gudmestad, A. (2008a). The acquisition of variation in second language Spanish: An agenda for integrating the studies of the second language sound system. *Journal of Applied Linguistics*, 5, 137–157.

Geeslin, K.L., & Gudmestad, A. (2008b). Comparing interview and written elicitation tasks in native and non-native data: Do speakers do what we think they do? In J. Bruhn de Garavito & E. Valenzuela (Eds.), *Selected proceedings of the 10th Hispanic Linguistics Symposium* (pp. 64–77). Somerville, MA: Cascadilla Press.

Geeslin, K. L., & Long, A. Y. (2014). *Sociolinguistics and second language acquisition: Learning to use language in context*. London: Routledge.

Geeslin, K., Linford, B., & Fafulas, S. (2015). Variable subject expression in second language Spanish. In A.M. Carvalho, R. Orozco, & N. Lapidus Shin (Eds.), *Subject pronoun expression in Spanish: A cross-dialectal perspective* (pp. 191–209). Washington, DC: Georgetown University Press.

Geeslin, K. L. & Schmidt, L. B. (2016, October). Does context make the heart grow fonder? Linking language acquisition, language attitudes and language experience. *Paper presented at the 2016 Hispanic Linguistics Symposium*, Washington, DC: Georgetown University.

George, A. (2014). Study abroad in central Spain: The development of regional phonological features. *Foreign Language Annals*, 47, 97–114.

Gudmestad, A. (2012). Acquiring a variable structure: An interlanguage analysis of second language mood use in Spanish. *Language Learning*, 62, 373–402.

Gurzynski-Weiss, L., Geeslin, K., Daidone, D., Linford, B., Long, A., Michalski, I., & Solon, M. (2018). Examining multifaceted sources of input: Variationist and usage-based approaches to understanding the L2 classroom. In A. Tyler, L. Ortega, M. Uno, & H. I. Park (Eds.), *Usage-inspired L2 instruction: Researched pedagogy*. Amsterdam: John Benjamins.

Gutiérrez, M., & Fairclough, M. (2006). Incorporating linguistic variation into the classroom. In R. Salaberry & B. Lafford (Eds.), *The art of teaching Spanish: Second language acquisition from research to praxis* (pp. 173–191). Washington, DC: Georgetown University Press.

Hansen, J.G. (2001). Linguistic constraints on the acquisition of English syllable codas by native speakers of Mandarin Chinese. *Applied Linguistics*, 22, 338–365.

Hay, J., & Drager, K. (2010). Stuffed toys and speech perception. *Linguistics*, 48, 865–892.

Howard, M. (2004). Sociolinguistic variation and second language acquisition: A preliminary study of advanced learners of French. *SKY Journal of Linguistics*, 17, 143–165.

Howard, M., Lemée, I., & Regan, V. (2006). The L2 acquisition of a phonological variable: The case of /l/ deletion in French. *Journal of French Language Studies*, 16, 1–24.

Hymes, D. (1971). Sociolinguistics and the ethnography of speaking. In E. Ardener (Ed.), *Social anthropology and language* (pp. 47–93). London: Routledge.

Jarvella, R., Bang, E., Jakobsen, A. L., & Mees, I. M. (2001). Of mouths and men: Non-native listeners' identification and evaluation of varieties of English. *International Journal of Applied Linguistics*, 11, 37–56.

Kanwit, M. (2017). What we gain by combining variationist and concept-oriented approaches: The case of acquiring Spanish future-time expression. *Language Learning*, 67(2), 461–498.

Kanwit, M., Geeslin, K.L., & Fafulas, S. (2015). Study abroad and the SLA of variable structures: A look at the present perfect, the copula contrast, and the present progressive in Mexico and Spain. *Probus*, 27, 307–348.

Kanwit, M., & Solon, M. (2013). Acquiring variation in future-time expression abroad in Valencia, Spain and Mérida, Mexico. In J.E. Aaron, J. Cabrelli Amaro, G. Lord, & A. de Prada Pérez (Eds.), *Selected Proceedings of the 16th Hispanic Linguistics Symposium* (pp. 206–221). Somerville, MA: Cascadilla Press.

Kennedy Terry, K.M. (2016). Contact, context, and collocation: The emergence of sociostylistic variation in L2 French learners during study abroad. *Studies in Second Language Acquisition*. Advance online publication. https://doi.org/10.1017/S0272263116000061

Kinginger, C., & Farrell, K. (2004). Assessing development of metapragmatic awareness in study abroad. *Frontiers: The Interdisciplinary Journal of Study Abroad*, 10, 19–42.

Knouse, S.M. (2012). The acquisition of dialectal phonemes in a study abroad context: The case of the Castilian theta. *Foreign Language Annals*, 45, 512–542.

Labov, W. (2001). *Principles of linguistic change: Social factors* (Vol. 2). New York, NY: Blackwell.

Ladegaard, H. (1998). National stereotypes and language attitudes: The perception of British, American and Australian language and culture in Denmark. *Language and Communication*, 18, 251–274.

Lafford, B.A., & Uscinski, I. (2013). Study abroad and second language Spanish. In K.L. Geeslin (Ed.), *The handbook of Spanish second language acquisition* (pp. 386–403). Chichester: Wiley-Blackwell.

Lambert, W., Hodgson, R., Gardner, R. & Fillenbaum, S. (1960). Evaluational reactions to spoken languages. *Journal of Abnormal and Social Psychology*, 60, 44–51.

Lemée, I. (2002). Acquisition de la variation socio-stylistique dans l'interlangue d'apprenants hibernophones de franc̜ais: Le cas de on et nous. *Marges Linguistiques*, 4, 56–67.

Li, X. (2010). Sociolinguistic variation in the speech of learners of Chinese as a second language. *Language Learning*, 60, 366–408.

Linford, B.G. (2016). *The second-language development of dialect-specific morpho-syntactic variation in Spanish during study abroad*. Unpublished PhD dissertation. Indiana University, Bloomington, IN.

Linford, B., Long, A., Solon, M. & Geeslin, K. (2016). Measuring lexical frequency: Comparison groups and subject expression in L2 Spanish. In L. Ortega, A.E. Tyler, H.I. Park, M. Uno (Eds.), *The usage-based study of language learning and multilingualism* (pp. 137–155). Washington, DC: Georgetown University Press.

Linford, B., Long, A.Y., Solon, M., Whatley, M., & Geeslin, K. (2016). Lexical frequency and subject expression in native and non-native Spanish. In S. Sassarego & F Tejedo-Herrero (Eds.), *Spanish language and sociolinguistic analysis* (pp. 197–219). Amsterdam: John Benjamins.

Linford, B., & Shin, N. L. (2013). Lexical frequency effects on L2 Spanish subject pronoun expression. In J. Amaro, G. Lord, A. de Prada Pérez, & J. Aaron, *Selected Proceedings of the of the 16th Hispanic Linguistics Symposium* (pp. 175–189). Sommerville, MA: Cascadillia Preceedings Project.

Long, A. Y. (2016). *The acquisition of sociolinguistic competence by Korean learners of Spanish: Development and use of the copula, subject expression, and intervocalic stops.* Unpublished PhD dissertation. Indiana University, Bloomington, IN.

Long, M. H. (2015). *Second language acquisition and task-based language teaching.* Malden, MA: Wiley & Sons.

Lyster, R. (1994). The effect of functional-analytic teaching on aspects of French immersion students' sociolinguistic competence. *Applied Linguistics*, 15, 263–287.

McIlrath, L., Lyons, A., & Munck, R. (Eds.). (2012). *Higher education and civic engagement: Comparative perspectives.* Houndmills: Palgrave Macmillan.

Mougeon R., Nadasdi, T. & Rehner, K. (2010). *The sociolinguistic competence of immersion students.* Bristol: Multilingual Matters.

Nagy, N., Blondeau, H., & Auger, J. (2002). Second language acquisition and "real" French: An investigation of subject doubling in the French of Montreal Anglophones. *Language Variation and Change*, 15, 73–103.

Ortiz Jiménez, M. (2013). Stigmatized linguistic identities and Spanish language teaching. *International Proceedings of Economics Development & Research*, 68, 129–135.

Raish, M. (2015). The acquisition of an Egyptian phonological variant by U.S. students in Cairo. *Foreign Language Annals*, 48, 267–283.

Ramírez, A. (1983). Bilingüismo y actitudes hacia variedades del español entre estudiantes de Texas y California. *Lingüística Española Actual*, 5, 249–268.

Regan, V. (2004). The relationship between the group and the individual and the acquisition of native speaker variation patterns: A preliminary study. *International Review of Applied Linguistics in Language Teaching*, 42, 335–348.

Regan, V. (2010). Sociolinguistic competence, variation patterns and identity construction in L2 and multilingual speakers. *Eurosla Yearbook*, 10, 21–37.

Regan, V., Howard, M., & Lemée, I. (2009). *The acquisition of sociolinguistic competence in a study abroad context.* Bristol: Multilingual Matters.

Rehner, K., Mougeon, R., & Nadasdi, T. (2003). The learning of sociolinguistic variation by advanced FSL learners. *Studies in Second Language Acquisition*, 25, 127–156.

Ringer-Hilfinger, K. (2012). Learner acquisition of dialect variation in a study abroad context: The case of the Spanish [θ]. *Foreign Language Annals*, 45, 430–446.

Salaberry, M. R. (2000). The acquisition of English past tense in an instructional setting. *System*, 28, 135–152.

Salgado-Robles, F. (2014). Variación dialectal por aprendientes de español en un contexto de inmersión en el extranjero: Un análisis cuantitativo del uso leísta en el discurso oral y escrito. *Lenguas Modernas*, 43, 97–112.

Scales, J., Wennerstrom, A., Richard, D. & Wu, S. H. (2006). Language learners' perceptions of accent. *TESOL Quarterly*, 40, 715–738.

Schmidt, L. B. (2009). The effect of dialect familiarity via a study abroad experience on L2 comprehension of Spanish. In J. Collentine, M. García, & F. Marcos Marín (Eds.), *Selected proceedings of the 11th Hispanic Linguistics Symposium* (pp. 143–154). Somerville, MA: Cascadilla Proceedings Project.

Schmidt, L. B. (2011). *Acquisition of dialectal variation in second language: L2 perception of aspiration of Spanish /s/.* Unpublished PhD dissertation. Indiana University, Bloomington, IN.

Schmidt, R. (1990). The role of consciousness in second language learning. *Applied Linguistics,* 11, 129–158.

Shirai, Y. & Andersen, R. W. (1995). The acquisition of tense-aspect morphology: A prototype account. *Language,* 71, 743–762.

Solon, M. (2017, April). *Acquisition of sociophonetic competence: Exploring contexts of acceptance of and preference for /d/ deletion.* Paper presented at the Linguistic Symposium on Romance Languages, University of Delaware, Newark, DE.

Solon, M., Linford, B., & Geeslin, K.. (accepted). Acquisition of sociophonetic variation: Intervocalic /d/ reduction in native and nonnative Spanish. *Revista Española de Lingüística Aplicada.*

Tagliamonte, S. A. (2012). *Variationist sociolinguistics: Change, observation, interpretation.* Malden, MA: Wiley-Blackwell.

Tsai, M. (2013). Rethinking communicative competence for typical speakers. *Pragmatics and Cognition,* 21, 158–177.

Valdman, A. (1988). Classroom foreign language learning and language variation: The notion of pedagogical norms. *World Englishes,* 7, 221–236.

Young, R. (1996). Form-function relations in articles in English interlanguage. In R. Bayley & D. R. Preston (Eds.), *Second language acquisition and linguistic variation* (pp. 135–175). Amsterdam: John Benjamins.

CHAPTER 2

# Speaking, interactional competencies, and mediated action

Rémi A. van Compernolle
Carnegie Mellon University

This chapter focuses on the development of interactional competence from a Vygotskian perspective. It is argued that interactional competence is a situated activity in which speakers draw on their historically rooted understanding of contextually appropriate communicative resources in order to create a shared conceptual space for interaction. One dimension of this shared conceptual space is the degree of social distance and power, as created through the use of such register features as second-person pronouns in European languages (e.g., French *tu* and *vous*). To show how this aspect of register, and therefore interactional competence, can develop in pedagogical context, I draw on recent studies of concept-based pragmatics instruction. Pedagogical implications and future research directions are presented in concluding.

## Introduction

This chapter examines the acquisition of second language (L2) speaking abilities in terms of the development of an aspect of interactional competencies (IC). Drawing on Vygotskian sociocultural psychology (Vygotsky, 1978, 1986), or sociocultural theory (SCT) of mind, I explore the ways in which speaking abilities are simultaneously a product and a driver of L2 development by focusing on one particular pragmatic feature of several European languages–second-person pronoun use (e.g., French *tu* and *vous*). The concept of mediated action (Wertsch, 1994; for L2 work on IC, see van Compernolle, 2015a) is invoked as a means of emphasizing the tension between the culturally constructed tools made available in one's environment and their contextualized use from moment to moment.

In breaking with some of the past research on IC that focuses exclusively on spoken interaction (e.g., the chapters contributed to Hall, Hellermann, & Pekarek Doehler, 2011, which all adopted conversation analysis as their method), this chapter takes a broader view that involves an expanded evidential basis for IC

https://doi.org/10.1075/aals.17.02com
© John Benjamins Publishing Company

development, including extra-communicative tasks (e.g., private speech and writing during verbalized reflections, problem-solving and awareness-raising tasks). In other words, I examine diverse sources of metalinguistic and linguistic data that can be used to understand IC development in pedagogical context. I draw data from two recent studies of sociopragmatics instruction (seen as a domain of IC) in French (van Compernolle, 201; van Compernolle & Henery, 2014) and another in Spanish (van Compernolle, Gomez-Laich, & Weber, 2016). Analytic focus is on the tension, identified above, between what IC resources are made available through the environment (i.e., pedagogy) and what learners actually do in interaction with others.

## Conceptual background

### Acquiring "speaking": Abstractness vs. situatedness

I want to begin my discussion of the mediated action perspective on IC and the acquisition of speaking by quoting Ortega's (2011) insightful observation on a central difference between traditional cognitivist-psycholinguistic perspective on L2 development and its alternatives. The difference, as Ortega sees it, relates to "their position as to whether knowledge exists separate from its context, leading to divergent goals of *abstractness* versus *situatedness*" (p. 168). Cognitivists "assume that knowledge can stand alone" (ibid.), and is therefore abstract, transferrable across contexts, and so on. By contrast, alternative perspectives, such as SCT and IC, conceive of "knowledge and learning as parts enmeshed in greater wholes" (ibid.), meaning that we have to understand how knowledge and learning are situated processes within specific contexts. It is also worth noting that acquisition for cognitivists typically refers to implicit knowledge of linguistic forms. SCT makes no such assumption. Indeed, SCT is not concerned with the implicit acquisition of formal linguistic knowledge or competence. Rather, SCT is a theory of consciousness; our focus is on how psychological processes may come to be intentionally controlled by cultural means, or "from the outside" as Vygotsky said (1978: 40).

If we understand speaking abilities as being mediated by the resources that become available in specific contexts, including in our prior experiences, we are compelled to see speaking abilities as situated in contexts rather than as individual competencies that can be acquired ready made and once and for all. This means that one's competence in speaking can change from one context to the next, from one moment to the next, as different resources are made available and relevant for our participation in specific forms of communicative activity. The development of speaking abilities therefore depends on one's experiences participating in specific communicative activities in which spoken language is used, on the one hand, and learning how, when, and for what purposes resources from one context may be more or less appropriate for use in another.

## Dimensions of IC

Mehan (1982) wrote over thirty years ago that IC is "interactional in two senses of the term. One, it is the competence necessary for effective interaction. Two, it is the competence that is available in the interaction between people" (p. 65). This is to say that while people certainly learn and appropriate particular interactional resources that underlie their ability to use spoken language effectively, their abilities are also afforded and constrained by the resources that become available in specific contexts. For example, my speaking abilities in my L2, French, are different in a classroom full of third-year undergraduate students from what they are in a conversation with my native speaker colleague whose office is next to mine. This has to do with the roles each interlocutor is performing (e.g., teacher-student, colleague and friend), and with these roles the expected patterns of speech (e.g., teacher talk vs. small talk/chit chat), but also with the repertoire of resources that interlocutors bring to the interaction. My students typically have less experience interacting in French than I do, and in a much more limited number of contexts, so the things I am able to do with them are mediated by a smaller subset of my resources than would be the case with my colleague next door. To be sure, as any teacher knows, my students are capable of doing things beyond their own individual capacities when interacting with me because I can help to provide relevant resources as we interact. And this, of course, is what teaching and learning are supposed to be all about. Following Young (2011), this means that "IC is not the knowledge or the possession of an individual person, but is co-constructed by all participants in a discursive practice, and IC varies with the practice and with the participants" (p. 428). Thus, Young continues, "IC is the construction of a *shared mental context* [emphasis mine] through the collaboration of all interactional partners" (ibid.).

The shared mental context referred to by Young (2011) involves the collaboratively constructed and emergent expectations for what to say and how to say it during the course of an interaction. While such expectations are certainly historically rooted in our previous experiences, they are remade anew, negotiated, and modified each time we interact. In other words, through participation in phenomenologically similar practices, we learn to reason our way through everyday interactions, and therefore develop expectations for how similar interactions should unfold in the future. These expectations fall along several dimensions, as outlined by Rine (2009), following the work of Hall (1993) and Young (2000): (1) topic management; (2) action sequencing; (3) participant frameworks; (4) turn-taking; and (5) register. Descriptions are given in Table 1.

**Table 1.** Components of interactional competence

| Component | Description |
| --- | --- |
| Topic management | What is talked about and what is not talked about, including who has the right to initiate and/or change topics |
| Action sequencing | The order of various speech acts and formulas that constitute an interactive practice |
| Participant frameworks | How coparticipants adopt relevant roles and ratify the roles of others during a given interaction |
| Turn-taking | The ways in which coparticipants construct and recognize relevant places to take a turn at talk, the rhythm of a given interaction |
| Register | The particular lexical, grammatical, phonological, etc. forms that are seen as appropriate to the interaction |

Source: van Compernolle (2015a: 173), based on Rine (2009: 37)

The focus of this chapter will be on the register component of IC. This is not to minimize the importance of the other dimensions described in Table 1, but simply because relevant work drawing on the concept of mediated action has focused on register, specifically sociopragmatics in French and Spanish, and examples will come from these studies. These examples help to illustrate the ways in which IC, of which register is a component, can develop in pedagogical contexts in which learning opportunities are metalinguistic (e.g., awareness-raising tasks) as well as linguistic (e.g., communicative interaction) in nature.

## IC and mediated action

The perspective on IC that I have used elsewhere (van Compernolle, 2015a) draws on the Vygotskian notion of mediation. Vygotsky (1978) argued that culturally constructed artifacts mediate higher forms of human psychological functioning, which include actions carried out in the material world. He argued that just as we might use a physical tool to accomplish some goal (e.g., hammering a nail), we use psychological tools to act in and with the environment around us. Language, for example, allows us to categorize, conceive of, and remember the world and objects, events, states, and so on in ways that transcend basic biologically endowed perception capacities (John-Steiner, 2007; Wertsch, 2007).

As Wertsch (1994) pointed out, however, mediation–and its related notions of internalization and appropriation–is not a question of acquiring psychological tools once and for all times. Rather, while mediation is indeed a psychological construct, it is only properly understood in relation to the contextualized, situated actions that are mediated by the use of relevant tools, or mediational means, because tools are not 'acquired' ready-made but must be recontextualized and remade anew in context.

> The essence of mediated action is that it involves a kind of tension between the mediational means as provided in the sociocultural setting, and the unique contextualized use of these means in carrying out particular, concrete actions.
>
> (Wertsch, 1994: 205)

IC is a form of mediated action because (a) it depends on the resources that have been made available in the sociocultural setting of prior interactions, which (b) may be made relevant and appropriate in one's current interactional setting, wherein (c) a unique contextualized use of relevant means is made.

## Developing IC through concept-based pragmatics instruction

### Background

As noted earlier (Table 1; Rine, 2009: 37), one dimension of IC is register, which relates to the particular lexical, phonological, grammatical, and pragmatic forms considered to be appropriate for the context in which communication is taking place. Note that there is an intersection here with other areas of study; namely, sociolinguistic competence and pragmatic competence (see van Compernolle, 2015b), which also deal with the contextual appropriacy of language.

Register denotes the ways in which language varies systematically in relation to the context in which it is used. Any setting therefore will be associated with certain choices of language, and less associated with others, leading to expectations of what might be appropriate for a given context. At the same time, the use of language indexes (Silverstein, 2003) the context, thereby creating, renewing, and possibly modifying it. An example is the grocery store check-out. The physical setting prompts a certain set of register resources for customer-employee interactive discourse (e.g., polite discourse, Sir/ma'am, grocery store jargon, etc.). Using the register in turn reifies the context as a certain kind of collaboratively achieved activity: the customer and the store clerk are "doing a check out." However, in the same setting, a different register would have the potential to index a change in the expected activity. If the customer and clerk know each other socially, more informal or familiar discourse, along with different kinds of topics (e.g., family well-being, weekend plans), would index the accomplishment of friendly chitchat rather than a check out. Note also that register participates in indexing qualities of social relationships and identities, or subject positions (Norton, 2000), which are negotiated interactionally.

In van Compernolle (2014a), I developed a framework for teaching register as a way to index social meaning potential.[1] Drawing on Vygotskian sociocultural theory, especially the work of Gal'perin (1992) and Davydov (2004) in general education and Negueruela (2003) in L2 pedagogy, I argued that instruction should center on holistic and systematic concepts that explained how categories of meaning were indexed through language choices.[2] Concept-based pragmatics instruction (CBPI) therefore focuses on meaning, using language forms, or register resources, that index particular meanings during communication to illustrate the meaning-making potential of language. The concepts I proposed included social indexicality, following Silverstein (2003), self-presentation, social distance, and power. An in-depth discussion of the framework is beyond the scope of the present chapter. Interested readers are referred to van Compernolle (2014a) for additional details as well as to recent extensions of CBPI to French and Spanish classrooms (van Compernolle & Henery 2014; van Compernolle et al., 2016). In what follows, I will provide only a cursory description of relevant aspects of the pedagogical framework as it applies to the development of register capacity as a dimension of IC.

## Orientation, execution, control

The lion's share of the CBPI framework focuses on developing learners' awareness of the meaning potential of language rather than speaking per se. While this might sound odd, especially in a volume dedicated to the acquisition of speaking,

---

1. Social meaning potential refers to the way in which language can carry social meaning in various ways in different contexts in the act of communication. As outlined in van Compernolle (2014a), this is to say that linguistic forms do not have fixed meanings. Instead, they have *potential* meanings, or indexical potential (Silverstein, 2003), in the social world. The particular meaning that is activated depends on the speakers and their experiences in the sociolinguistic world (Johnston & Kiesling, 2008). CBPI aims to help learners gain a foothold into the indexical meaning potential of the language they are studying, rather than teaching them rather fixed, or static, "meanings" of linguistic forms.

2. Concept-based instruction in general, as outlined especially by Negueruela (2003), centers on holistic concepts that illustrate categories of meaning. Concepts are explained verbally (or in writing) along with visual aids, such as diagrams, flow charts, or pictures. Students engage in several types of tasks, including verbalizing their understanding of the concepts, completing problem-solving activities, and communicating in the L2 with the aid of the concepts. The point of the approach is to lead learners to orient to the meanings they wish to create in communication as a basis for selecting relevant linguistic forms.

there is good reason. As Gal'perin (1989, 1992) pointed out, all mental actions are subserved by three functions. The first is an *orientation*, or planning, function, which involves assessing the circumstances of one's actions and identifying relevant mediational means (e.g., selecting appropriate forms). The second is the *execution* of the orientation in the material world, or the action itself. The third is a *control* function, which monitors the execution in relation to the orientation and circumstances that might be in flux, thereby necessitating a modification of the orientation and execution. Note that the orientation function is central in Gal'perin's framework because it underlies both the execution and control of any action. As such, it is the most important function to focus on in pedagogy (see Lantolf & Thorne, 2006 and Lantolf & Poehner, 2014 for discussion of Gal'perin and concept-based instruction in L2 settings).

In CBPI, concepts such as self-presentation, social distance, and power are used to illustrate how language indexes social meaning. This serves as a powerful orientation to language use and to adjusting one's register in a way that meets social expectations and/or participates in shifting expectations in interactive discourse. Learning tasks, including verbalization, problem solving, and communication, are designed to help link learners' developing conceptual knowledge to their communicative practices. In what follows, I will provide illustrations of this process from three exemplar studies.

### Exemplar 1. van Compernolle (2014a)

The original illustration of CBPI was provided in van Compernolle (2014a). Eight intermediate-level US university learners of French participated in an extracurricular tutoring program that involved six weekly one-on-one meetings with a tutor. During the tutoring sessions, students engaged in a series of tasks, including reading concept-based explanations of pragmatics, verbalizing their understanding of relevant concepts, applying the concepts to solve communication problems, and performing scenarios based on DiPietro's (1987) strategic interaction method. Excerpts of video-recorded interactions with one of the learners, Susan, are provided below to illustrate these tasks.

Excerpt 1 shows Susan verbalizing her understanding of the French second-person pronouns *tu* and *vous* in relation to the concept of power. In particular, Susan was reflecting on the meaning of a pedagogical diagram depicting asymmetrical *tu/vous* use. The diagram (see Appendix A) showed a woman standing above a man; the woman was shown using *tu* but receiving *vous* in return. The diagram was meant to highlight that an unequal power relationship existed and was being emphasized by the asymmetrical second-person address pattern (i.e., the woman had more power so she could use *tu* but expect to be called *vous*).

Excerpt 1.

 1  Susan:  *tu* and *vous*
 2          I feel like would be such an awkward awful situation
 3          like if you're addressing someone
 4          like your employer as *vous*
 5          and all they're saying back to you is *tu* this *tu* that
 6  Tutor:  and what's happening
 7          what's being created there
 8  Susan:  a clear distribution of power
 9  Tutor:  right
10  Susan:  that they're above you
11          and you're below
12          and that's it
13  Tutor:  exactly

Susan was creating an orientation to communication here, noting that asymmetrical *tu/vous* use would be "awkward" and "awful" (line 2). When the tutor asked her to elaborate (lines 6–7), she recalled the concept explanation (from other materials she encountered earlier): "clear distribution of power" (line 8) and "they're above you and you're below" (lines 10–11). This is the kind of orienting knowledge that Susan could put to use in spoken communication, as part of her developing IC (i.e., how to negotiate an appropriate register with her interlocutor in relation to *tu/vous* address). This is also the kind of understanding that can create a "shared mental context" between interlocutors that Young (2011:428), cited earlier, referred to.

In a subsequent task, Susan was asked to use the concepts she was appropriating to help her choose pragmatic forms that would create relevant meanings in a series of social-interactive situations. Excerpt 2 shows her concept-based reasoning for the following situation:

> You are headed downtown to meet a group of friends for lunch when you happen to run into a classmate, Christophe. He's about your age and you've known him for a few months, although you haven't really hung out with him outside of school.

Excerpt 2.

 1  Susan:  my intention would be to show that I'm relaxed around him
 2  Tutor:  okay
 3  Susan:  um that there's no
 4          it's a

| | | |
|---|---|---|
| 5 | | what was it |
| 6 | | total equality |
| 7 | Tutor: | okay |
| 8 | Susan: | that it's not a power situation |
| 9 | | which one was that ((shifts gaze to diagrams)) |
| 10 | | was it that one ((pointing to distance diagram)) |
| 11 | | or that one ((pointing to power diagram)) |
| 12 | Tutor: | um (uh) this one ((pointing to power diagram)) |
| 13 | | diagram four |

Of particular interest is Susan's reference to the concept of power in lines 3–8. She described her preference to show her interlocutor that there was "total equality" (line 6) and "that it's not a power situation" (line 8). This particular orientation to the situation led her in turn to choose the familiar *tu* form, and at the same time to expect *tu* in return (not shown in Excerpt 2).

In a following tutoring session, Susan performed oral strategic interaction scenarios (DiPietro, 1987) with the tutor in which she had to plan her communicative actions (cf. orientation) and then execute the plan. Note here that, as outlined in van Compernolle (2014a: chap. 6), the execution also involved a two-tiered control function: both the student and the tutor were responsible for control over performance inasmuch as if the student encountered difficulty, the tutor could shift from being the scenario-defined interlocutor to fulfilling a teacher role by intervening to help the learner regain control over performance (see also van Compernolle, 2013a, 2013b, 2014b, in press). One such example is given in Excerpt 3, taken from van Compernolle (2014a: 169), which shows the opening of a scenario in which a potential employer (the tutor) was interviewing Susan for a job. In a planning stage of the scenario, she had opted to use *vous* with the interviewer to create an appropriate degree of social distance and to signal deference to his more powerful social position.

Excerpt 3. From van Compernolle (2014a: 169) (Transcription conventions provided in Appendix B)

| | | |
|---|---|---|
| 1 | Tutor: | ah bonjour Susan. comment allez-vous. |
| | | *oh hello Susan how are you [vous]* |
| 2 | Susan: | ehh + pas mal. et toi ? |
| | | *not bad and you [tu]* |
| 3 | Tutor: | ((looks at Susan with raised eye brow)) |
| 4 | Susan: | mm et <u>vous</u>. ((in a low, serious tone)) |
| | | *mm and you [vous]* |
| 5 | Both: | ((laughing)) |
| 6 | Susan: | <u>GEEZ</u>. |

7 Tutor:  uhhuh, ((laughing))

8 Susan:  <u>AHHH</u>.

9 Tutor:  ((laughs)) donc. + moi  ça va, merci. ((scenario moves forward))
           *so me fine thanks*

Despite Susan's general orientation to the scenario as requiring social distance and deference to the employer's power through the use of *vous*, she was not able to put this into practice. In line 2, Susan responded to the tutor's greeting, which included a *vous* form (line 1), with a *tu* form in the tag question *et toi?* 'and you?'. The raised eyebrow from the tutor (line 3) was enough to direct Susan's attention to her mistake, which she then corrected (line 4), before the two interlocutors continued the scenario.

One of the important findings of the van Compernolle (2014a) study was that despite their developing awareness and knowledge of appropriate forms, many learners had previously developed unanalyzed chunks for spoken interaction. Part of developing IC, in terms of control over register, therefore involved becoming aware of the unanalyzed chunks and reflecting on them, thereby making the chunk analyzable and open to register-appropriate variation. Susan's comments about the infelicitous use of *et toi?* 'and you?' from Excerpt 3 provide evidence of her own increasing awareness of her chunking, or what she referred to as "habit".

Excerpt 4.  From van Compernolle (2014a: 170)

 1 Susan:  <u>oka</u>y. so I <u>screw</u>ed <u>up</u> right in the beginning. I was like *et <u>toi</u>?*
           ((laughs))

 2 Tutor:  uhhuh ((laughs)) you don't get the job.

 3 Susan:  <u>crap</u>. um probably you get so used like <u>drill</u>ed in your <u>head</u>.

 4        like *ça va? ça va bien. et <u>toi</u>?* (('how are you?' 'fine' 'and you?'))

 5 Tutor:  mhm

 6 Susan:  so it was just like it wasn't + that I wasn't <u>think</u>ing about it,

 7        it was out of habit. it just + <u>came out</u>.

 8 Tutor:  right.

 9 Susan:  so <u>that's</u> + going to be something I have to think about.

10        […] I'm <u>so so so</u> used to being like *et toi?* (xxx)

11        I've been used to saying that.

As I argued in van Compernolle (in press), the approach to linking conceptual awareness of categories of meaning to appropriate forms entails a simultaneous focus on meaning and form (FonMF). In other words, it is not enough to simply know what forms can mean, just as it is insufficient to know how to use forms without understanding their meaning potentials; both are required. Indeed, the goal of CBPI is to orient learners first and foremost to the meanings they wish to create in communication with others (e.g., social distance vs. closeness), and then to link those intended meanings to relevant forms. The concept of mediated action (Wertsch, 1994) is relevant for describing how FonMF develops IC. Categories of meaning and illustrative forms are made available in the sociocultural environment through pedagogy, and these meanings and forms are known to the learners (i.e., metalinguistic awareness), but a tension exists between what they know (and, by extension, their orientation to communication) and what they do in performance (i.e., execution). FonMF is an attempt at mediating between awareness and performance–that is, between orientation and execution. The results of the van Compernolle (2014a) study, as also summarized and discussed in van Compernolle (in press), showed development in students spoken performance. FonMF resulted in learners being able to match their scenario performances to their orientations, which suggested that they had not only developed their conceptual awareness of sociopragmatics to orient to interaction but also their ability to self-regulate (i.e., the control function) during the execution of spoken-interactive discourse. Additional examples are provided below.

*Exemplar 2. van Compernolle & Henery (2014)*

The study by van Compernolle and Henery (2014) extended the CBPI framework to a second-semester US university-level classroom. The framework was adapted in order to complement the existing curriculum over the course of about eight weeks. This mainly involved tailoring the content of tasks to match the course's themes (e.g., a scenario involving eating at a restaurant when food was the theme of a unit). Another modification was the use of text-based synchronous computer-mediated communication (i.e., real-time chat) for performing scenarios in lieu of spoken interaction. The main reason for doing so was that, given the proficiency level of the students, extended oral discourse was not feasible; however, the students could engage in text-based interaction since online processing demands are reduced in such contexts. The argument is that by reducing the processing demands of the task, learners can deliberately link their conceptual awareness to their performances, which has the potential to support their orientation to, and control over, spoken-interactive communication in the future.

In general, the findings of the study supported earlier work (van Compernolle, 2014a) and showed that CBPI was feasible in a classroom setting and would result in IC development. Space does not permit an in-depth discussion of the results, so only one important example from the study will be discussed here. Excerpt 5 is taken from a scenario performed by two students, Adan and Katie, that involved an interaction between a travel agent (Adan) and a student traveler (Katie). In the planning stage of the scenario, Adan had noted that he might prefer to use an informal form of address (i.e., second-person *tu*) in order to reduce social distance; however, he had also indicated that the more formal *vous* might also be appropriate "to express my professionalism." By contrast, Katie had planned to use the *vous* form in order to maintain social distance. Note that the two students had not seen each other's plans prior to the scenario performance. The turns reproduced in Excerpt 5 are from the opening of the scenario.

Excerpt 5.  From van Compernolle & Henery (2014:571)

| Adan (Travel Agent) | Katie (Student/traveler) |
| --- | --- |
| 1    Bonjour Katie, qu'est ce que je peux t'aider?<br>[Hello Katie, what can I help you [T] with?] | |
| 2 | Je voudrais une salle pas cher a Paris…quelles sont **vos** [V] suggestions? C'est pour moi et une amie.<br>[I would like an inexpensive room in Paris… what are your [V] suggestions? It's for me and a friend.] |
| ((5 lines not shown where Adan lists hotel options)) | |
| 3    Quel chambre **voulez vous** [V]<br>[Which room would you [V] like?] | |

In turn 1, Adan addressed Katie with a *tu* form. In response, however, Katie stuck to her plan and used *vous* (turn 2). In turn 3, then, Adan produced a *vous* form, which he maintained for the remainder of the scenario. Van Compernolle and Henery (2014) argued the following:

> [Adan] noticed and reciprocated Katie's use of [*vous*] after his initial opening with [*tu*], an implicit shift that demonstrates Adan's sensitivity to his interlocutor's choice of pronoun. This is an especially important dimension of pragmatic abilities because social relationships are interactional in nature. In other words, it is not just about one speaker's "appropriate" choice of language, but how co-participants (tacitly) construct the qualities of their relationships through language use.
>
> (p.572)

This interactive, and indeed *adaptive*, dimension is centrally important to the development of IC. Knowing what kinds of interactive practices might be appropriate or personally desirable for a given context in the abstract is meaningless and useless if one is not able to negotiate and modify one's use of interactive practices in situated communication.

*Exemplar 3. van Compernolle, Gomez-Laich, & Weber (2016)*

The third exemplar study (van Compernolle et al., 2016) was carried out in an introductory Spanish classroom designed for so-called true beginners (i.e., students with no Spanish learning background). As with the van Compernolle and Henery (2014) study, the CBPI enrichment program was integrated into the curriculum and task contents and themes aligned with relevant chapter units. Because the learners had no experience in Spanish in principle, no speaking or interactive chat tasks were used for performance tasks. Instead, written discourse completion tasks (W-DCTs) were chosen because they allowed learners to focus on producing discourse with ample planning time. I will return to this issue later in the discussion.

Generally speaking, the findings corroborated the earlier studies. Significant quantitative gains and important qualitative changes were observed in students' understanding of how register (in this case, address forms in Spanish) was an important aspect of creating social identities and social relationship qualities in interaction. There were, however, mixed findings with regard to learners' abilities to use relevant forms in performance, as evidenced in W-DCT data. The tasks prompted learners to produce a speech act (e.g., asking a question) and then explain their performance. Following the multi-week intervention, there were a number of "mismatches" between actual language use (i.e., form) and intended use (i.e., explanations of performance) in the W-DCT data. Table 2 provides several representative examples given by van Compernolle et al. (2016).

The mismatches identified in the data suggested that while learners had certainly developed high-quality orientations to performance, they continued to struggle with the execution, likely because no specific form-focused practice was integrated as part of the pedagogy. In other words, the learners knew what they wanted to do in interactive settings, but they did not always know how to do what they wanted to do. Van Compernolle et al. (2016) concluded by suggesting additional tasks in which the focus would be on marked *tú* and *usted* in verbal morphology (i.e., where second-person is overt, since Spanish is a pro-drop language) and in a wide range of verb tenses.

## IC as the *source and driver* of development

So far, I have discussed IC in terms of learners' orientations to communication and their ability to execute and control their orientations in spoken interaction (van Compernolle, 2014a), text-based chat (van Compernolle & Henery, 2014), and W-DCTs (van Compernolle et al., 2016). In this section, I want to address the

**Table 2.**  Examples of mismatches in W-DCT data

| W-DCT utterance | Student explanation | Mismatch |
|---|---|---|
| Lo siento, pero no puedo. Tengo que asistir a otros actividades. ¿Puedo almorzar **contigo** al día siguiente? *'I'm sorry, but I can't. I have other things to do. Can I have lunch with you tomorrow?'* | First, the man is my boss, so he's at a more powerful position. Second, he invites me to have lunch with him, but I can't make it and want to change the time, so I am actually asking him for a favor. In this situation, I should use *usted* rather than *tú*. | The *tú* form *contigo* is used but is explained as *usted*. |
| Hola. ¿Practica deportes? *'Hi. Do you play sports?'* | I would use *tú* because my friend's fiancé is in the same generation with us and I have a good relationship with my friend. I would like to create a casual atmosphere and a casual relationship with her fiancé. So I would use *tú* and the verb should be *practica*. | The *usted* form of the verb *practica* is used, but is explained as *tú*. |
| ¿Cómo estás **usted**? *'How are you?'* | The use of *usted* is meant to convey that the professor is elder to me. | Both a *tú* form (*estás*) and *usted* are used here, but is explained as *usted*. |

*Note.* Examples are from van Compernolle et al. (2016: 354).

role of IC as a source and driver of development in CBPI. This is to say that while CBPI certainly has the goal of developing IC (e.g., register abilities), IC underlies the construction of learning opportunities. This is particularly relevant to learning to execute and control one's orientation to communication in spoken interactions, such as in the strategic interaction scenarios described in van Compernolle (2014a) (and see van Compernolle, 2013a, 2015a for discussion of IC's role in driving development).

Here, I want to draw on an example discussed in van Compernolle (2013a), taken from a strategic interaction scenario in French (see van Compernolle, 2014a) performed by a learner, Mary, and her teacher, shown in Excerpt 6. The scenario was part of a dynamic assessment (DA) of her development. The reader will note that DA involves teaching as part of the assessment of learner abilities in order to invoke change in competencies (Lantolf & Poehner, 2014; Poehner, 2008). The focus of this exchange is on Mary's struggle to control the use of negative constructions. French has two options for verbal negation: (1) a standard, or formal, two-particle construction involving the preverbal particle *ne* and a second post-verbal negative word, such as *pas* 'not'; and (2) an everyday, or informal, construction in which the *ne* is omitted. Mary, like virtually all classroom learners of French, had only ever been taught the more standard two-particle construction. As part of the CBPI enrichment program, she was learning to omit the *ne* in order to vary the register of her speech as appropriate. In this scenario, which involved two roommates and age peers looking for a new apartment, Mary had opted to omit the *ne* because it was more appropriate in terms of register. However, in line 5, she produced a negative construction with *ne*, at which point the tutor (line 7) initiated a mediation sequence (van Compernolle, 2013a) to assist her in regaining control over the execution of her performance (cf. the concept of orientation, discussed above).

Excerpt 6. From van Compernolle (2013a: 344–345) (Transcription conventions provided in Appendix C)

```
 1  T:  donc euh::: <on peut pas marcher,
        so   uh        we can't    walk
 2      (0.8)
 3  M:  a(h)h::  ↓um non.
        ah         um no
 4      (.) ((M looks down at SD))
 5      {<on ne peut pa:s marcher. à[: la-]
         we [NEG] cannot walk    to   the
 6      ((M continues to look down at SD))}
 7  T:                          {[wait.]
 8      ((makes "rewind" gesture))}
 9      [        (.)       ]
10      [((M looks up at T))]
11  T:  <do you want to sa:y
12      (.)
13      on ne peut pa:s,
        we cannot walk
14      (0.4)
15      <what do you want to say.
16  M:  oh. (.) um. (4.2) hh (li-) <I guess-
17      °just I'm saying (that)° we: ca::n't wa:lk. =
18  T:  = o↑ka::[y, ]
19  M:         [there.] =
20  T:  = <so what do you ha-
21      just think about that, a little bit,
22      (.)
23      what did you just say,
24      (0.6)
25  M:  ↑OH. (.) on ne (.) pouvons pas.
        oh       we [NEG] cannot
26      (0.4)
27      er=
28  T:  =h ↑(h)m::::,
29      (2.2)
30  M:  O↑H:↓: on (0.4) peut p(h)a[:.]
        oh     we           can't
31  T:                           [ah]::.
32      there yo[u go:. so-]
33  M:          [ <°p o u ]vons pas.°
        can't
34  T:  on peu:t pas.
        we can't
35      (0.6)
36      ri:ght,
37      (0.4)
```

```
38  M:  on peut pas.
        we can't
49  T:  on peut pas.
        we can't
40  M:  ok↑ay.
41      (.)
42      on peu:t pa:::s (0.2) um (tch) (.) marcher,
        we can't              um           walk
```

The analysis presented in van Compernolle (2013a) emphasizes Mary's IC in relation to her knowledge of how to participate in a DA of her abilities within the
context of a strategic interaction scenario. Thus, there is a dual focus here: on the
one hand, the scenario aimed to develop Mary's IC in terms of her ability to control negative constructions in register-appropriate ways and, on the other, she had
to develop her IC in relation to what participation in DA, and what the teacher's
intent was when he intervened, entailed. Indeed, Mary had to attempt three cor-
rections before omitting the *ne*: (1) she focused on content (lines 16–17); (2) she
tried to change the morphology of the verb; and (3) she realized *ne* was the issue.
As summarized in van Compernolle (2013a):

> This mediation sequence is important because it served as the initial opportunity
> for Mary to develop control over her use of verbal negation, the object of media-
> tion. It should be noted that the assistance provided by the tutor in this excerpt
> was strategic rather than directive: it pushed Mary to make successive attempts at
> resolving the problem (i.e., content > verbal morphology > *ne*). Mary's eventual
> production of the appropriate form was not attributable to Mary alone, but rather
> to the cooperative interaction between her and the tutor (i.e., *inter*psychological
> functioning). In other words, Mary was offered with just enough support to allow
> her to work to assume most of the responsibility for identifying the object of
> mediation and correcting it herself. As such, this mediation sequence also repre-
> sents a locus for the potential development of Mary's interactional competence as
> a DA participant–that is, learning that mediation sequences are initiated by the
> tutor in response to an infelicitous use of a pragmalinguistic form.        (p. 346)

van Compernolle (2013a) went on to show how Mary's IC as a DA participant
developed alongside her control over negative constructions. In this sense, her
development of register-related IC resources (e.g., *ne*) was driven by her IC in
engaging in DA scenarios: Mary and her tutor had to establish a "shared mental
context" (Young, 2011:428) for the conduct of DA (i.e., IC), which in turn led to
the creation of learning opportunities specifically focused on controlling negative
constructions.

## Conclusion

In this chapter, I have focused on the relationship between developing knowledge of IC resources through CBPI and developing control over relevant resources in language performance. Drawing on the Vygotskian concept of mediated action (Werstch, 1994; van Compernolle, 2015a for L2 interaction), I argued that IC was a historically rooted and at the same time contextually contingent activity achieved between people in interaction. This is to say that IC development involves, on the one hand, learning which resources (e.g., register-appropriate forms) are available and how they can be used appropriately, and, on the other, one's competence in using resources that are made relevant in particular, contextualized interactions (cf. orientation, execution, and control functions; Gal'perin, 1989, 1992). It is for this reason that the concept of IC is preferred over the notion that speaking is a discrete skill, and that situatedness is preferable to abstractness in thinking about competence, and L2 development more generally (Ortega, 2011). IC is also an important driver of development, inasmuch as competence in participating in relevant learning opportunities is required for further development to occur (van Compernolle, 2013a).

As noted earlier, IC develops not only in and through spoken interaction but it can also develop through learning opportunities involving awareness-raising tasks, computer-mediated communication, and written performance. Indeed, as noted in van Compernolle and Henery (2014) and van Compernolle et al. (2016), learner abilities need to be taken into account, and tasks tailored to their emerging capacities, in order to provide relevant and appropriate opportunities for development. This argument holds a number of interesting opportunities for research as well as pedagogical practice.

From its inception (van Compernolle, 2014a), an underlying assumption of the CBPI framework is that conceptual knowledge should be linked to performance in a deliberate way; namely, this means building up control over the execution of one's orientation through a series of tasks involving reflection, then problem-solving, then language use. What has yet to be examined, however, is how different language use tasks, such as W-DCTs (van Compernolle et al., 2016), text-based chat (van Compernolle & Henery, 2014), and strategic interaction scenarios (van Compernolle, 2014a) might be used within a single pedagogical program as a means of developing spoken-interactive abilities. One might imagine, for instance, sequencing these tasks such that online processing demands are gradually increased. For example, W-DCTs would provide ample opportunity to reflect on and control language use, while text-based chat can introduce a more interactive, yet still somewhat slowed down, communicative context, before learners are expected to orient to situations and execute and control performance in speech. There is neurolinguistic justification for the approach, as outlined by Paradis (2009) and suggested in van Compernolle (2014a): learners typically rely on metalinguistic (i.e., declarative) knowledge during language production, and this use of metalinguistic knowledge may be speeded up (Paradis, 2009), or accelerated (van Compernolle, 2014a), to the point that it is functionally equivalent to implicit competence. If this is indeed the case, sequencing tasks from "slow" to "fast" processing demands could be a way, in essence, of scaffolding the speeding up process. To be sure, this is simply an idea, and one that requires empirical investigation in classroom contexts.

Additional directions for research and pedagogical practices involve expanding CBPI to include domains of IC other than register. Indeed, van Compernolle (2011) and Young (2011) have both argued that concept-based approaches to instruction could be beneficial to IC development in general. Van Compernolle's (2011) study actually included specific recommendations for teaching learner to negotiate turn-taking in interaction and how to initiate and complete conversational repair action sequences. To date, however, these recommendations have yet to be taken up in the literature, but they have the potential to provide much needed insight into the nature of IC development in contexts where the development of IC is an explicit pedagogical focus.

# References

Davydov, V. V. (2004). *Problems of developmental instruction: A theoretical and experimental psychological study* (Trans. P. Moxay). Moscow: Akademyia Press.

Di Pietro, R. J. (1987). *Strategic interaction: Learning languages through scenarios.* Cambridge: Cambridge University Press.

Gal'perin, P. I. (1989). Organization of mental activity and the effectiveness of learning. *Soviet Psychology*, 27, 65–82.

Gal'perin, P. I. (1992). Stage-by-stage formation as a method of psychological investigation. *Journal of Russian and East European Psychology*, 30, 60–80.

Hall, J. K. (1993). The role of oral practices in the accomplishment of our everyday lives: The sociocultural dimension of interaction with implications for the learning of another language. *Applied Linguistics*, 14, 145–167.

Hall, J. K., Hellermann, J., & Pekarek Doehler, S. (Eds.). (2011). *L2 interactional competence and development.* Bristol: Multilingual Matters.

John-Steiner, V. P. (2007). Vygotsky on thinking and speaking. In H. Daniels, M. Cole, & J. V. Wertsch (Eds.), *The Cambridge companion to Vygotsky* (pp. 136–152). Cambridge: Cambridge University Press.

Johnstone, B., & Kiesling, S. F. (2008). Indexicality and experience: Exploring the meaning of /aw/-monophthongization in Pittsburg. *Journal of Sociolinguistics*, 12, 5–33.

Lantolf, J. P., & Poehner, M. E. (2014). *Sociocultural theory and the pedagogical imperative in L2 education,* New York, NY: Routledge.

Lantolf, J. P., & Thorne, S. L. (2006). *Sociocultural theory and the genesis of second language development*. Oxford: Oxford University Press.

Mehan, H. (1982). The structure of classroom events and their consequences for student performance. In P. Gilmore & A. A. Glatthorn (Eds.), *Children in and out of school: Ethnography and education* (pp. 59–87). Washington, DC: Center for Applied Linguistics.

Negueruela, E. (2003). *A sociocultural approach to teaching and researching second language: Systemic-theoretical instruction and second language development*. Unpublished doctoral dissertation. The Pennsylvania State University, University Park.

Norton, B. (2000). *Identity and language learning: Social processes and educational practice*. London: Longman.

Ortega, L. (2011). SLA after the social turn: Where cognitivism and its alternatives stand. In D. Atkinson (Ed.), *Alternative approaches to second language acquisition* (pp. 167–180). New York, NY: Routledge.

Paradis, M. (2009). *Declarative and procedural determinants of second languages*. Amsterdam: John Benjamins.

Poehner, M. E. (2008). *Dynamic assessment: A Vygotskian approach to understanding and promoting second language development*. Berlin: Springer.

Rine, E. F. (2009). *Development in dialogic teaching skills: A micro-analytic case study of a pre-service ITA*. Unpublished PhD dissertation, The Pennsylvania State University.

Silverstein, M. (2003). Indexical order and the dialectics of sociolinguistic life. *Language and Communication*, 23, 193–229

van Compernolle, R. A. (2011). Responding to questions and L2 learner interactional competence during language proficiency interviews: A microanalytic study with pedagogical implications. In J. K. Hall, J. Hellermann, & S. Pekarek Doehler (Eds.), *L2 interactional competence and development*. Bristol: Multilingual Matters.

van Compernolle, R. A. (2013a). Interactional competence and the dynamic assessment of L2 pragmatic abilities. In S. Ross & G. Kasper (Eds.), *Assessing second language pragmatics* (pp. 327–353). Houndmills: Palgrave Macmillan.

van Compernolle, R. A. (2013b). Concept appropriation and the emergence of L2 sociostylistic variation. *Language Teaching Research*, 17, 343–362.

van Compernolle, R. A. (2014a). *Sociocultural theory and L2 instructional pragmatics*. Bristol: Multilingual Matters.

van Compernolle, R. A. (2014b). Profiling second language sociolinguistic development through dynamically administered strategic interaction scenarios. *Language and Communication*, 37, 86–99.

van Compernolle, R. A. (2015a). *Interaction and second language development: A Vygotskian perspective*. Amsterdam: John Benjamins.

van Compernolle, R. A. (2015b). The emergence of sociolinguistic competence in L2 classroom interaction. In N. Markee (Ed.), *Handbook of classroom discourse and interaction* (pp. 265–280). London: Wiley-Blackwell.

van Compernolle, R. A. (In press). Focus on meaning and form: A Vygotskian perspective on task and pragmatic development in dynamic strategic interaction scenarios. In M. Ahmadian & M. P. G. Mayo (eds), *Recent trends in task-based language learning and teaching*. Berlin: Mouton de Gruyter.

van Compernolle, R. A., & Henery, A. (2014). Instructed concept appropriation and L2 pragmatic development in the classroom. *Language Learning*, 64, 549–578.

van Compernolle, R. A., Gomez-Laich, M. P., & Weber, A. (2016). Teaching L2 Spanish sociopragmatics through concepts: A classroom-based study. *Modern Language Journal*, 100, 341–361.

Vygotsky, L. S. (1978). *Mind in society: The development of higher psychological processes.* Cambridge, MA: Harvard University Press.

Vygotsky, L. S. (1986). *Thought and language.* Cambridge, MA: The MIT Press.

Wertsch, J. V. (1994). The primacy of mediated action in sociocultural studies. *Mind, Culture, and Activity*, 1, 202–208.

Wertsch, J. V. (2007). Mediation. In H. Daniels, M. Cole, & J. Wertsch (Eds.), *The Cambridge companion to Vygotsky* (pp. 178–192). Cambridge: Cambridge University Press.

Young, R. F. (2000). Interactional competence: Challenges for validity. Paper presented at a joint symposium on 'Interdisciplinary Interfaces with Language Testing'. Annual meeting of the American Association for Applied Linguistics and the Language Testing Research Colloquium, March 11, 2000, Vancouver, British Columbia, Canada.

Young, R. F. (2011). Interactional competence in language learning, teaching, and testing. In E. Hinkel (Ed.), *Handbook of research in second language teaching and learning* (Vol. 2, pp. 426–443). London: Routledge.

## Appendix A.   Power diagram

**Relative status?**

## Appendix B.    Simple transcription conventions

| | |
|---|---|
| + | short pause |
| ++ | long pause |
| +++ | very long pause |
| (2.0) | timed pause (2.0 seconds or more) |
| . | full stop marks falling intonation |
| , | slightly rising intonation |
| ? | raised intonation (not necessarily a question) |
| (word) | single parentheses indicate uncertain hearing |
| (xxx) | unable to transcribe |
| ((comment)) | double parentheses contain transcriber's comments or descriptions |
| - | abrupt cutoff with level pitch |
| <u>underline</u> | underlining indicates stress through pitch or amplitude |
| = | latched utterances |
| [. . .] | indicates that a section of the transcript has been omitted |
| [ | onset of overlapping speech |
| ] | end of overlapping speech |
| CAPITALS | capital letters indicate markedly loud speech |

## Appendix C.    Conversation analysis transcription conventions

| | |
|---|---|
| [ | Onset of overlapping speech |
| ] | End of overlapping speech |
| = | Latching (i.e., no gap between utterances) |
| (.) | Micropause (less than 0.2 sec) |
| (2.0) | Timed pause (longer than 0.2 sec) |
| <u>word</u> | Underlined words (or parts of words) indicates stress |
| :: | Sound lengthening. Multiple colons indicate more prolongation |
| - | Abrupt cut off |
| . | Falling intonation |
| , | Slightly rising/continuing intonation |
| ¿ | Mid-rising intonation |
| ? | Rising intonation (not necessarily a question) |
| ↑ | Markedly higher pitch relative to preceding talk |
| ↓ | Markedly lower pitch relative to preceding talk |
| WORD | Markedly loud sound relative to surrounding context |
| °word° | Markedly soft sound relative to surrounding context |
| #word# | Creaky voice |
| h | Audible outbreath (multiple *h*s mean longer outbreath) |
| .h | Audible inbreath (multiple *h*s mean longer inbreath) |
| w(h)ord | Breathiness, as in laughter during speech |
| <word> | Slower speech, relative to surrounding context |
| >word< | Faster speech, relative to surrounding context |
| <word | Quick start or syncopated speech |
| ( ) | Empty parentheses indicate inaudible speech |
| (word) | Unclear speech. For errors in French leading to unclear or indecipherable speech, the transcription is a phonetic approximation of the word or string of sounds. |
| (( )) | Transcriber's notes, comments, descriptions, etc. |
| {word ((comment))} | Braces indicate the synchronization of speech and nonverbal behavior, described in double parentheses. |
| → | Right-pointing arrow before an utterance indicates a line of interest in the discussion. |

# CHAPTER 3

# Gesture and speaking a second language

Gale Stam
National Louis University

Speaking in a second language involves not just speech; it also involves gesture (Stam, 2014). To not consider gesture in second language speaking is to ignore an integral part of language and interaction. When we view language as only speech, we view only one aspect of language and thought, the verbal aspect. We ignore gesture, the imagistic aspect. We take only a static view of language and ignore the dynamic aspect as David McNeill (2012) has pointed out. Speaking is not a static activity; it is an action. This chapter discusses why gestures need to be taken into account when looking at speaking in a second language.

## Introduction

Wilhelm von Humboldt (1836) viewed language and thought as an inseparable unit. For him, language was instrumental in conceptualization, and he saw each language as giving its speakers a particular "world-view" (p. 60).

> Man lives primarily with objects, indeed, since feeling and acting in him depend on his presentations, he actually does so exclusively, as language presents them to him. By the same act whereby he spins language out of himself, he spins himself into it, and every language draws about the people that possess it a circle whence it is possible to exit only by stepping over at once into the circle of another one.
>
> (von Humboldt, 1836/1999:60)

What von Humboldt is saying is that the language one speaks influences how one thinks and that this has important implications for learning another language and speaking in a second language (L2) because it involves thinking in a new way.

Speaking is a complex bilateral activity (Clark & Krych, 2004; Levelt, 1993) that requires thought, planning, and execution as well as self- and other-monitoring to determine if the message is being understood. It is both an individual action and "a collective action" (Holtgraves, 2002:7), a social and cultural one. It takes place in a socio-cultural environment (Vygotsky, 1986). Furthermore it is affected by the type of activity the speaker and the interlocutor are involved in – for exam-

https://doi.org/10.1075/aals.17.03sta

ple a class presentation, an informal conversation, or cooking; the context, what is said before and after as well as the situation, whether it is formal or informal; participants – their knowledge, their proficiency, their status, and their degree of familiarity; settings – where the interaction is taking place; goals – the purpose of the interaction; and rules – how the interaction should be conducted (Gumperz, 1972; Holtgraves, 2002; Hymes, 1974; Mead, 1934). For second language learners, this environment may be the classroom or the community, but wherever it takes place, it involves linguistic and social conventions, which often differ from those of the L2 learner's native language.

To understand speaking in another language, we need to look at more than just speech because the act of speaking itself is multimodal. It involves *kinesics* – eye contact, facial expressions, gestures, head movements, and posture; *proxemics* – personal space and touching; and *chronemics* – use of time; and conversational silence (Dausendschön-Gay, 2003; Sime, 2008; Stam & McCafferty, 2008). The work of Condon and Ogston (1967, 1971) illustrates this point. Condon and Ogston studied body movement during conversation using slow motion frame-by-frame film and made two observations about body movement in regard to speech that are relevant for speaking and listening in another language. One is that there is self-synchrony in the speech and body movement of the speaker, and the other is that there is interactional synchrony in the speech and body movement of the speaker and listener.

> As a normal person speaks, his body "dances" in precise and ordered cadence with the speech as it is articulated. The body moves in patterns of change which are directly proportional to the articulated pattern of the speech stream.
> (Condon & Ogston, 1971: 153)

> A hearer's body was found to "dance" in precise harmony with the speaker. When the units of change in their behavior are segmented and displayed consecutively, the speaker and hearer look like puppets moved by the same set of strings.
> (Condon & Ogston, 1971: 158)

Although all the multimodal aspects are important in understanding speaking in an L2, this chapter focuses on co-speech gestures and why they need to be considered in examining L2 speaking. It is organized in the following manner. First, I discuss what co-speech gestures, speech-linked gestures, and emblems are. Next, I discuss studies that illustrate the importance of gesture for understanding and facilitating L2 speaking. Then, I discuss areas where further research is needed and teaching implications.

## Co-speech gestures

When we speak, we move our hands. These spontaneous movements of our hands that accompany speech are called co-speech gestures or gesticulations (Stam, 2013), and speakers are generally unaware that they are producing them. Co-speech gestures are, of course not the only type of gestures we make when we speak. However, they are a particular type of gesture that differs from other types of gestures in several ways (Kendon, 2004; McNeill, 1992, 2005). First, co-speech gestures are synchronous with speech. Second, they tend to occur with new, con-trastive, or focused information – elements high in communicative dynamism. Third, co-speech gestures and speech perform the same pragmatic functions. Fourth, co-speech gestures cannot be understood without their accompanying speech. In other words, co-speech gestures and speech form a unit and comple-ment each other (Kendon, 2000). Sometimes they indicate the same entity, and sometimes co-speech gestures indicate something that is present in the speaker's thought but is not expressed in speech (Stam, 2013).

McNeill (1992, 2005, 2012) has proposed that co-speech gesture is a part of language just as speech is and that speech and gesture arise from the same under-lying process, form a single-integrated system, and develop together over time. Together, speech and co-speech gestures provide us with a more complete picture of speakers' thinking, both their verbal (speech) and imagistic (gesture) thinking, than speech does alone (McNeill & Duncan, 2000). This view of language goes beyond the synchronic view of language as a static entity, by adding a dynamic dimension – imagery and gesture – to the synchronic one.

> language is more than … lexicosyntactic forms … . It is also imagery. This imagery is in gesture, and is inseparable from language. … Taking seriously that language includes gesture as an integral component changes the look of every-thing. We see language in a new way, as a dynamic "language-as-action-and-being" phenomenon, not replacing but joining the traditional static (synchronic) "language-as-object" conception that has guided linguistics for more than a century. (McNeill, 2012:p.xi)

Co-speech gestures do not have only one function. They have both cognitive and communicative functions, and they often perform these functions simultaneously. Speakers gesture when they are having difficulty with speech production or to lighten their cognitive load, and they gesture to communicate information to their interlocutors (for a review of these functions, see Stam, 2013; Stam & McCafferty, 2008). It is important to note that speakers do not necessarily produce gestures all the time (Kendon, 1997). Whether or not speakers gesture and how they gesture is affected by such factors as common ground between the participants (Bavelas,

2007; Clark, 1992; Galati & Brennan, 2013; Gerwing & Bavelas, 2004; Holler & Stevens, 2007; Holler & Wilkin, 2009; Jacobs & Garnham, 2007; Wilkin & Holler, 2011), identity of the interlocutor (Stam & Tellier, 2017; Tellier & Stam, 2012; Tellier, Stam, & Bigi, 2013), interlocutors' understanding of what has been said (Bavelas, 2007; Hoetjes, Krahmer, & Swerts, 2015), location of the speaker and interlocutor (Özyürek, 2002), and task (Stam, 2016; Tabensky, 2008).

Co-speech gestures can be analyzed according to their semiotic properties in terms of how they refer to something, point to something, highlight parts of the discourse, and show interaction (Stam, 2013). Thus, they can be analyzed according to their degree of *"iconicity, metaphoricity, deixis, 'temporal highlighting' (beats), social interactivity'* (McNeill, 2005:41). Both gestures with iconicity and metaphoricity refer to something. The difference between them is that gestures with iconicity indicate concrete actions or objects, e.g., two hands rotating indicating *rolling*, whereas those with metaphoricity indicate abstract ideas, e.g., two hands facing each other holding an *idea*. Pointing gestures are gestures with deixis. They point to the location of an entity or time. Temporal highlighting gestures are beat gestures, quick vertical or horizontal hand movements aligned with the speech rhythm that highlight information: they indicate repairs, introduce new information, and summarize action. Beat gestures can be superimposed on gestures with iconicity, metaphoricity, and deixis for emphasis. Gestures with social interactivity indicate interaction between speakers and listeners, such as when speakers finish a turn and extend their hand to their listener for the listener to reply (Stam, 2013). It is important to note that just as gestures are multifunctional, they are also multidimensional, and many gestures exhibit more than one semiotic property. In other words, a gesture can have both iconicity and deixis or both metaphoricity and social interactivity (McNeill, 2005; Stam, 2013).

Empirical research on co-speech gestures has shown that these gestures provide researchers with more information about speakers' thinking and conceptualizations than speech alone does. For instance, gestures show transitions to the two-word stage in first language acquisition (e.g., Iverson & Goldin-Meadow, 2005; Özçalışkan & Goldin-Meadow, 2005, 2009), speakers' conceptualizations during narration (e.g., McNeill, 1992, 2005; McNeill & Duncan, 2000), and whether L2 learners are thinking in their L2 or not when speaking their L2 (e.g., Gullberg, 2006, 2011; Stam, 1998, 2008, 2015).

## Speech-linked gestures and emblems

There are two other types of gestures that are relevant for understanding and encouraging L2 speaking: speech-linked gestures and emblems (Stam, 2013). These gestures are produced with some conscious awareness.

Like co-speech gestures, speech-linked gestures occur with speech. However, their timing is different. They are asynchronous with speech and fill a speech gap, a grammatical slot in the sentence. Speech-linked gestures complete the sentence such as in the following utterance: "Sylvester went [gesture of an object flying out laterally]" (McNeill, 2005: 5). Speech-linked gestures may occur when learners do not have the vocabulary to finish the sentence or when teachers leave a blank and perform a gesture for learners to supply the missing words.

Emblems are the gestures that most people think of when they hear the term gesture. These are culturally specific, conventionalized, translatable gestures, such as the *thumbs up* or *okay* gesture in English that may occur with or without speech (Stam, 2013, 2014). Because an emblem is conventionalized, its form and meaning is well known to members of a cultural group. However, because it is culturally specific, the form may have different meanings in different cultures. Emblems are learned gestures that are an important way of expressing oneself in a particular language and culture and can and should be taught to second language learners.

## Importance of gesture for understanding and facilitating L2 speaking

Over the past thirty years, there have been a growing number of empirical L2 studies that have examined speech and gestures to see what light gesture sheds on L2 acquisition and L2 teaching (for reviews, see e.g., Gullberg & McCafferty, 2008; Gullberg, de Bot, & Volterra, 2008; Stam, 2013; Stam & McCafferty, 2008). These studies have looked at learners' and teachers' gestures in controlled experiments and in naturalistic interactions both inside and outside the classroom. Among the topics that have been investigated are assessment, bilingual development, communicative competence, emblems, learners' gestures and their functions (communication strategies, lexical searches and retrieval, thinking for speaking), teachers' gestures and their functions, and the role of gesture in facilitating comprehension and learning (see Stam, 2013, for a more detailed description). In this section I will discuss assessment, communicative competence, emblems, and learners' gestures and their functions and how these topics relate to L2 speaking.

## Assessment, communicative competence, and emblems

The idea that L2 communicative competence is more than just linguistic competence and that it affects the assessment of learners' speaking ability is not a new one. Acknowledging that L2 learners need to demonstrate nonverbal competence in addition to linguistic competence, several researchers (e.g., Antes, 1996; Pennycook, 1985; von Raffler-Engel, 1980; Wylie, 1985), have recommended the teaching of emblems and nonverbal behavior, e.g. kinesics and proxemics, in the L2 classroom. Furthermore, Jungheim has advocated for the testing of second language learners' nonverbal ability, their ability "to use and interpret a variety of nonverbal behavior or cues appropriately for the target language and culture" (Jungheim, 1995:150–151).

Several researchers (Gullberg, 1998; Nambiar & Goon, 1993; Neu, 1990; Jenkins & Parra, 2003; Stam 2006a) have investigated whether gesture and other non-verbal communication have an effect on the oral proficiency assessments of L2 learners and found that it did. Gullberg (1998), looking at the difference between ratings in an audio-only and a video-condition, found that oral proficiency was rated significantly higher in a video-condition when gestures could be seen than in the audio-only condition. She also found that when gestures could be seen, narrative skills were rated higher. In addition, Nambiar and Goon (1993), comparing the rating of oral proficiency interviews in an audio-only and a face-to-face condition, found that the scores were significantly higher in the face-to-face condition. In both of these cases, the raters benefited from more information about the learners – the speech of the L2 speakers, their visible speech (mouth movements) and their gestures (Drijvers & Özyürek, 2016). Furthermore, investigating how learners' gestures and nonverbal behavior impact oral proficiency interview ratings, Neu (1990), Jenkins and Parra (2003), and Stam (2006a), found that when the learners' gestures and nonverbal behavior were closer to those of the target language and culture, they were rated higher, and when they were not, they were rated lower regardless of their verbal performance. These studies clearly demonstrate that learners' gestures have an effect on how their oral proficiency is perceived by raters whether the raters themselves are aware that they are taking them into account or not. In other words, not just learners' speech, but also their gestures are being assessed by the raters in rating learners' fluency.

## Learners' gestures and their functions

The gestures of L2 learners have been looked at in terms of their frequency, their function, and the light they shed on L2 conceptualization. For instance, a number of studies (e.g., Gullberg, 1998; Hadar, Dar, & Teitelman, 2001; Marcos, 1979;

Stam, 2006a) have examined the effect of language fluency on L2 gesture frequency and found that L2 learners produce more gestures while speaking their L2 than their first language (L1). They also found that both L2 proficiency and language order affected L2 gesture frequency. Learners who speak first in their L2 and then in their L1 produce more gestures in their L2 than those speakers who speak first in their L1 and then in their L2 (Sainsbury & Wood, 1977; Stam, 2006a).

L2 speakers' gestures serve both communicative and cognitive functions just as L1 speakers' gestures do and are affected by the tasks they are engaged in (Stam, 2016; Tabensky, 2008). The gestures convey additional information to interlocutors that is not present in speakers' speech, and this has implications for understanding and facilitating L2 speaking. For example, Stam (2008) showed that when a learner's speech was just looked at (Example 1), it was clear that she was having trouble narrating what she had seen in a cartoon, but it did not tell us what she was thinking. However, when her speech and gesture were looked at together (Example 2), it became obvious that the learner was trying to express Tweety throwing a bowling ball. This is important because with this additional information, teachers can provide learners with the vocabulary they need to express themselves.

(1)   and <uhm> the Tweety / / <uhm> /[1]
      <mmm> / / / <mhff> #
      the Tweety has a / a bowling ball                           (Stam, 2008: 252)

(2)   and <uhm> t[he Tweety / / <uh<u>m</u>>]
      iconic: both hands at upper right and left, move away from body and down
      and repeat movement <Tweety throwing the bowling ball>
      [ / <mmm> ]
      metapragmatic: left hand rises to nose, index finger touches nose, and
      retracts<trying to find the words>
      [ / **/ /** ] <mhff> #
      iconic (repetition to reduced repetition of previous iconic): both hands at
      upper right and left, move away from body and down and repeat as a smaller
      movement <Tweety throwing the bowling ball>
      [[the Twe**ety has**] [**a /**] [**bo**<o>**wling ba** <u>**ll /**</u> ] ]
      a                b        c
      a.   iconic: both hands move to their respective sides and up to upper
           chest<Tweety holding bowling ball + shape of bowling ball>
      b.   aborted iconic: both hands continue from previous movement, move up
           to neck, out to respective sides, and back to neck<bowling ball>

---

1.   In the transcription < > indicates filled pause and elongation of vowel, / an unfilled pause, #
a breath pause, and * a repair, repetition, or self-correction. Brackets are around the entire gesture phrase, the stroke of the gesture is in bold, and holds are underlined.

  c. iconic: both hands continue from previous movement, move up slightly
     open to their respective sides, then down to lower chest, and
     hold<showing shape of bowling ball>                    (Stam, 2008: 252)

Gestures also help speakers with the organization and control of information
and task and with lexical retrieval problems (Stam, 2013). For example, Gullberg
(1998), investigating learners' use of gestures as communication strategies, found
that learners use gestures to deal with expressive problems related to fluency,
grammar, and lexical difficulties. Moreover, Stam (2001, 2012) found that the
types of gestures learners produced during lexical searches, lexical retrievals, and
lexical failures varied depending on whether learners were trying to retrieve a
word or were asking the interlocutor for help. The searches that resulted in lexical retrieval often had superimposed beats on an iconic gesture, and during the
retrieval of the word, there was a larger beat on the retrieved word. It is important
for L2 teachers to be aware of the difference in L2 learners' gestures when they are
having lexical retrieval problems so that they can help learners express themselves
when necessary.

Perhaps most importantly, gestures have been looked at for the additional
information they shed on learners' conceptualizations while speaking (Stam,
2016). The majority of these studies have been carried out on the topic of thinking
for speaking (Stam, 2014). L2 thinking for speaking studies investigate typological
differences between languages in the expression of motion events, for example,
languages that express directionality with a verb (verb-framed) and those that
express directionality with a satellite (satellite-framed) and what happens when
speakers of one typological language learn another typological language (see
Stam, 2015). Some of these studies have looked at only the speech or writing of
L2 learners (see Cadierno 2013; Stam, 2010, 2015 for reviews), while others have
examined both speech and gesture. The studies that examine both speech and gesture in L2 learners' narrations of motion events use the timing of gestures showing
directionality (path) to determine whether the learners are thinking for speaking
in their L1, their L2, or a combination of the two languages when they narrate a
motion event in their L2 (Stam, 2015).

In this regard, Stam (2008) clearly demonstrated that it is not sufficient to
look at only learners' speech, but that it is necessary to look at their gestures
because she found that advanced L2 learners of English produced grammatically
correct sentences that described the motion event appropriately, but the timing
of their gestures indicated that they were not thinking for speaking in their L2.
For example, she showed that a native speaker of English and an advanced Spanish speaking L2 learner of English produced the following utterances (Example 3)
in speech, both of which are grammatically correct with the appropriate use of

verbs and satellites. She stated that based on speech alone, it would seem that the L2 learner is describing the motion event like a native English speaker and thinking for speaking in her L2. However, if the speakers' gestures are also examined (**Example 4**), it's clear that based on the synchrony of the learner's gestures, she is not thinking for speaking in her L2 like a native speaker of English. She had path gestures on the subject of the sentence *the cat* (a), the verb *went* (b) following a Spanish pattern, and the satellite and article *through the* (c) following an English pattern, and her gestures were very segmented unlike the native speaker whose two gestures on the satellites *up* and *through*, an English pattern, involved continuous movement.

(3)   Comparison of Speech – Cat climbing up inside the drainpipe
**Native English speaker**
and / / he goes / up through the pipe this time #                 (Stam, 2008: 243)
**Advanced L2 English learner**
he * the cat went / / through the * / / / the pipe /                 (Stam, 2008: 243)

(4)   Comparison of Speech and Gesture – Cat climbing up inside the drainpipe
**Native English speaker**
a<a>nd / / he goe[[ss / **up/ th| rough** <u>the</u> pipe]] this time #
                                   a               b

   a.   iconic: right hand at low right waist moves from right to left to next to left thigh <Sylvester moves into lower part of the pipe> PATH + GROUND

   b.   iconic: right hand "O" pops open to loose curved hand and moves up vertically from next to left thigh to left side lower chest level<Sylvester moves up inside pipe> PATH + GROUND                 (Stam, 2008: 248)

**Advanced L2 English learner**
<sub>RH</sub>[[he* **the cat**] [**went //**] [**through the***][////][the<e> **pipe** <u>/ and * but</u> the*]]/
<sub>LH</sub>[ [he* **the cat** ][**went //**]]through   the* / / / the <e> pipe / and* but the* /
              a            b            c           d         e

   a.   iconic: right hand at right, left hand, "O" at left waist<Sylvester entering the drainpipe>PATH

   b.   iconic: right hand at right chest moves up to right side of face, left hand, "O" at waist lowers to lap as right hand rises<Sylvester going up inside drainpipe>PATH

   c.   iconic: right hand at right side of face moves in toward body and moves up to forehead changing hand orientation to palm toward down, fingers toward left <Sylvester going through the drainpipe>PATH

   d.   iconic: right hand at nose level and moves up to top of head then retracts to nose level<pipe>GROUND

e.  iconic (reduced repetition of previous gesture) right hand at upper chest
    moves up in toward body to chin level and down away from body to
    upper chest, small circular movement, and holds<pipe>GROUND
    N.B. Gestures 'd' and 'e' occur on a metalinguistic level with a word
    search and finding of the word, respectively.          (Stam, 2008:249)

The results of the L2 speech and gesture thinking for speaking studies have been
mixed in terms of whether learners are able to shift to L2 thinking for speaking patterns. Some studies (e.g., Kellerman & van Hoof, 2003; Negueruela et al.,
2004; Yoshioka, 2008; Yoshioka & Kellerman, 2006) found no shift from L1 to L2
thinking for speaking patterns in the learners' L2 narrations while others (Brown
& Gullberg, 2008; Choi & Lantolf, 2008 Lewis, 2012; Stam, 1998, 2006a, 2006b,
2008) found that the learners' narrations contained aspects of both their L1 and
their L2 thinking for speaking patterns and that these changed over time (Stam,
2010, 2015, 2017). Furthermore, Brown and Gullberg (2008) found that learners'
L2 also affected their L1 thinking for speaking patterns and that there was bidirectional cross-linguistic transfer. Looking at speech alone would not give us this
information because in each case, learners produced grammatically correct utterances with appropriate motion event descriptions in their L2.

## Summary

All of the above studies make it clear that if we look at only speech, we miss an
important amount of information about learners' speaking: their communicative
competence including their ability to use emblems, how their speaking is actually
being assessed, what are the functions of their gestures during speaking, and their
conceptualizations–how they are thinking for speaking while speaking in their L2.
More research is needed in all these areas so that we can better understand L2
learners' speaking and how it is perceived by L1 speakers.

## Other areas for further research

In addition to the areas that have already been researched, studies are needed on
the topics of beat gestures, emblems, and head movements as they are relevant for
L2 teaching of speaking.

Beat gestures

Beat gestures are important in second language speaking as they are aligned with the rhythm, the prosody, of a language and, consequently, vary from language to language. However, there has been a paucity of research on where and how frequently speakers of various languages produce beats and their relevance for second language speakers.

For example, McClave (1994, 1998a) investigated the occurrence of beats in the spontaneous conversations of two dyads of English speakers (male-male and female-female). She found that there was no significant correlation between rising and falling hand/arm movements and rising and falling pitch. She also found that there was a tendency for stress and stroke to co-occur and that beats were organized in a rhythmic manner and "occur on both stressed and unstressed syllables and during pauses" (McClave, 1994:60). In addition, in the spontaneous conversations of dyads and triads of native English speakers, Loehr (2004, 2007) investigated how gesture and intonation are integrated rhythmically and found that the head, hands, and voice all worked together "much like a jazz piece" (Loehr, 2004:iii). He raised the point that as English was a stress-timed language, it would be interesting to also look at a syllable-timed language to see how the rhythmic patterns might differ (Loehr, 2007). Furthermore, McCafferty (2006) examined the beat gestures of a Taiwanese learner of English during an interaction with a native speaker of English. He found that the learner used beat gestures as a way to break down words into syllables and gain control of prosody in English.

Although these studies are interesting, they only give us information about beats in English, and the information is limited. We do not know what the rate of producing beat gestures is in different languages, how this affects L2 learners' rate of producing beats in their L2, and whether this has an impact on how L2 learners are evaluated in terms of their L2 speaking fluency. Beats need more systematic research as they may hold the key to how prosody manifests itself visually and how L2 learners' speaking is perceived.

First, we need research on when native speakers of various languages produce beat gestures in alignment with speech. We need to know how often they produce them, whether the beat gestures align with the prosody of the language, how this differs for syllable-timed and stressed-time languages, and how beat gestures relate to what speakers are stressing in their discourse. Then we need systematic cross-linguistic comparisons of the languages that we have L1 data on so that we can see what the differences are in order to facilitate teachers' and learners' awareness of these differences between learners' L1 and L2 and how they affect L2 speaking.

## Emblems

Emblems are another area that needs further research. Although there have been some reviews and studies on emblems, (e.g, Calbris, 1990; Ekman & Friesen, 1969; Kendon, 1981; Morris et al., 1979; Ricci Bitti & Poggi, 1991) and some languages have published emblem repertoires (e.g., Brookes, 2004; Payrató, 1993), there is a need for many more. For L2 learners to function and express themselves fully in the language and culture of their L2, they need to know what the emblems are in the L2 and what the appropriate contexts are for using them. This means that research needs to be conducted on what emblems are used and when they are used in all languages so that clear emblem glossaries can be developed for languages that do not have them and emblems can be added to L2 teaching materials.

## Head movements

The term gesture is generally used to refer to movements of the hands and arms that accompany speech, but gestures can also occur on other body articulators such as the head, legs, and feet (McNeill, 2005). To date, head movements are just beginning to be analyzed. For instance, research has been conducted on head movements as indicators of inclusivity, intensification, uncertainty, negation, deixis, repairs, and direct speech in English, French, Bulgarian, Arabic, Korean, and African-American English Vernacular (e.g., Calbris, 2011; Harrison, 2014; Kendon, 2002; McClave, 1998b, 2000, 2001; McClave et al., 2007). However, no research has been conducted on the head movements of second language speakers and what they indicate. Much research is needed in this area:

First, it is necessary to establish base lines for the head movements of L1 speakers of additional languages. For example, some of the questions that need to be answered are the following: (1) When do speakers of a particular language move their heads when speaking? (2) Do they always do it in the same direction and in the same manner? (3) Do they move their head with negatives or when they switch from reported to direct speech? (4) What do speakers of another language do? Second, it is necessary to systematically analyze the head movements of L2 speakers to see how they compare with the base line data for both their L1 and L2. This is important to see if L2 speakers are unconsciously moving their heads in an L1 manner when they are speaking their L2, which could affect how their speaking of the L2 is perceived by native English speakers. After this is known, it might be possible to include head movements along with emblems and beats in L2 language curriculum to facilitate learners' speaking.

## Teaching of beat gestures, emblems, and head movements in the L2 classroom

Possible ways of teaching beat gestures, emblems, and head movements in the L2 classroom are discussed in this section.

### Beat gestures

Once we have data on beat gestures, it would be possible for L2 teachers to model beat gestures in the L2 and have students practice them in the classroom. In addition, teachers can videotape the learners speaking in the L2 before they have a lesson on beat gestures, provide the lesson, have the learners practice the beat gestures and discuss their impressions of producing the gestures, reinforce the lesson another day with additional practice, and encourage the learners to practice at home. Then the teachers could videotape the learners again after a month, make a copy of the videotapes and give it to the learners to watch at home with the assignment of writing down differences they noticed in their production of beat gestures. What they noticed could then be discussed in class, and examples could be shared.

### Emblems

One way to add emblems to teaching materials to build learners' awareness of their usage would be to develop videotapes where L1 speakers of a language use emblems in appropriate situations. These videotapes could be shown in the classroom and discussed. After this, L2 learners could be given an assignment to observe the use of emblems on TV or in the community and to bring back examples to the classroom. Following this, the examples could be presented in the classroom, and the appropriate and inappropriate use of emblems observed could then be discussed. Finally, learners could be given a speaking assignment that lends itself to the use of emblems and given a list of the emblems that are appropriate. They could then engage in the assignment with instructions to use the emblems. Afterwards, the teacher could discuss with the students what emblems they used and why. The teacher could then provide feedback if the emblem that was used was appropriate for the context.

### Head movements

A way to add head movements into the L2 classroom to facilitate L2 speaking would be for the L2 teacher to discuss and model head movements with inclusivity, intensification, uncertainty, negation, deixis, repairs, and direct speech in speaking the L2. The students could then practice these head movements in different speaking contexts. After this is done, the teacher could point out and discuss differences in head movements in the learners' L1 and their L2 and encourage students to pay attention to their head movements so that they become more aware of how they move their head when speaking.

## Conclusion

What does it mean to speak another language? If we take von Humboldt's (1836/1999) perspective that speaking another language involves stepping into another circle of both language and thought, then we need to consider what that actually means. Speaking is a bilateral action (Clark & Krych, 2004) that involves both a speaker and a listener. It occurs in a sociocultural context (Vygotsky, 1986) and is not a unimodal phenomenon involving just speech and the mouth. It is a multimodal phenomenon, which includes the entire body (Condon & Ogston, 1971). Extremely important in this activity are two types of gestures that speakers make: co-speech gestures and emblems. Co-speech gestures are important because they are an integral part of language just as speech is (McNeill, 1992, 2005), and emblems are important because they are the codified gestures of a particular languaculture (Agar, 1994) that learners need to master. Research to date has shed some light on the role and importance of gestures in understanding speaking in a second language. However, it is just a beginning. If we are to embrace, language and speaking in their entirety, we need many more studies. Only then, will we unlock the secrets that analysis of co-speech gesture along with speech can reveal about speaking a second language.

## References

Agar, M. (1994). *Language shock: Understanding the culture of conversation*. New York, NY: William Morrow & Co.

Antes, T. A. (1996). Kinesics: The value of gesture in language and in the language classroom. *Foreign Language Annals*, 29(3), 439–448.

Bavelas, J. (2007). Face-to-face dialogue as a micro-social context. In S. D. Duncan, J. Cassell, & E. T. Levy (Eds.), *Gesture and the dynamic dimension of language: Essays in honor of David McNeill* (pp. 127–146). Amsterdam: John Benjamins.

Brookes, H. (2004). A repertoire of South African quotable gestures. *Journal of Linguistic Anthropology*, 14(2), 186–224. https://doi.org/10.1525/jlin.2004.14.2.186

Brown, A., & Gullberg, M. (2008). Bidirectional crosslinguistic influence in L1-L2 encoding of manner in speech and gesture: A study of Japanese speakers of English. *Studies in Second Language Acquisition*, 30(2), 225–251.

Cadierno, T. (2013). Thinking for speaking in second language acquisition. In C. A. Chapelle (Ed.), *The encyclopedia of applied linguistics*. Oxford: Blackwell. https://doi.org/10.1002/9781405198431.wbeal1213

Calbris, G. (1990). *The semiotics of French gestures*. Bloomington, IN: Indiana University Press.

Calbris, G. (2011). *Elements in meaning in gesture*. Amsterdam: John Benjamins.

Choi, S., & Lantolf, J. P. (2008). Representation and embodiment of meaning in L2 communication: Motion events in the speech and gesture of advanced L2 Korean and L2 English speakers. *Studies in Second Language Acquisition*, 30(2), 191–224.

Clark, H. H. (1992). *Arenas of language use*. Chicago, IL: The University of Chicago Press.

Clark, H. H., & Krych, M. A. (2004). Speaking while monitoring addressees for understanding. *Journal of Memory and Language*, 50, 62–81.

Condon, W. S., & Ogston, W. D. (1967). Segmentation of behavior. *Journal of Psychiatric Research*, 5(3), 221–235.

Condon, W. S., & Ogston, W. D. (1971). Speech and body motion synchrony of the speaker-hearer. In D. L. Horton & J. J. Jenkins (Eds.), *Perception of language* (pp. 150–184). Columbus, OH: Charles E. Merrill.

Dausendschön-Gay, U. (2003). Producing and learning to produce utterances in social interaction. *EUROSLA Yearbook*, 3, 207–228.

Drijvers, L., & Özyürek, A. (2016). Visual context enhanced: The joint contribution of iconic gestures and visible speech to degraded speech comprehension. *Journal of Speech, Language, and Hearing Research*, 60, 212–222. https://doi.org/10.1044/2016_JSLHR-H-16-0101.

Ekman, P., & Friesen, W. V. (1969). The repertoire of nonverbal behavior: Categories, origins, usage, and coding. *Semiotica*, 1, 49–98.

Galati, A., & Brennan, S. E. (2013). Speakers adapt gestures to addressees' knowledge: Implications for models of co-speech gesture. *Language and Cognitive Processes*. https://doi.org/10.1080/01690965.2013.796397.

Gerwing, J., & Bavelas, J. (2004). Linguistic influences on gesture's form. *Gesture*, 4(2), 157–195.

Gullberg, M. (1998). *Gesture as a communication strategy in second language discourse. A study of learners of French and Swedish*. Lund: Lund University Press.

Gullberg, M. (2006). Handling discourse: Gestures, reference tracking, and communication strategies in early L2. *Language Learning*, 56(1), 155–196.

Gullberg, M. (2011). Thinking, speaking and gesturing about motion in more than one language. In A. Pavlenko (Ed.), *Thinking and speaking in two languages* (pp. 143–169). Bristol: Multilingual Matters.

Gullberg, M., & McCafferty, S. G. (2008). Introduction to gesture and SLA: Toward an integrated approach. *Studies in Second Language Acquisition*, 30, 133–146.

Gullberg, M., de Bot, K., & Volterra, V. (2008). Gestures and some key issues in the study of language development. *Gesture*, 8(2), 149–179.

Gumperz, John J. (1972). The speech community. In P. P. Giglioli (Ed.), *Language and social context* (pp. 219–231). Harmondsworth, UK: Penguin.

Hadar, U., Dar, R., & Teitelman, A. (2001). Gesture during speech in first and second language: Implications for lexical retrieval. *Gesture*, 1(2), 151–165.

Harrison, S. (2014). The organization of kinesic ensembles associated with negation. *Gesture*, 14(2), 117–140.

Hoetjes, M., Krahmer, E. & Swerts, M. (2015). On what happens in gesture when communication is unsuccessful. *Speech Communication*, 72, 160–175.

Holler, J., & Stevens, R. (2007). The effect of common ground on how speakers use gesture and speech to represent size information. *Journal of Language and Social Psychology*, 26(1), 4–27.

Holler, J., & Wilkin, K. (2009). Communicating common ground: How mutually shared knowledge influences speech and gesture in a narrative task. *Language and Cognitive Processes*, 24(2), 267–289.

Holtgraves, Thomas M. (2002). *Language as social action: Social psychology and language use*. Mahwah, NJ: Lawrence Erlbaum Associates.

Hymes, Dell H. (1974). *Foundations of sociolinguistics: An ethnographic approach*. Philadelphia, PA: University of Pennsylvania Press.

Iverson, J. M., & Goldin-Meadow, S. (2005). Gesture paves the way for language development. *Psychological Science*, 16, 367–371.

Jacobs, N., & Garnham, A. (2007). The role of conversational hand gestures in a narrative task. *Journal of Memory and Language*, 56, 291–303.

Jenkins, S., & Parra, I. (2003). Multiple layers of meaning in an oral proficiency test: The complementary roles of nonverbal, paralinguistic, and verbal behaviors in assessment decisions. *The Modern Language Journal*, 87(1), 90–107.

Jungheim, N. O. (1995). Assessing the unsaid: The development of tests of nonverbal ability. In J. D. Brown & S. O. Yamashita (Eds.), *Language testing in Japan* (pp. 149–165). Tokyo: The Japan Association for Language Teaching.

Kellerman, E., & van Hoof, A-M. (2003). Manual accents. *International Review of Applied Linguistics*, 41, 251–269.

Kendon, A. (1981). Geography of gesture. *Semiotica*, 37, 129–163.

Kendon, A. (1997). Gesture. *Annual Review of Anthropology*, 26, 109–128.

Kendon, A. (2000). Language and gesture: unity or duality? In D. McNeill (Ed.), *Language and gesture* (pp. 47–63). Cambridge: Cambridge University Press.

Kendon, A. (2002). Some uses of the head shake. *Gesture*, 2(2), 147–182.

Kendon, A. (2004). *Gesture: Visible action as utterance*. Cambridge: Cambridge University Press.

Levelt, W. J. M. (1993). *Speaking: From intention to articulation*. Cambridge, MA: The MIT Press.

Lewis, T. (2012). The effect of context on the L2 thinking for speaking development of path gestures. *L2 Journal*, 4, 247–268.

Loehr, D. P. (2004). *Gesture and intonation*. PhD dissertation. Georgetown University.

Loehr, D. (2007). Aspects of rhythm in gesture and speech. *Gesture*, 7(2), 179–214.

Marcos, L. R. (1979). Hand movements and nondominant fluency in bilingual. *Perceptual and Motor Skills*, 48, 207–214.

McCafferty, S. G. (2006). Gesture and the materialization of second language prosody. *International Review of Applied Linguistics*, 44, 195–207.

McClave, E. (1994). Gestural beats: The rhythm hypothesis. *Journal of Psycholinguistic Research*, 23(1), 45–66.

McClave, E. (1998a). Pitch and manual gestures. *Journal of Psycholinguistic Research*, 27(1), 69–89.

McClave, E. (1998b). Cogniive and interactional functions of head movements. In S. Santi, I. Guaïtella, C. Cavé, & G. Konopczynski (Eds.), *Oralité et gestualité: Communication multimodale, interaction* (pp. 365–370). Paris: L'Harmattan.

McClave, E. (2000). Linguistic functions of head movements in the contest of speech. *Journal of Pragmatics*, 32, 855–878.

McClave, E. (2001). Head movements in Arabic, Bulgarian, Korean and African American English: What's cognitive and what's cultural? In S. Santi, I. Guaïtella, C. Cavé, & G. Konopczynski (Eds.), *Oralité et gestualité: Communication multimodale, interaction* (pp. 560–564). Paris, France: L'Harmattan.

McClave, E., Kim, H., Tamer, R., & Mileff, M. (2007). Head movements in the context of speech in Arabic, Bulgarian, Korean, and African-American Vernacular English. *Gesture*, 7(3), 343–390.

McNeill, D. (1992). *Hand and mind*. Chicago, IL: The University of Chicago Press.

McNeill, D. (2005). *Gesture and thought*. Chicago, IL: The University of Chicago Press.

McNeill, D. (2012). *How language began: Gesture and speech in human evolution*. Cambridge: Cambridge University Press.

McNeill, D., & Duncan, S. D. (2000). Growth points in thinking-for-speaking. In D. McNeill (Ed.), *Language and gesture* (pp. 141–161). Cambridge: Cambridge University Press.

Mead, George H. (1934). *Mind, self & society*. Chicago, IL: The University of Chicago Press.

Morris, D., Collett, P., Marsh, P., & O'Shaughnessy, M. (1979). *Gestures their origins and distribution*. London: Jonathan Cape.

Nambiar, M. K., & Goon, C. (1993). Assessment of oral skills: A comparison of scores obtained through audio recordings to those obtained through face-to-face evaluation. *RELC Journal: A Journal of Language Teaching and Research in Southeast Asia*, 24(1), 15–31.

Negueruela, E., Lantolf, J. P., Rehn Jordan, S., & Gelabert, J. (2004). The "private function" of gesture in second language speaking activity: A study of motion verbs and gesturing in English and Spanish. *International Journal of Applied Linguistics*, 14(1), 113–147.

Neu, J. (1990). Assessing the role of nonverbal communication in the acquisition of communicative competence in L2. In R. Scarcella, E. S. Andersen, & S. D. Krashen (Eds.), *Developing communicative competence in a second language* (pp. 121–138). Rowley, MA: Newbury House.

Özçalışkan, Ş., & Goldin-Meadow, S. (2005). Gesture is at the cutting edge of early language development. *Cognition*, 96(3), B101–B113.

Özçalışkan, S., & Goldin-Meadow, S. (2009). When gesture-speech combinations do and do not index linguistic change. *Language and Cognitive Processes*, 24(2), 190–217.

Özyürek, A. (2002). Do speakers design their cospeech gestures for their addressees? The effects of addressee location on representational gestures. *Journal of Memory and Language*, 46, 688–704.

Payrató, L. (1993). A pragmatic view on autonomous gestures: A first repertoire of Catalan emblems. *Journal of Pragmatics*, 20(3), 193–116. http://doi.org/10.1016/0378-2166(93)90046-R

Pennycook, A. (1985). Actions speak louder than words: Paralanguage, communication and education. *TESOL Quarterly*, 19(2), 259–282.

Ricci Bitti, P. E., & Poggi, I. (1991). Symbolic nonverbal behavior: Talking through gestures. In R. S. Feldman & B. Rimé (Eds.), *Fundamentals of nonverbal behavior* (pp. 433–457). Cambridge: Cambridge University Press.

Sainsbury, P., & Wood, E. (1977). Measuring gesture: Its cultural and clinical correlates. *Psychological Medicine*, 7, 63–72.

Sime, D. (2008). "Because of her gesture, it's very easy to understand" – Learners' perceptions of teachers' gestures in the foreign language class. In S. G. McCafferty, & G. Stam (Eds.), *Gesture: Second language acquisition and classroom research* (pp. 259–279). New York NY: Routledge.

Stam, G. (1998). Changes in patterns of thinking about motion with L2 acquisition. In S. Santi, I. Guaïtella, C. Cavé, & G. Konopczynski (Eds.), *Oralité et gestualité: Communication multimodale, interaction* (pp. 615–619). Paris: L'Harmattan.

Stam, G. (2001). Lexical failure and gesture in second language development. In C. Cavé, I. Guaïtella, & S. Santi (Eds.), *Oralité et gestualité: Interactions et comportements multimodaux dans la communication* (pp. 271–275). Paris: L'Harmattan.

Stam, G. (2006a). *Changes in patterns of thinking with second language acquisition.* PhD dissertation. University of Chicago.

Stam, G. (2006b). Thinking for speaking about motion: L1 and L2 speech and gesture. *International Review of Applied Linguistics, 44*(2), 143–169.

Stam, G. (2008). What gestures reveal about second language acquisition. In S. G. McCafferty & G. Stam (Eds.), *Gesture: Second language acquisition and classroom research* (pp. 231–255). New York, NY: Routledge.

Stam, G. (2010). Can a L2 speaker's patterns of thinking for speaking change? In Z. Han & T. Cadierno (Eds.), *Linguistic relativity in SLA: Thinking for speaking* (pp. 59–83). Clevedon: Multilingual Matters.

Stam, G. (2012). Gestes et recherche de mots en langue seconde. In R. Vion, A. Giacomi & C. Vargas (Eds.), *La corporalité du langage: Multimodalité, discours et écriture. Hommage à Claire Maury-Rouan* (pp. 55–71). Aix en Provence: Publications de l'Université de Provence.

Stam, G. (2013). Second language acquisition and gesture. In C. A. Chapelle (Ed.), *The encyclopedia of applied linguistics.* Oxford: Blackwell. https://doi.org/10.1002/9781405198431.wbeal1049.

Stam, G.. (2014). Why gesture! *AL Forum –The Newsletter of the Applied Linguistics Section,* TESOL, September 2014. <http://newsmanager.commpartners.com/tesolalis/issues/2014-08-27/7.html>

Stam, G. (2015). Changes in thinking for speaking: A longitudinal case study. *The Modern Language Journal, 99,* 83–99. https://doi.org/10.1111/j.1540-4781.2015.12180.x

Stam, G. (2016). Gesture as a window onto conceptualization in multiple tasks: Implications for second language teaching. *Yearbook of the German Cognitive Linguistics Association (GCLA), 4,* 289–314

Stam, G. (2017). Verb framed, satellite framed or in between? A L2 learner's thinking for speaking in her L1 and L2 over 14 years. In I. Ibarretxe-Antuñano (Ed.), *Motion and space across languages: Theory and applications* (pp. 329–365). Amsterdam: John Benjamins.

Stam, G., & McCafferty, S. G. (2008). Gesture studies and second language acquisition: A review. In S. G. McCafferty, & G. Stam (Eds.), *Gesture: Second language acquisition and classroom research* (pp. 3–24). New York, NY: Routledge.

Stam, G., & Tellier, M. (2017). Gestures: The sound of silence: How gestures in pauses can enhance interaction. In R. B. Church, M. W. Alibali, & S. D. Kelly (Eds.), *Why gesture? How the hands function in speaking, thinking and communicating* (pp. 353–378). Amsterdam: John Benjamins.

Tabensky, Alexis. (2008). Expository discourse in a second language classroom: How learners use gesture. In S.G. McCafferty & G. Stam (Eds.), *Gesture: Second language acquisition and classroom research* (pp. 298–320). New York, NY: Routledge.

Tellier, M., & Stam, G. (2012). Stratégies verbales et gestuelles dans l'explication lexical d'un verbe d'action. In V. Rivière (Ed.), *Spécificités et diversité des interactions didactiques* (pp. 357–374). Paris: Riveneuve éditions.

Tellier, M., Stam, G., & Bigi, B. (2013). Gesturing while pausing in conversation: Self-oriented or partner-oriented? *Proceedings from TiGeR 2013*, Tilburg Gesture Research Meeting, 19–21 June.

von Humboldt, W. (1836/1999). *On language: On the diversity of human language construction and its influence on the mental development of the human species*, Edited by M. Losonsky, Translated by P. Heath. Cambridge: Cambridge University Press.

von Raffler-Engel, W. (1980). Kinesics and paralinguistics: A neglected factor in second language research. *Canadian Modern Language Review*, 36(2), 225–237.

Vygotsky, L.S. (1986). *Thought and language*. Cambridge, MA: The MIT Press.

Wilkin, K. & Holler, J. (2011). Speakers' use of 'action' and 'entity' gestures with definite and indefinite references. In G. Stam & M. Ishino, (Eds.), *Integrating gestures: The interdisciplinary nature of gesture* (pp. 293–307). Amsterdam: John Benjamins.

Wylie, L. (1985). Language learning and communication. *The French Review*, 58(6), 777–785.

Yoshioka, K. (2008). Linguistic and gesture introduction of ground reference in L1 and L2 narrative. In S.G. McCafferty & G. Stam (Eds.), *Gesture: Second language acquisition and classroom research* (pp. 211–230). New York, NY: Routledge.

Yoshioka, K., & Kellerman, E. (2006). Gestural introduction of ground reference in L2 narrative discourse. *International Review of Applied Linguistics*, 44, 173–195.

CHAPTER 4

# L2 talk as social accomplishment

Søren W. Eskildsen & Numa Markee
University of Southern Denmark | University of Illinois

This position paper builds on ethnomethodological conversation analysis to make a number of interrelated, empirically derived claims about speaking a second language and learning to do it as a social endeavor. We will show that: (1) language is primarily action, that linguistic units are primarily designed and used for and learned as actions in situ; (2) language is occasioned and environmentally contingent, and speaking is turn-taking that presupposes an ability to monitor other people's talk; and (3) language, learning and cognition are socially distributed, co-constructed, embodied and embedded in local situations. They are each other's ongoing continuations or extensions, made visible by verbal and bodily behavior. They rely on other people's actions in situ as language is co-constructed and language-as-action emerges.

## Introduction

This chapter builds on ethnomethodological conversation analysis (EMCA) to make a number of interrelated, empirically derived claims about speaking a second language and learning to do it as a social endeavor. Our point of departure is that language is primarily a repertoire for social action, and that language, cognition, and learning are locally occasioned, situated, embodied, and socially distributed phenomena. We will unpack these issues as the chapter unfolds and dive straight into our investigation with an empirical example which showcases the key points of the chapter; the socially visible and distributed nature of language, learning, and cognition, the occasioned nature of turns-at-talk, and the view of language as primarily a resource for social action.

In the Extract (1) which comes from a corpus of Danish L2 data recorded by foreign students studying Danish at the University of Southern Denmark, Thomas (a Dane) begins telling Petra (a German) about a spa hotel which is to be built in their town (line 1). Prior to this turn, they have been talking about another big construction project in the same town.

https://doi.org/10.1075/aals.17.04esk
© John Benjamins Publishing Company

**Extract 1**[1]

```
01 THO:   de har tænkt sig å lave ehm: stor- sån stort fancy e:h badehotel
          they plan to build        big-  a kind of big fancy spa hotel
02        (1.6)
03 THO:   ved du  hva  det  er
          do  you know what that is
04        (0.5)
05 PET:   nej
          no
06        (0.5)
07 THO:   hotel↗
          hotel↗
08 PET:   ja  det ⌈ved jeg↘
          yes i    know that↘
09 THO:         ⌊bade↗
                 spa
10        (0.8)
11 THO:   de har tænkt sig å lave sån svømmehal og fancy: badeland og sån ⌈nåed
          they plan to build a kind of swimming pool and fancy water park and
          stuff
12 PET:                                                                   ⌊°oh
13        god° a:h d- ↑a::h↘ ja
                             yes
14 THO:   ⌈😊a:::::h😊↘
15 PET:   ⌊det er det samme på tyHsk heh .hh heh ⌈nogen gang er det så let
          it's the same in german               sometimes it's so easy
16 THO:                                          ⌊heh heh
17 THO:   en gang imellem sir det li: klik å ⌈så er den der↘
          sometimes it just clicks           and then you have it
18 PET:                                      ⌊jer
                                              yeah
19 THO:   ⌈*jer*⌉
           yeah
20 PET:   ⌊*jer*⌋
           yeah
```

In the turn at line 1, Thomas makes use of a "sån X"-construction[2] which in spoken Danish is typically used in a first-pair part of an adjacency pair calling for an alignment-signaling response (Pedersen 2014). However, as can be seen in the long pause in line 2, no response is forthcoming which Thomas treats as a display of non-understanding on Petra's part. Next, Thomas initiates repair as he asks Petra if she knows what a "badehotel" ("spa hotel") is (line 4). Following another pause, Petra simply says *nej* ("no") (line 6). Another pause ensues, following which Thomas repeats the final part of the Danish compound, *hotel*, expressed with rising intonation (line 8); this is enough for the turn to be interpreted by Petra as a question requiring a response. She confirms that she knows *hotel* (line 9). Thomas then repeats the first part of the compound, *bade* (line 10), which literally means *bathe* or *swim*, again with rising intonation. This time, no answer seems to be

---

1. Transcription conventions after references.
2. Rougly equivalent to "a kind of X" in English.

forthcoming from Petra (line 11), and Thomas begins elaborating on the kind of hotel to be built, one which includes a fancy waterpark (line 12). Petra overlaps toward the end of Thomas' turn with a low-volume *oh god* which is an assessment of what Thomas is saying. Immediately following the assessment, she produces two *a:h*s, change-of-state tokens (Heritage 1984a), the latter said with a distinctive pitch raise which then falls to normal range, and a yes-token, which completes her change-of-state displays as claims of understanding (lines 12–13). Next, she shows her understanding by making an accountable reference to the corresponding word for *bade* in her mother tongue, German (it is the same, *baden*) and comments that "sometimes it's so easy" (line 15). Thomas' prolonged *ah* in a smiley voice (line 14), an exaggerated repetition of Petra's change-of-state tokens, suggests that he recognized Petra's action, and his next action, his comment that "sometimes it just clicks and then you have it" (line 17), further attests to this as it describes how understanding runs off. The two *yes*-tokens at the end, showing the co-participants' alignment, close down the sequence (lines 19–20).

The extract shows the two speakers collaborating in the face of challenged intersubjectivity. In this case, Thomas reacted to a silence in a place in the conversation where an expression of epistemic alignment was expected. Thomas' turn, in other words, occasioned a response which, because it is not there, is notably absent (Schegloff 1972). Notable absence applies to second pair parts that are not forthcoming but treated as accountable actions; although there is no verbal response, the absence of the expected response is also a response. We may infer, on the basis of the assessment later (*oh god*, line 12), that Petra is aware of the interactional preference for a second pair part in this sequential position, so her silence in line 3 occasions the next action: Thomas' repair-initiation in the form of a comprehension check ("do you know what badehotel is"). Note that it is only by recourse to Thomas' repair initiation that we interpret his understanding of the absent response from Petra. This is an important point; sometimes known as an emic perspective (Firth & Wagner 1997), in a conversation analytic approach our proof lies in the participants' orientations to actions and phenomena.

These first three lines also bring to light the view of language as primarily action that we pursue and explicate empirically in this paper: Thomas' first turn is the beginning of a story-telling, Petra's non-response is an action that occasions repair, and the next action from Thomas is a comprehension check. Our understanding of this, however, is different from that found in the interaction hypothesis (cf. discussion in Eskildsen 2018). We will elaborate on this point in due course; suffice it to say here that because cognition is collaborative and socially displayed and distributed (Firth & Wagner 2007; Kasper 2009; Koschmann 2011, 2013) it is the visible reaction by the interactional co-participant that makes a particular action what it is. In other words, it is the lack of affirmation from Petra that makes Thomas' action recognizable and accountable as a comprehension check.

Thomas' action is not to teach the L2 speaker, but to achieve intersubjectivity; Petra needs to understand *badehotel* to understand what they are talking about. Her eventual displays of comprehension run off as a claim of understanding (change-of-state tokens) and an account of understanding (reference to her own language) that authorizes it. Then Thomas contributes to their emergent perspective on the interaction as an achievement of understanding, as he proclaims that "sometimes it just clicks" and new knowledge falls into place.

The interaction reveals how people envision, conceptualize and talk about comprehension processes in social encounters. There is arguably more *recognition* than learning involved here, although if one assumes learning to be a lengthy process of appropriating semiotic resources (Eskildsen & Wagner 2015), the distinction between recognizing and learning becomes blurred. What we can ascertain is that Petra engages in learning behavior by displaying and accounting for an observable change in epistemic state (Markee 2008) and that Thomas aligns with it by displaying his recognition of the account. In any case, people make it their real-time thinking visible to co-participants, and as such the learning of the new item as an act of relating it to previous knowledge becomes the responsibility of both interactants; instigated by the person learning but approved by the person already in the know. In this case, both participants make it publicly visible that they think of the situation as learning which makes it even clearer that cognition is socially anchored and shared (Kasper 2009).

Cognition is also embedded in the unfolding social practice; when Petra utters her change-of-state tokens, Thomas knows immediately what she is now understanding, and when Petra says "it is the same in German", Thomas also knows that it harks back to the word "badehotel" – even though Petra does not explicitly say any of these things. Perhaps more controversially we will also argue that this is an example of extended cognition; through language-as-action Petra and Thomas constantly display what they are currently thinking, and this results in a practice of explaining and understanding that is fundamentally co-achieved and which cannot be reduced to any one of its constituent turns-at-talk. The cognition that is revealed through turns-at-talk is only understood through an understanding of the particular turns-at-talk as social actions.

In the next section we will provide an overview of our theoretical footing and how it relates to current SLA research before moving on to presenting our empirical material.

## Background

### Interaction and SLA research

The natural point of departure for a discussion of speaking skills in second language acquisition (SLA) is the primordial purpose of speaking, which is social interaction. Humans learn to speak in, through, and for interaction. This implies that our linguistic capabilities are inherently intertwined with those of other people; the local contexts in which we deploy and learn linguistic utterances are made up of other people doing the same thing reciprocally (Eskildsen & Cadierno 2015). This has consequences for views on interaction, language, learning, and cognition as we will show.

Interaction is widely accepted as key to second language (L2) learning in many branches of research, such as conversation analytic SLA (CA-SLA) and research on L2 interactional competence (e.g., Brouwer & Wagner 2004; Firth & Wagner 1997, 2007; Hall, Hellermann, & Pekarak Doehler 2011; Hellermann 2008; Kramsch 1986; Markee 2000; Kasper 2009; Pallotti & Wagner 2011; Pekarek Doehler & Pochon-Berger 2015; Eskildsen & Theodórsdóttir 2017); socio-cultural and socio-cognitive approaches to SLA (e.g., Atkinson 2002; Hall & Verplaetse 2000; Lantolf 2011; Lantolf & Thorne 2006; Thorne & Hellermann 2015; van Compernolle 2015; Watson-Gegeo 2004); second language socialization studies (e.g.,Duff & Talmy 2011; Kanagy 1999; Zuengler & Cole 2005), usage-based approaches (e.g., Ellis 2015; Ellis & Larsen-Freeman 2006; Hall, Cheng, & Carlson 2006; Eskildsen 2012, 2015; Eskildsen & Cadierno 2015), and of course cognitive-interactionist research based on Long's Interaction Hypothesis (e.g., Long 1996; Mackey 2013).

Although the research listed here, even with only a fraction mentioned, is too rich and varied to be discussed in any way that would do justice to all its findings, it seems to make sense to mention them here and try to capture in very general terms what co-affiliates them. Apart from Long's framework, which is essentially about input processing (Block 2003; Mackey 2013; cf. discussion in Eskildsen 2018), there are shared assumptions, especially about the nature of cognition and language learning, among the branches of research listed above. Language learning and the cognitive processes that go into it are viewed as fundamentally embodied, socially situated, and socially shared; they cannot in any meaningful way be abstracted away from contextualized usage. Even the more cognitively oriented approaches embrace the notion that cognition is both embodied and socially shared (MacWhinney 1999, 2005; de Bot & Larsen-Freeman 2011; Ellis 2014; Ortega 2014; Roehr-Brackin 2015).

There is, then, a field-historical point to be made. As pointed out in numerous places over the last two decades, SLA was, for some time, perceived primarily as a cognitive science (e.g., Markee 1994; Firth & Wagner 1997; Block 2003; Doughty & Long 2003; Atkinson 2011). The 1990s saw a discussion, at times hostile, between proponents of theory culling and theory proliferation, and instead of reconciliation there was a "never the twain shall meet" air to the scene; the field was splitting up into a mainstream, cognitivist branch centered around input processing vis à vis the Interaction Hypothesis (Long 1996; Mackey 2013) and a series of what came to be known as alternative approaches to SLA (Atkinson 2011). The scene is changing; while the Interaction Hypothesis continues to live on in the same form since Long (1996), producing variations on the insight that interaction in terms of negotiation for meaning plays a supportive role in L2 learning (Gass 2003, 2015; Gass & Mackey 2007; Fujii & Mackey 2009; Mackey 2013), the so-called alternative approaches are producing a wealth of diverse insights. This is attested by the richness of the literature mentioned above and related recent position papers and book-length publications that move the field forward such as Hulstijn et al.'s (2014) attempt to bridge the gap between cognitive and social SLA, May's (2014) edited collection exploring the role of multilingualism in applied linguistics, Cadierno & Eskildsen's (2015) edited volume on usage-based approaches to SLA, van Compernolle & McGregor's (2016) edited volume on authenticity and interaction in L2 learning, the Douglas Fir Group position paper on a transdisciplinary framework for SLA (2016), and forthcoming edited volumes on CA advances in classroom L2 research (Kunitz, Sert, & Markee, forthcoming) and language learning in the wild (Hellermann et al., forthcoming).

It is therefore archaic to distinguish between a mainstream, cognitivist SLA and an esoteric social SLA (cf. Swain & Deters 2007). Especially since Firth and Wagner (1997) called for a reconceptualized SLA and urged the field to expand the database beyond the classroom and reconsider the role of language use in language learning, SLA has complexified and diversified. It has now come to sustain a multitude of approaches, theories, methodologies, and empirical ecologies that each go hand in hand with particular epistemologies and research interests. Now, 20 years later, CA-SLA is an established research paradigm whose results are being published not only in the *Journal of Pragmatics, The Modern Language Journal, International Review of Applied Linguistics,* and *Applied Linguistics* but also in *Language Learning* (Hauser 2013; Markee & Kunitz 2013; Burch 2014; Eskildsen & Wagner 2015), one of the most widely read and influential journals in the field of SLA. For us the social embeddedness of cognition, language, and learning and the interest we take in conversation as the primordial site of human sociality (Schegloff 1987) makes CA and its ethnomethodological roots the most relevant theoretical and epistemological starting point.

## Ethnomethodology and conversation analysis[3]

We now move on to briefly outline ethnomethodology (EM) and conversation analysis (CA). Following Garfinkel (1967), EM is a radically emic (participant-relevant) form of sociology that emerged in the 1960s (other key references on EM include: Button 1991; Button et al. 1995; Francis & Hester 2004; ten Have 2004; and Heritage, 1984b). More specifically, in contrast with the etic (researcher-relevant) methods then commonly used in sociology to elucidate how independent variables such as socio-economic status might explain, say, ultimate educational achievement, Garfinkel sought to develop a commonsense, members' understanding of how they accomplished, for themselves and for others, the unremarkable actions of everyday life in real time. EM thus represented a rather significant break with the ontological and epistemic certainties of the day.

The most well-known spin-off of EM to this day is CA. CA seeks to explain how various interactional practices – specifically, turn taking, repair, sequence and preference organization (see ten Have 2007; Hutchby & Wooffitt 2008; Sacks, Schegloff, & Jefferson 1974; Schegloff 1979, 2007; Schegloff, Jefferson, & Sacks 1977; Schegloff et al. 2002) – specify the underlying architecture of *talk-in-interaction*. This latter term (coined by Schegloff 1987) subsumes: 1) ordinary conversation, which is viewed as the default speech exchange system in CA; and (2) institutional talk of various kinds (see Drew & Heritage 1992; Heritage & Clayman 2010). So, for example, classroom talk is a speech exchange system in which the practices of ordinary conversation are systematically modified to enact various courses of institutionally relevant action (cf. e.g., Markee 2000; McHoul 1978; Mehan 1979; 1990; Seedhouse 2004). From a methodological perspective, CA uses audio or (preferably) video recordings of naturally occurring talk-in-interaction as primary data, from which secondary data consisting of transcripts that are worked up to various degrees of granularity are constructed (see Jefferson 2004 for the default system for transcribing talk only, and Goodwin 2013 and Mondada 2016 as two important recent examples of how embodied talk is being transcribed nowadays). These transcripts enable researchers to analyze the most transient, microscopic details of talk-in-interaction at leisure.

## Socially distributed cognition

There are at least three different ways in which cognition can be said to be socially distributed. Following Robbins and Aydede (2009), we can talk about *embedded* mind, *embodied* mind and *extended* mind. The construct of embedded mind ulti-

---

3. This section is revised and updated from Markee (2011).

mately derives from the ground-breaking work of Hutchins (1995) on cognition "in the wild". Hutchins was one of the first researchers to develop an interactional account of how cognition is embedded in larger social, often technological contexts. Thus, Hutchins showed empirically how simultaneous, real time decision-making on the bridge of a US warship is distributed across multiple parties who have different responsibilities and obligations, and who use different navigational and communication tools to collaboratively steer this ship out of trouble. The concept of embodied cognition – that is, how the mind is shaped by the body – is traceable to (among others) the philosopher of mind Gallagher (2005). In the multi-modal CA literature that is closer to our present concerns (see, for example, Goodwin 2000a, 2000b, 2003a, 2003b, 2007, 2013; Mondada 2014a, 2014b, 2014c, 2016; Mortensen 2011; Neville 2015; Seo & Koshik 2012) we can see how eye-gaze, pointing and other gestures are routinely choreographed with talk by participants to achieve multi-semiotic displays of cognition-done-as-behavior in real time. The argument made by these and other authors is that, if we are to understand how interaction observably works from an emic perspective, these different layers of semiosis cannot be isolated one from another. Rather, they must be understood as a unified whole. In recent work, Eskildsen and Wagner (2013, 2015, in press) have shown how such situated, embodied sense-making work plays into long-term L2 learning of particular linguistic-interactional resources.

Finally, there is extended cognition, which is undoubtedly the most controversial category in the trinity of socially distributed cognition (see, for example, Rupert's 2011 very dense critique of Clark 2008). Extended cognition has to do with how participants achieve particular courses of action whose sum is greater than its individual parts. These courses of action are inherently *inter*actional; they are the result of the work people carry out together to reach intersubjectivity which, in essence, is what drives interaction. Interaction is a collaborative achievement irreducible to any one particular contribution, turn-at-talk, or individual mind. Learning to speak crucially concerns learning to navigate in this interactional reality of monitoring other people's behavior and using constantly calibrated and recalibrated semiotic resources to act, behave, and respond in ways that make sense to others.

## Empirical data

### Showcasing embedded, embodied, and extended cognition

Let us now take a look at some empirical, interactional examples of how participants achieve these different categories of socially distributed mind in and through observable talk. The first examples are taken from Markee and Kunitz (2013), who were originally concerned with showing how planning – a traditionally individual cognitive construct (see R. Ellis 2005, 2009) – may be understood as socially distributed activity. Here, we analyze the interactional work three students (John, Mary and Lucy who were taking Italian as a foreign language at an American University; all names are pseudonyms) do to figure out the grammatical gender, masculine, of the Italian word "ristorante". At the beginning of their planning talk (which is spread out over three different sessions), the three students incorrectly assume that this word is a feminine noun. However, just prior to Extract 2, Lucy questions whether John is right in his on-going assertions that "ristorante" is feminine. Note that, up to this point, the way in which all three students have been referring to the gender of this word is by talking about either "la ristorante" or "il ristorante" – i.e. by using the gender marked (feminine and masculine) pronouns, respectively, that mean "the" in Italian. John at first resists Lucy's re-analysis of the gender of "ristorante," but finally proposes to break the deadlock by invoking the indisputable, and external, epistemic authority of an online, bilingual English-Italian dictionary (WebReference), to which the students observably have real time access on Mary's laptop (screen shot, Picture 1).

**Extract 2**

```
57          (3.6)
58 MAR:     °restaurant↘°
59          (1.2)
```

Picture 1

```
60 JOH:     it's MAsculine↘ you're right↘
```

Here we see examples of *socially embedded* and *extended* cognition. More specifically, in lines 57–59, Mary is searching for the WebReference website on her laptop and eventually finds the entry for "restaurant/ristorante" shown above. And in line 60, John not only emphatically recognizes that "ristorante" is a " *Ma*sculine" noun but that Lucy was correct all along in making this claim. This fragment therefore illustrates how: (1) the three speakers use tools in their environment (specifically, Mary's laptop, and the WordReference website) as locally relevant aide-memoires that: (2) effectively extend cognition beyond the confines of the individual skull by: (3) talking these socially embedded resources into relevance in and through their talk. Moreover, John's brief switch from their previous vernacular discussion of gender (i.e., whether the word is "la ristorante" or "il ristorante") to the more technically grammatical term "masculine" seems to be occasioned by the technologically mediated representation of the grammar, "ristorante *m*". However, as we will now see, the students quickly revert to their more vernacular way of talking about grammar in Extract 3. This fragment illustrates what *embodied* and *extended* cognition look and sound like.

### Extract 3

```
61        (1.0)
62 MAR:   s:o:
```
                                              Picture 2

```
63        (0.5)
64 LUC:   uh⌈m ⌉
65 JOH:    ⌊il⌋ risto⌈ran°te° ⌉
66 MAR:            ⌊b/i/enve⌋nu ⌈ti:⌉
67 JOH:                       ⌊nos⌋tro↘
68 LUC:   alli: (.) nostro:: o:r yeah (.) u::h=
69 JOH:   =a:l
70 LUC:   ⌈a:l⌉
71 MAR:   ⌊al ⌋
72 LUC:   (h)t(h) a(h)l no(h)⌈stro⌉
73 MAR:                      ⌊rist⌋oran°te::°
74        (0.3)
75 MAR:   p̲asta hut
76        (0.3)
77 JOH:   p̲asta hut
```

In this extract (which follows immediately after Extract 2), the students are simultaneously: (1) *summarizing* what they have just learned about the gender of the word "ristorante" (line 65, in which John switches back to talking about "il ristorante") and (2) *rehearsing* the final version of a script line ("bienvenuti al nostro ristorante Pasta Hut/welcome to our restaurant Pasta Hut;" lines 66–77) that they will use in a skit to be presented in their final in-class presentations. Notice that the emic analysis that Mary is doing a summary of what they have just learned in lines 61–64 involves two separate but converging pieces of evidence. First, she produces the word "so" in line 61, which, in this particular sequential context, verbally looks back to the interaction in Extract 2 and essentially says: "we all now agree on this point." But, in addition, this analysis also invokes Mary's simultaneous *embodied* action of leaning back (Picture 2) as she says "so," which constitutes another locally relevant layer of semiosis that visually reinforces the idea that the current course of social action has just been completed. Finally, note that the production of the final script line ("bienvenuti al nostro ristorante Pasta Hut") that occurs in lines 66–77 looks forward to anticipated action. Furthermore, the social course of action of rehearsal is achieved as *extended-mind-in-action* through the interactional resources of repair and collaborative completions of each other's turns as the participants collectively struggle to formulate their final script line for later use.

## Collaborative word searches[4]

The prior section demonstrated empirically the embedded, embodied, and extended nature of cognition in a planning activity. We now extend this insight to bear on other learning and teaching practices, starting with word searches. While word searches were also prominent in the planning activities discussed above (see Markee & Kunitz 2013), they constitute a general and very frequent collaborative interactional practice that concerns how speakers initiate and carry out repair in the face of lacking vocabulary. Repair is a well-described phenomenon; it is the interactional organization of orienting to problems in understanding and restoring intersubjectivity (Schegloff et al. 1977; Schegloff 1992). Word searches can be carried out through the use of a lingua franca and/or explicitly marked through a request for help (e.g. *how do you say (x)?, is it ok to say X?*), or implicitly marked through turn-design (e.g. pauses and try-marking through rising intonation) (Brouwer 2003; Kurhila 2006; Mori 2010; Eskildsen 2011; Mortensen 2011; Theodórsdóttir & Eskildsen 2011). As such, word searches have been shown to be collaborative learning activities and recently, with the appropriate longitudinal data, they have been documented to have repercussions for long-term language learning (Eskildsen 2018). It should be noted, however, that word searches are not exclusive to L2 speakers (Brouwer 2003; Goodwin & Goodwin 1986; Hayashi 2003). By implication, not all word searches constitute L2 learning activities. This depends on the ensuing interaction. In the following we will show how a word search unfolds as collaborative learning activities. In Extract 4, from the same database as Extract 1, the participants are Tina (TIN) and Mona (MON) (German students of L2 Danish) and Anne-Mette (ANM) (Danish student of L2 German). They are talking about where they live, and at lines 1–2 Tina is telling the others that she would like to move to a particular student dorm, but when she is about

---

4. The introduction to word searches and the analysis of Extract 4 are based on Eskildsen (2018).

to give the reason she runs into trouble, makes a noise of being annoyed in smiley voice, and begins laughing.

### Extract 4

```
01 TIN: jeg vil os gerne flytte til slettestrand kollegiet (1.2) fordi jeg har
02      ikke (1.2) ehm (1.9) ehm (2.8) ☺orh☺ hehhehheh .hhh=

        i would also like to move to slettestrand dorm    because i have
        not
03 T/M: =°kitchen↗°
04      (0.9)
05 ANM: køkken↗
        kitchen↗
06 TIN: køkken jeg ikke en: køkken (0.5) og jeg vil gerne (.) ha en: (1.1) (jaer)
07      (2.1) i: min: eh værelse↗ (1.6) jeg vil gerne ehm have et køkken
        kitchen i not a: kitchen        and i would like    to have on:e (yes)
              in: my:    room↗        i would like to have a kitchen
08 ANM: ja↗
        yes↗
09 TIN: ja hmf
        yes
10 MON: ja jeg bor i slettestrand kollegiet hehhehheh .hh og jeg har en køkken heh
11      heh heh heh heh heh .hh det er rigtig godt så vi kan ø:h køkken sammen
12      (.) å: det verbum↗
        yes I live in slettestrand dorm       and I have a kitchen
                                     it is really good so we can kitchen together
              an:d that verb↗
13      (0.9)
14 ANM: så vi ka: (.) <-lave mad->
        so we can:        cook
15 MON: oh ⌈så vi ⌉ kan lave mad sammen jahaer .hh
        oh so we can cook together yehes
16 ANM:   ⌊sammen⌋
           together
```

The item missing from Tina's turn is then provided by either Tina or Mona – the low volume makes it difficult to discern their voices (line 3). It is delivered with rising intonation which passes the floor to a next speaker. Following a pause, Anne-Mette responds by delivering the item in Danish, *køkken*, also with rising intonation (line 5). Tina accepts "køkken" as the solution to her word search and then explains, using the new word "køkken" twice, that she does not have a kitchen but would like to have one (lines 6–7). This is the reason why she would like to move to another student dorm and her turn initiated in lines 1–2 is now complete. Anne-Mette then signals listenership and Tina yields the floor (lines 8–9). Then, at line 11, Mona also displays having noticed "køkken" as she declares that she lives in the dorm in question and that she does have a kitchen (lines 10–12). As such she displays alignment with Tina's story but she also moves the story further as she assesses the living situation as "really good" because they can cook together. That results in another word search for the Danish word for "cook", "lave mad" (literally "make food"), which Anne-Mette provides upon request from Mona (line 14). Mona picks it up and finishes her turn (line 15).

Here we have an L2 speaker, Tina, who goes from not having a word available to getting it and using it. Whether produced by Tina or Mona, it is the occurrence of "kitchen" that occasions Anne-Mette's candidate response, *køkken*, which then leads to Tina's repetition and use of the item. These turns constitute and establish the activity as a word search; i.e., it does not belong to any one participant. Rather, it is a collaborative sense-making activity, carried out to achieve and maintain intersubjectivity and following general turn-taking procedures in story-tellings that are paused while the word search is carried out and continued when it is resolved (Brouwer 2003, 2004).

The collaborative nature of interaction is particularly evident in the search for "lave mad", the Danish word for "cook". Here, Anne-Mette builds on Mona's syntactic structure when she provides "lave mad", packaged in Mona's format "så vi kan lave mad" ("so we can cook"). She even reuses "sammen" ("together") in overlap with Mona's display of noticing "lave mad" – a term which Mona had also used in her turn leading to the word search. This implies that the ownership of language implied by *input* and *output* in much cognitivist SLA is empirically misguided (Firth & Wagner 2007; cf. discussion in Eskildsen 2018). Of course, this is just one empirical example of the distributed nature of language and cognition and as such it may be dismissed by critics as exotic. There are three things to say to this: (1) while there is power in numbers, setting a numerical threshold for when a phenomenon is pervasive is in principle arbitrary; (2) the collaborative way in which things are demonstrably done consists of members' mundane methods of accomplishing intersubjectivity, and from an emic perspective such methods are never exotic; and (3) the fact is that interactional practices, including word searches, are at heart collaborative and dependent on participants' publicly noticeable recognition of each other's turns-at-talk as particular actions that are current displays of thinking. This runs as an undercurrent through the examples shown so far – and will also be evident in the remaining empirical examples. The way language is too often predicated, as an individually owned monolith, is the obscure and exotic way; if we agree that interaction is the driving force for L2 learning, then we should take next (implicational) step and concern ourselves with what it is, namely a collaborative thing which defies dissection into discernible parts owned and controlled solely and exclusively by any one particular individual.

## Collaborative completion

The next Extract (5) showcases collaborative completion, a practice that has been documented as a frequent feature in naturally occurring talk (Goodwin 1979; Lerner 1991; Jacoby & Ochs 1995). The extract comes from an oral proficiency interview with a Spanish speaking learner of L2 English.[5] ROS is the L2 learner

Rosa and INT is the American interviewer. They are talking about Rosa's unemployment. Prior to the extract, Rosa has been telling the interviewer how difficult it is to get a job within her field of expertise. In line 1, the interviewer asks Rosa if her previous work place might be an option.

**Extract 5**

```
01 INT:    and you don't wanna go back to the bank or < -anything- > ↘
02 ROS:    .hhh ↑we:ll (.) hh you know when you're unemployed hh heh heh ⌈heh
03 INT:                                                                  ⌊you'll do
04         anythin⌈g heh hmhm
05 ROS:          ⌊yeah ⌈heh heh⌉
```

The interviewer designs her question as a (negative) declarative with slightly falling intonation to which the preferred response is usually a confirmatory alignment (Stivers 2010), which in this case, especially considering the "or anything" at the end, would be a "no"-response (Heritage & Robinson 2011). Rosa, however, does not align with the confirmatory request; producing a dispreferred response, indicated by the turn-initial *well*, she begins to contradict it instead (line 2), saying *you know when you're unemployed* and laughing. The response is thus incomplete, waiting for the interviewer to complement it. This is not only because it is an unfinished "when-then"-construction without a "then"-part, it is also because Rosa has already invited the interviewer to chip in by way of the turn-initial "you know" (Östman 1981; Fox Tree, & Schrock 2002). Accordingly the interviewer supplies the pending "then"-part, *you'll do anything* and joins the laughter (lines 3–4). After that, Rosa continues, first by acknowledging their co-achieved agreement, *yeah*, and then (not shown here) by exemplifying what "anything" might be (computers, accounting).

This extract shows the intricate collaborative work that speaking in interaction is. The co-participants are constantly monitoring each other's on-going turns at talk and displaying alignment with each other. The collaborative completion in the "when-then"-turns is crucial to our points here because not only does it show how cognition works beyond the individual, it also shows that people are aware of this and may draw on it as a resource. Rosa might have finished the entire "when-then"-construction herself, but she does not; rather, she invites her co-participant to complete the action. Her accepting response, in turn, shows that this was, indeed, where she wanted to go. Collaborative achievements and other kinds of doing distributed cognition are, in other words, mundane methods for achieving intersubjecvitity.

---

5.  We thank Gale Stam for permission to use the data here and Rineke Brouwer for analytical insights. For more information about Rosa, please see Stam (2015).

## Embedded, embodied, and extended cognition in learning over time

The final set of data (Extracts 6a–e) shows the full ecology of embedded, embodied and extended cognition involved in the teaching and learning of two expressions, "it is incorrect" and "let me help you". The data come from the Multimedia Adult English Learner Corpus, which consists of audio-visual recordings of classroom interaction in a U.S. English as a second language context (Reder 2005). The focal student in the data is Carlos, an adult Mexican Spanish-speaking student in the class (cf. e.g. Eskildsen 2015, 2016), and the extracts are all from his first 8 months in class.

In Extract 6a Gabriel is writing on the whiteboard. The situation is portrayed in Picture 3. In lines 1–2, two of the students produce "no no no" and "no E", respectively. We know that these utterances work as assessments from Gabriel's reaction (he stops writing and looks toward the teacher, line 3) and from the teacher's response (lines 4–7). She corrects the students' way of doing the assessment, targeting her expression at Alejandro's turn (line 1). His "no no no" is uttered with falling intonation and stretched vowels which makes it sound impatient or tired. The teacher (line 4) indexes Alejandro's talk by asking a rhetorical question ("who said...?") and reenacting and exaggerating his epistemic stance by repeating the "nos" in a sing-song fashion and posing with her hands on her hips, a posture which can indicate that issues need to be dealt with (Pease & Pease 2006). Abandoning the posture and placing her left hand on her heart, perhaps indicating a more empathetic stance, she then offers an alternative candidate expression "oh no I don't think so let me help you". This results in heavy repair and repetition work on the part of the students (lines 8–12).

**Extract 6a**

Picture 3

```
01 ALE:   n:no: no: no:↘
02 THA:   no E
03 GAB:   stops writing, turns around, looks in dir. of teacher (pic 4)
```

Picture 4

```
04 TEA:   *tseh (.) who said *£no: no: no: no: ⌈no:£
          *turns around        *begins hands-on-hips pose (pic 5)
```
Picture 5

```
05 MUL:                                   ⌊eh ⌈heh heh heh heh heh .hh⌉
06 TEA:                                       *⌊how abou:t £o:h        ⌋ no=
                                              *terminates hands-on-hips pose
07 TEA:   =*I don't think so let me help you:↘£
          *places left hand on torso over her heart (pic 6)
```
Picture 6

```
08 UNI:   what what
09 CAR:   wha- one more ⌈time
10 TEA:                 ⌊let me help you
11 MUL:   ((attempts at repeating "let me help you"))
12 TEA:   let me help you
13 CAR:   o:⌈h
14 TEA:     ⌊*come↘
               *gestures "come"
15 CAR:   ⌈let me-              ⌉let me- let me ⌈help you
16 TEA:   ⌊who's going to help him⌋*
                             *TEA summons THA by gesturing (pic 7)
```
Picture 7

```
17 UNI:                                    ⌊let me help you
18 THA:   ⌈gets up .hh heh walks to Gabriel
19 CAR:   ⌊help you
20 TEA:   <-let me help ⌈you->
```

```
21 CAR:                ⌊help you
22 TEA:  let me help you (1.0) let me help you
```

Our focal student, Carlos, then expresses a hearable change-of-state token (Heritage 1984a) indicating that he has now understood something (line 13). In overlap the teacher is moving on to the next activity, namely selecting a student, Thamarin, to correct Gabriel's writing. She does this while still orienting to the students', in particular Carlos', rehearsing and dissecting the new phrase (lines 14–22). Ultimately (not shown), the teacher specifically tells the students not to say "no no no you're wrong" before she writes what transpires as the key phrase, "let me help you", on the whiteboard.

The extract illustrates many of our points. The teacher's displayed understanding of Alejandro's "no no no no" as an epistemic stance marker through her posture shows her embodied understanding of the turn as a particular action. She then presents the students with an alternative, more situationally appropriate action that not only works as an epistemic stance marker ("oh I don't think so") but also as a display of an intention to help restore epistemic equilibrium ("let me help you"). This is done in a highly embodied fashion where the teacher first reenacted Alejandro's turn and then changed her posture to one that seems to correspond better with a more empathetic stance.

Ten minutes later Carlos draws the teacher's attention to something he finds questionable on the whiteboard (lines 1–4, Extract 6b). Carlos is sitting in the front row and the teacher is right in front of him, so she can see his actions. At line 1 he utters a soft "no" and accompanies it with a thinking face. The teacher launches her next question in overlap with which Carlos begins moving his hand away from his face, abandoning the thinking face. The teacher then cuts off her turn-so-far and orients to Carlos' actions, as displayed through her *yes* and shift in eye-gaze (line 2). Carlos begins pointing and the teacher shifts her gaze to the whiteboard (lines 2–3); through this, we know that Carlos is pointing to something on the whiteboard which they have thus co-established as their joint attentional focus.

**Extract 6b**

```
01 CAR: °no-° puts r. hand to mouth, thinking-face (pic 8)
```

Picture 8

```
02 TEA: do  %you go to bed- *yes¤→
            %CAR begins moving r. hand toward TEA/whiteboard (pic 9)
                        *establishes mutual eye-gaze w. CAR (pic 10)
                            ¤CAR begins pointing gesture (pic 11)
                    Picture 9
```

Picture 9

Picture 10

Picture 11

```
03 CAR:  %I'm not sure is- whis correct
         %TEA shifts gaze to whiteboard, following CAR's pointing (pic 12)
                        Picture 12
```

Picture 12

```
04 TEA: ↑oh takes eraser, shifts gaze to CAR/class (pic 13)
            Picture 13
```

```
05 CAR: *ai- ⌈A M↗⌉
        *abandons pointing gesture
06 LIN:      ⌊A M↘⌋
07 TEA:  okay (.) so: ⌈*we say let %me #help you heh ¤heh heh heh heh heh  heh.hh=
```

```
                              *looks toward where she wrote the phrase (pic 14)
                   Picture 14
```

```
08 CAR:                    ⌊*is e:h-
                           *begins pointing gesture (pic 15)
                                    %CAR points in dir of TEA's gaze (pic 16)
                                        #TEA reestablishes mutual gaze w. CAR (pic 17)
                                              ¤CAR abandons pointing
                                                        gesture
                   Picture 15
```

```
                   Picture 16
```

```
                                        Picture 17
```

```
09 TEA: = *.hh hokay⌄ (.) so what is ⌈it⌄
             *puts eraser to board, looks in dir of CAR/class (pic 18)
                   Picture 18
```

```
10 MUL:                              ⌊( ⌈ )
11 CAR:                                 ⌊eh⌄ (.) e:h let me help you ⌈.hh-⌉
12 TEA:                                                            ⌊okay⌋
13      come ⌈and help me heh heh heh heh hh okay  ⌉
14 CAR:      ⌊*e:h is correct the:: A M no the P M ⌋ (.) is: (.) ⌈A M ⌉
              *begins pointing gesture
15 TEA:                                                    *⌊okay⌋=
                   *erases
16 TEA: =(1.5) A M *thank you very much⌄
                   *writes AM
```

```
17 TEA:  *before you say let me help you you can say (2.5) <-it is in::correct->
         *writes "it is incorrect" above "let me help you" (pic 19)
                                        Picture 19
```

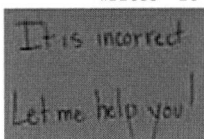

```
18 MU/C: it is incorrect incorrect
19 TEA:  it is incorrect okay let me help you very good okay
```

Still pointing, Carlos begins verbalizing his epistemic stance towards what is written (line 3). As the transcription reveals, Carlos does not do this entirely by conventional linguistic means, but there is not orientation to this on the part of the participants.[6] The teacher utters a high-pitch change-of-state token, reaches for the whiteboard eraser, and shifts gaze back to Carlos (line 4). In response, Carlos abandons his pointing gesture and simply says "AM" in overlap with another student (lines 5–6). The teacher then shifts her focus away from the current correcting and begins orienting, verbally and bodily, to "let me help you", the phrase from the prior interaction which she wrote on the other side of the whiteboard (line 7). In overlap, however, Carlos seemingly continues the correcting activity, saying "is e:h" and initiating a new pointing gesture towards the whiteboard (line 8). He abandons this turn and instead shows alignment with the teacher as he points in the direction where she is currently looking. She then shifts her gaze back to Carlos and Carlos abandons the pointing. These embodied actions serve to establish a joint attentional focus and intersubjectivity.

Carlos takes the teacher's next action (line 9) as an elicitation of the phrase they just co-indexed as their focus as he provides "let me help you" as a response (line 11). The teacher, however, does not respond to his action as a delivery of an elicited item but instead she responds to it as an offer of assistance that she accepts (lines 12–13). Carlos then begins doing the correcting from PM to AM (line 14). The teacher makes the correction and thanks him (line 16).

The teacher's next move (line 17) is to teach the class to say "it is incorrect" before they say "let me help you". She then writes this new phrase beneath the previous one on the whiteboard. Ultimately, the students repeat "it is incorrect" following which the teacher, yet again, repeats both "it is incorrect" and "let me help you" followed by positive feedback (lines 18–19).

The teacher has now taught the class to use *it is incorrect* and *let me help you* when correcting / helping others with the task at hand. Another ten minutes later, the teacher is instructing the students to listen to and correct each other if they

---

6. The "whis" in Carlos' turn in the transcript is an attempt at representing orthographically what he says.

make mistakes in the use of "yes I am/no I'm not" and "yes I do/no I don't" (lines
1–2, Extract 6c). She does this in an embodied fashion; she enacts "listening" by
putting her hand to her ear, but she also enacts her example, shaking her head and
flipping her wrist downwards in a rejection gesture upon saying "no I'm not" (line
2). In her example, "no I'm not" is a wrong answer because her question was "do
you work". Therefore her high-pitched "huh" together with her head movement,
pushing her chin forward, work as an embodied, enacted repair-initiation.

**Extract 6c**

```
01 TEA:  and *listen to your partner's answer↘ if I say do you work and you say=
              *puts r. hand to r. ear (pic 20)
               Picture 20
```

```
02       =*mm %no I'm not ¤↑.hhuh
            *shakes head (pic 21)
               %flips wrist downwards (pic 22)
                       ¤pushes chin forward (pic 23)
                   Picture 21
```

```
                 Picture 22
```

```
             Picture 23
```

```
03       (2.4)
```

```
04 ROS:   °do you work↗°
05 CAR:   what dyou say
06        (0.8)
07 TEA:   ⌈do you-⌉
08 CAR:   ⌊is inco⌋rrect↘ smiles
09 TEA:   hhyou heh -> whaddoyou⌈say < - ⌉ *it's incor%rect↘ (.)  < -let me %help you- > =
                                          *makes pose, moves hips (pic 24)
                                                    %changes
                                                    pose
                                                    (pic 25)
```

Picture 24

Picture 25

```
10 CAR:                            ⌊hehheh⌋
                                                  %CAR nods
11 TEA:   =very good okay .hh do ⌈you work↗        ⌉
12 CAR:                          ⌊*let me help you ⌋
                                  *looks toward phrase on board (pic 26)
                                  Picture 26
```

At first intersubjectivity is challenged, as one student does a soft repeat of the question (line 4) and Carlos initiates repair (line 5). He then, in overlap with the teacher, says "is incorrect" (line 8) and gives a smile which causes the teacher to laugh (line 9) before she acknowledges his answer by repeating it. Through Carlos' response and the teacher's acceptance of it we now know what her action in lines 1–2 was. The teacher then moves on to re-index their joint teaching/learning moment from before by relating "it's incorrect" to "let me help you" (line 9). Carlos shows recognition and understanding of this through a repeat of "let me help you" and a gaze in the direction of where the teacher wrote the phrase on the whiteboard.

We note with interest that the teacher does a funny pose with an air of superiority upon the repeat of "it's incorrect". Perhaps she is enacting that it is pragmatically awkward to point out other people's mistakes that bluntly. When she utters "let me help you" she changes her pose to a more inviting one as she extends her hand, palm open upwards, towards Carlos on "help".

In an interaction four days later, Carlos displays having noticed a mistake in his own writing on the board by announcing *the my is incorrect* and getting up to correct it; "the my" is a common way for him to say "mine" (line 1, Extract 6d). The teacher does an open-class repair initiator and Carlos repeats his prior turn (lines 2–3) while pointing (presumably to his writing on the whiteboard) and walking to the whiteboard.

**Extract 6d**

```
01 CAR:   ?well? the my is incorrect gets up
02 TEA:   what↗
03 CAR:   the my is incorrect begins, walks board, pointing
04 TEA:   yours is not correct↗ okay correct it then↘ very good
```

The teacher's next action may work as a comprehension check and an embedded repair; her emphasis on "yours" suggests that her focus is on Carlos' erroneous pronoun, but Carlos does not respond and the teacher makes a quick transition, by way of "okay", to her next action, namely to encourage Carlos to correct his writing (line 4).

**Extract 6e**

```
01 STE:   *that's ⌈%I:: that's I⌉
          *points to Rosario's writing, facing ROS, moving closer to her (pic 27)
              %ROS puts cap on pen, moves backwards (pic 28)
```

Picture 27

Picture 28

```
02 CAR:        ⌊*hhh let me- ⌋
               *gets up, walks to whiteboard
```

```
03 STE:   eh ⌜heh *heh heh .hh⌝
                 *reaches towards ROS (pic 29)
                 Picture 29
```

```
04 CAR:      ⌊let me help her⌋
05 STE:   o%ka⌜y⌶ steps closer to ROS (pic 30)
             %ROS looks past teacher towards CAR who is approaching (pic 30)
                 Picture 30
```

```
06 ROS:      ⌊no #teacher
                 #evades TEA, signals giving pen to CAR (pic 31)
                 Picture 31
```

```
07 STE:   hh heh ⌜hah hah hah hah hah .hh        ⌝
08 CAR:          ⌊let me %help her heh heh heh⌋
                        %ROS gives pen to CAR (pic 32)
```

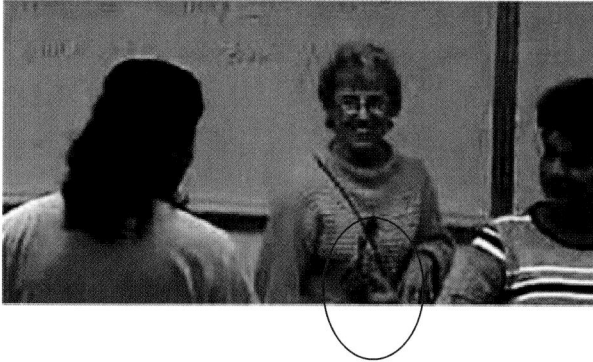

Picture 32

09 STE:    o:kay◞

The substitute teacher continues to try to help Rosario, moving in closer to her, but Rosario physically evades the teacher and signals handing over the pen to Carlos who is on his way (lines 3–6). She does the signaling by way of a head-nod and slight flip of the wrist toward Carlos. Carlos then repeats his request for permission, *let me help her*, which the teacher accepts post festum – i.e. it follows after Rosario has given Carlos the pen (lines 8–9) – following which Carlos makes the correction. We note that Carlos accomplishes three things through the use of "let me help her": he displays understanding of the trouble in the situation (Rosario's skills and the insufficiency of the teacher's guidance), and he asks the teacher to grant him permission to help while displaying to Rosario's his willingness to help. Rosario's and the teacher's next actions confirm this as they, respectively, give Carlos the pen and acknowledge his right to help.

## Discussion and conclusion

We have shown, through fine-grained analyses of particular L2 practices, that L2 talk is a social accomplishment. Language, cognition, and learning are fundamentally embedded in the local circumstances of talk-in-environment and distributed across participants and, as the video data further showcase, inherently embodied. While all our data to varying degrees lend testimony to these observations, as also pointed out throughout the analyses, they probably materialize at their clearest in Extracts 6a-e, so this section will draw mostly on these.

These final data showed how a teacher taught her students the two phrases *it's incorrect* and *let me help you* in a highly contextualized fashion, in environments where she explicitly linked the expressions to particular actions of pointing out mistakes and volunteering to correct the mistakes. She has afforded the L2 students opportunities to use specific semiotic resources for specific actions in specific environments. Carlos learns and uses these expressions in these recurring environments around activities that occasion the uses. He displays the interactional competence in the classroom as community of practice to be able to volunteer, write on the communal board, correct himself and others, and help others. Through an understanding of those practices he learns the linguistic tools, taught by the teacher, to index and / or express the upcoming action. Whether or not other teachers would have preferred to teach other linguistic tools for accomplishing these particular actions is irrelevant to our point which is that language is here taught and learned as a semiotic resource for social action (Eskildsen in press).

These data also showcase the complex ecology of situated language learning. The co-participants continuously display that they are navigating the environment and using resources within it. Cases in point include the teacher's repeated orientations to the whiteboard and the phrases she wrote there. Cognition is, in other words, deeply embedded in and contingent upon the materiality and configuration of the local space. We know this not because we can see the writing on the board, but because of participants' visible orientations; i.e., the participants constantly display their current thinking through verbal and bodily actions. They do not just speak; they enact, point, nod, shift gaze etc. Cognition is, then, not only embedded, it is also embodied and socially shared. On a methodological note we therefore make a call for increased awareness of the importance of using video data for microanalytic research. The use of audio only, while advantageous because it is less intrusive (or at least used to be, before the advent of small, high-quality videorecorders such as GoPro), has obvious epistemological limitations; we simply lose access to the environment and the embodied behavior that play such essential roles in learning-in-interaction.

In addition to showing the embedded and embodied nature of cognition, we also see here examples of extended cognition; through language-as-action the co-participants, notably the teacher and Carlos, accomplish teaching, explaining, understanding, and learning in a way that is fundamentally co-constructed and which cannot be reduced to any one of its constituent turns-at-talk. This was also found to apply to the word search practices analyzed earlier. Cognition emerges as distributed across participants and fundamentally contingent upon their actions in the service of achieving and maintaining intersubjectivity. The teaching and learning of language-as-a-semiotic-resource-for-social-action achieved in these final excerpts ultimately rest on contingencies in the local ecology (cognition is embedded), bodily actions (cognition is embodied), and fundamentally collaborative practices that are irreducible to any one particular contribution, turn-at-talk, or individual mind (cognition is socially shared and extended beyond the individual). Learning to speak therefore crucially concerns learning to navigate local ecologies, to monitor other people's behavior, and to use constantly recalibrated semiotic resources to act, behave, and respond in ways that make sense to others.

Through a range of data from different settings, surrounding different phenomena, we have shown the locally situated nature of speaking and learning how to speak and how this learning is fundamentally dependent on particular others. We have argued that speaking and learning to speak is fundamentally socially anchored, that language is primarily action, that it is occasioned and socially distributed and co-constructed, that language learning is a socially displayed activity, and that learning and cognition are socially distributed. A case in point is Carlos' learning of the two situated, indexical expressions "it is incorrect" and "let me help you". That case demonstrated the crucial importance of recurrence and meaningful (re-)use in a community of practice to learning as L2 speakers appropriate new semiotic-resources-for-social-action in the L2. Pedagogical measures should therefore be taken to raise L2 learners' awareness of the actional reality and potential of the bits and pieces of language they are picking up.

Having argued that language learning is locally contextualized, that language emergence is situated, occasioned, socially shared and locally contingent, and that understanding and learning an L2 is grounded in understanding of social practices (Wagner 2015), we call for an epistemology of SLA research that views language, learning, and cognition as essentially socially distributed. This continues the work of others who have made similar points over the years (e.g., Markee, 1994, 2000, 2011; Firth & Wagner, 1997, 2007; Kasper 2009; Mori & Hasegawa 2009; Markee & Kunitz 2013; Burch 2014; Eskildsen et al. in press; Kunitz & Skogmyr Marian 2017) but the data we have shown here, coming from a multitude of settings, shows the prevailing nature of socially distributed cognition empirically. It should not be denied that social practices simply envelop language and cognition; L2 learners learn to act in situated, locally calibrated ways that adapt to their co-participants. This is what speaking is all about.

# References

Atkinson, D.. (2002). Toward a sociocognitive approach to second language acquisition. *The Modern Language Journal* 86 (4): 525–545.

Atkinson, D. (2011). A sociocognitive approach to second language acquisition. In *Alternative Approaches to Second Language Acquisition*, D. Atkinson (ed.), 143–166. New York, NY: Taylor and Francis.

Block, D.. (2003). *The Social Turn in Second Language Acquisition*. Edinburgh, UK: Edinburgh University Press.

Brouwer, C. E. (2003). Word searches in NNS-NS interaction: Opportunities for language learning? *The Modern Language Journal*, 87 (4): 534–545.

Brouwer, C. E. (2004). On doing pronunciation. In *Second Language Conversations*, R. Gardner, & J. Wagner (eds.), 93–113. London: Continuum.

Brouwer, C. E., & Wagner, J.. (2004). Developmental issues in second language conversation. *Journal of Applied Linguistics* 1: 29–47.

Burch, R. A. (2014). Pursuing information. A conversation analytic perspective on communication strategies. *Language Learning* 64 (3): 651–684.

Button, G. (1991). *Ethnomethodology and the Human Sciences*. Cambridge: Cambridge University Press.

Button, G., Coulter, J., Lee, J. R.E., & Sharrock, W. (1995). *Computers, Minds and Conduct*. Cambridge: Polity Press.

Cadierno, T. & Eskildsen, S. W. (eds.) (2015). *Usage-based Perspectives on Second Language Learning*. Berlin: Mouton de Gruyter.

Clark, A. (2008), *Supersizing the Mind: Embodiment, Action and Cognitive Extension*. Oxford: Oxford University Press.

de Bot, K. & Larsen-Freeman, D. (2011). Researching second language development from a dynamic systems perspective. In *A Dynamic Approach to Second Language Development: Methods and Techniques*, M. H. Verspoor, K. de Bot & W. Lowie (eds.), 5–23. Amsterdam: John Benjamins.

Doughty, C. & M. H. Long (eds.). (2003). *The Handbook of Second Language Acquisition*. Malden, MA: Blackwell.

Douglas Fir Group, the. (2016). A transdisciplinary framework for SLA in a multilingual world. *The Modern Language Journal* 100 (Supplement): 19–47.

Drew, P. & Heritage, J. (1992). *Talk at Work*. Cambridge: Cambridge University Press.

Duff, P. A. & Talmy, S. (2011). Language socialization Approaches to second language acquisition. In *Alternative Approaches to Second Language Acquisition*, D. Atkinson (ed.), 95–116. New York: Taylor and Francis.

Ellis, N. C. (2014). Cognitive *and* social language use. In Studies in Second Language Acquisition 36: 397–402. [Special Issue *Bridging the Gap. Cognitive and social approaches to research in second language learning and teaching*, J. Hulstijn, R. F. Young, & L. Ortega (eds.).]

Ellis, N. C. (2015). Cognitive and social aspects of learning from usage. In *Usage-based Perspectives on Second Language Learning*, T. Cadierno, & S. W. Eskildsen (eds.), 49–74. Berlin: Mouton de Gruyter.

Ellis, N. C., & Larsen-Freeman, D. (2006). Language emergence: Implications for applied linguistics. Introduction to the special issue. *Applied Linguistics* 27 (4): 558–589.

Ellis, R. (2005). Planning and task-based performance. In *Planning and Task Performance in a Second Language*, R. Ellis (ed.), 3–34. Amsterdam: John Benjamins.

Ellis, R.. (2009). The differential effects of three types of task planning on the fluency, complexity, and accuracy in L2 oral production. *Applied Linguistics* 30: 474–509.

Eskildsen, S. W. (2011). The L2 inventory in action: Conversation analysis and usage-based linguistics in SLA. In *L2 Learning as Social Practice: Conversation-Analytic Perspectives*, G. Pallotti & J. Wagner (eds.), 337–373. Honolulu, HI: University of Hawai'i, National Foreign Language Resource Center.

Eskildsen, S. W. (2012). L2 negation constructions at work. *Language Learning* 62(2): 335–372.

Eskildsen, S.W.. (2015). What counts as a developmental sequence?: Exemplar-based L2 learning of English questions. *Language Learning* 65(1): 33–62.

Eskildsen, S. W. (2016). The emergence of creativity in L2 English – a usage-based case-study. In *Multiple Perspectives on Language Play*, N. Bell (ed.), 281–316. Berlin: Mouton de Gruyter.

Eskildsen, S. W. (2018). "We're Learning A Lot of New Words": Encountering New L2 Vocabulary Outside of Class. *The Modern Language Journal.*

Eskildsen, S. W. (In press). L2 constructions and interactional competence: Subordination and coordination in English L2 learning. In *What Is Applied Cognitive Linguistics? Answers from Current SLA Research*, A. Tyler & C. Moder (eds.). Berlin: Mouton de Gruyter.

Eskildsen, S. W. (forthc). "Let me help you": Learning to do and correct public writing in the L2 classroom. In Kunitz, S., Sert, O. & Markee, N. (eds.), *Emerging Issues in Classroom Discourse and Interaction: Theoretical and Applied CA Perspectives on Pedagogy*. Dordrecht: Springer.

Eskildsen, S. W. & Cadierno, T. (2015). Advancing usage-based approaches to L2 studies. In *Usage-based perspectives on second language learning*, T. Cadierno & S. W. Eskildsen (eds.), 1–18. Mouton de Gruyter.

Eskildsen, S. W., Cadierno, T. & Li, P. (2015). On the development of motion constructions in four learners of L2 English. In *Usage-based perspectives on second language learning*, T. Cadierno & S. W. Eskildsen (eds.), 207–232. Berlin: Mouton de Gruyter.

Eskildsen, S. W. & Theodórsdóttir, G. (2017). Constructing L2 learning spaces: Ways to achieve learning inside and outside the classroom. *Applied Linguistics* 38(2): 143–164.

Eskildsen, S. W. & Wagner, J. (2013). Recurring and shared gestures in the L2 classroom: Resources for teaching and Learning. European *Journal of Applied Linguistics* 1: 139–161

Eskildsen, S. W. & Wagner, J. (2015). Embodied L2 construction learning. *Language Learning* 65: 419–448.

Eskildsen, S. W. & Wagner, J. (in press). From trouble in the talk to new resources –The interplay of bodily and linguistic resources in the talk of a novice speaker of English as a second language. In *Documenting Change across Time: Longitudinal Studies on the Organization of Social Interaction*, S. Pekarek Doehler, E. González-Martínez, & J. Wagner (eds.). Basingstoke: Palgrave Macmillan.

Firth, A., & Wagner, J. (1997). On discourse, communication, and (some) fundamental concepts in SLA research. *The Modern Language Journal* 81 (3): 285–300.

Firth, A. & Wagner, J. (2007). S/FL learning as a social accomplishment: Elaborations on a "reconceptualised" SLA. *The Modern Language Journal* 91: 800–819.

Fox Tree, J. E. & Schrock, J. C. (2002). Basic meaning of *you know* and *I mean*. *Journal of Pragmatics* 34: 727–747.

Francis, D. & Hester, S. (2004). *An Invitation to Ethnomethodology: Language, Society and Interaction*. London: Sage.

Fujii, A., & Makey, A. (2009). Interactional feedback in learner-learner interactions in a task-based EFL classroom. *International Review of Applied Lingusitics* 47: 267–301.

Gallagher, S. (2005). *How the Body Shapes the Mind*. Oxford: Oxford University Press.

Garfinkel, H. (1967). *Studies in Ethnomethodogy*. Englewood Cliffs: Prentice Hall.

Gass, S. (2003). Input and Interaction. In *The Handbook of Second Language Acquisition*, C. Doughty & M. H. Long (eds.), 224–255. Malden, MA: Blackwell.

Gass, S. (2015). Comprehensible input and output in classroom interaction. In *The Handbook of Classroom Discourse and Interaction*, N. Markee (ed.), 182–197. Malden, MA: Blackwell.

Gass, S., & Mackey, A. (2007). Input, interaction and output in second language acquisition. In *Theories in Second Language Acquisition. An Introduction*, B. VanPatten & J. Williams (eds.), 175–199. Mahwah, NJ: Lawrence Erlbaum.

Goodwin, C. (1979). The interactive construction of a sentence in natural conversation. In *Everyday Language: Studies in Ethnomethodology*, G. Psathas (ed.), 97–121. New York, NY: Irvington Publishers.

Goodwin, C. (2000a). Action and embodiment within situated human interaction. *Journal of Pragmatics* 32: 1489–1522.

Goodwin, C. (2000b). Practices of seeing: visual analysis: an ethnomethdological approach. In. *Handbook of Visual Analysis*, T. van Leeuwen & J. Carey (eds.), 157–182. London: Sage.

Goodwin, C. (2003a). Pointing as situated practice. In *Pointing: Where Language, Culture and Cognition Meet*, S. Kita (ed.), 217–241. Mahwah, N.J.: Lawrence Erlbaum.

Goodwin, C. (2003b). The body in action. In *Discourse, the Body, and Identity*, J. Coupland & R. Gwyn (eds.), 19–42. Mahwah, N.J: Lawrence Erlbaum.

Goodwin, C.. (2007). Participation, stance and affect in the organization of activities. *Discourse and Society* 18: 53–73.

Goodwin, C. (2013). The co-operative, transformative organization of human action and knowledge. *Journal of Pragmatics* 43: 8–23.

Goodwin, C. & Goodwin, M. (1986). Gesture and coparticipation in the activity of searching for a word. *Semiotica* 62: 51–75.

Hall, J.K., Cheng, A., & Carlson, M.T. (2006). Reconceptualizing multicompetence as a theory of language knowledge. *Applied Linguistics* 27 (2): 220–240.

Hall, J.K., Hellermann, J. & Pekarek Doehler, S. (eds.) (2011). *L2 Interactional Competence and Development*. Clevedon: Multilingual Matters.

Hall, J.K. & Verplaetse, L.S. (2000). The development of second and foreign language learning through classroom interaction. In *Second and Foreign Language Learning through Classroom Interaction*, J.K. Hall, & L.S. Verplaetse (eds.), 1–20. Mahwah, NJ: Lawrence Erlbaum.

Hauser, E. (2013). Stability and change in one adult's second language english negation. *Language Learning* 63 (3): 463–498.

Hayashi, M. (2003). Language and the body as resources for collaborative action: Astudy of word searches in Japanese conversation. *Research on Language and Social Interaction* 36 (2): 109–141.

Hellermann, J. (2008). *Social Actions for Classroom Language Learning*. Clevedon: Multilingual Matters.

Hellermann, J., Eskildsen, S.W., Pekarek Doehler, S. & Piirainen-Marsh, A. (eds.). (forthc.). *Conversation Analytic Research on L2 Interaction in the Wild: The Complex Ecology of Learning-In-Action*. Dordrecht: Springer.

Heritage, J. (1984a). A change-of-state token and aspects of its sequential placement. In *Structures of Social Action*, J.M. Atkinson & J. Heritage (eds.), 299–345. Cambridge, UK: Cambridge University Press.

Heritage, J. (1984b). *Garfinkel and Ethnomethodology*. Cambridge: Polity Press.

Heritage, J. (2012). Epistemics in action: Action formation and territories of knowledge. *Research on Language and Social Interaction* 45 (1): 1–29.

Heritage, J. & Clayman, S. (2010). *Talk in Action: Interactions, Identities and Institutions*. Malden, MA: Wiley-Blackwell.

Heritage, J. & Robinson, J. D. (2011). 'Some' vs 'any' medical issues: Encouraging patients to reveal their unmet concerns. In *Applied Conversation Analysis: Changing Institutional Practices*, C. Antaki (ed.), 15–31. Basingstoke: Palgrave Macmillan.

Hulstijn, J., Young, R. F. & Ortega, L. (eds.). (2014). Bridging the Gap. Cognitive and Social Approaches to Research in Second Language Learning and Teaching. *Special issue of Studies in Second Language Acquisition.*

Hutchby, I. & Wooffitt, R. (2008). *Conversation Analysis*, (2nd edition). Cambridge: Polity Press.

Hutchins, E. (1995). *Cognition in the Wild*. The MIT Press, Cambridge, MA.

Jacoby, S. & Ochs, E. (1995). Co-construction: An introduction. *Research on Language and Social Interaction* 28: 171–183.

Jefferson, G. (2004). Glossary of transcript symbols with an Introduction. In *Conversation Analysis: Studies from the First Generation*, G. H. Lerner (ed.), 13–23. Philadelphia: John Benjamins.

Kanagy, R. (1999). Interactional routines as a mechanism for L2 acquisition and socialization in an immersion context. *Journal of Pragmatics* 31: 1467–1492.

Kasper, G. (2009). Locating cognition in second language interaction and learning: Inside the skull or in public view? *International Review of Applied Linguistics* 47: 13–36.

Kasper, G., & Wagner, J. (2011). A conversation-analytic approach to second language acquisition. In *Alternative Approaches to Second Language Acquisition*, D. Atkinson (Ed.), 117–142. New York: Taylor & Francis.

Kasper, G., & Wagner, J. (2014). Conversation Analysis in Applied Linguistics. *Annual Review of Applied Linguistics* 34: 171–212.

Koschmann, T. (2011). Understanding understanding in action. *Journal of Pragmatics* 43: 435–437.

Koschmann, T. (2013). Conversation analysis and learning in interaction. In *Conversation Analysis*, K. Mortensen, & J. Wagner (eds.). In *The Encyclopedia of Applied Linguistics*, C. A. Chapelle (ed.), 1038–1043. Oxford, UK: Wiley-Blackwell.

Kramsch, C. (1986). From language proficiency to interactional competence. *The Modern Language Journal* 70 (4): 366–372.

Kunitz, S., Sert, O. & Markee, N. forthc. *Emerging Issues in Classroom Discourse and Interaction: Theoretical and Applied CA Perspectives on Pedagogy.* Dordrecht: Springer.

Kunitz, S. & Skogmyr Marian, K. (2017). Tracking immanent language learning behavior over time in task-based classroom work. *Tesol Quarterly.* 51: 507–535.

Kurhila, S. (2006). *Second Language Interaction.* John Benjamins, Amsterdam.

Lantolf, J. P. (2011). Sociocultural theory. A dialectical approach to L2 research. In *Handbook of Second Language Acquisition* S. M. Gass, & A. Mackey (eds.), 57–72. New York, NY: Routledge.

Lantolf, J. P., & Thorne, S. L. (2006). *Sociocultural Theory and the Genesis of Second Language Development.* Oxford: Oxford University Press.

Lerner, G. (1991). On the syntax of sentences-in-progress. *Language in Society* 20 (3): 441–458.

Long, M. H. (1996). The role of the linguistic environment in second language acquisition. In *Handbook of second language acquisition*, W. C. Ritchie, & T. K. Bhatia (eds.), 413–468. San Diego, CA: Academic Press.

Mackey, A. (2013). *Input, Interaction, and Corrective Feedback in L2 Learning.* Oxford: Oxford University Press.

MacWhinney, B. (1999). The emergence of language from embodiment. In *The Emergence of Language*, B. MacWhinney (ed.), 213–256. Mahwah, NJ: Lawrence Erlbaum.

MacWhinney, B. (2005). The emergence of grammar from perspective. In *Grounding Cognition. The Role of Perception and Action in Memory, Language, and Thinking*, D. Pecher & R. A. Zwaan (eds.), 198–223. Cambridge, UK: Cambridge University Press.

Markee, N. (1994). Toward an ethnomethodological respecification of second-language acquisition studies. In *Research Methodology in Second-Language Acqusition*, E. E. Tarone, S. M. Gass & A. D. Cohen (eds.), 89–116. Hillsdale, NJ: Lawrence Erlbaum.

Markee, N. (2000). *Conversation Analysis*. Mahwah, NJ: Lawrence Erlbaum.

Markee, N. (2008). Toward a learning behavior tracking methodology for CA-for-SLA. *Applied Linguistics* 29 (3): 404–427.

Markee, N.. (2011). Doing, and justifying doing, avoidance. *Journal of Pragmatics* 43: 602–615.

Markee, N. & Kunitz, S. (2013). Doing planning and task performance in second language acquisition: An ethnomethodological respecification. *Language Learning* 63 (4): 629–664.

May, S. (ed.). (2015). *The multilingual turn: Implications for SLA, TESOL and bilingual education*. New York: Routledge.

McHoul, A. W. (1978). The organization of turns at formal talk in the classroom. *Language in Society* 7: 183–213.

McHoul, A. W. (1990). The organization of repair in classroom talk. *Language in Society* 19: 349– 377.

Mehan, H. (1979). *Learning Lessons*. Cambridge, MA: Harvard University Press.

Mondada, L. (2014a). The local constitution of multimodal resources for social interaction. *Journal of Pragmatics* 65: 137–156.

Mondada, L. (2014b). Pointing, talk and the bodies: Reference and joint attention as embodied interactional achievements. In *From Gesture in Conversation to Visible Utterance in Action*, M. Seyfeddinipur & M. Gullberg (eds.), 95–124. Amsterdam: Benjamins.

Mondada, L. (2014c). Bodies in action: Multimodal analysis of walking and talking. *Language and Dialogue* 4: 357–403.

Mondada, L.. (2016). Challenges of multimodality: Language and the body in social interaction. *Journal of Sociolinguistics* 20: 336–366.

Mori, J. (2010). Learning language in real time: A case study of the Japanese demonstrative pronoun "are" in word-search sequences. In *Pragmatics in language learning, vol 12*, G. Kasper, H. t. Nguyen, D. Yoshimi & J. K. Yoshioka (eds.), 15–42. Honolulu: University of Hawai'i, National Foreign Language Resource Center.

Mori, J, & Hasegawa, A. (2009). Doing being a foreign language learner in a classroom: Embodiment of cognitive states as social events. *International Review of Applied Linguistics* 47: 65–94.

Mortensen, K. (2011). Doing word explanation in interaction. In *L2 Learning as Social Practice: Conversation-Analytic Perspectives*, G. Pallotti & J. Wagner (eds.), 135–162. Honolulu, HI: University of Hawai'i, National Foreign Language Resource Center.

Nevile, M. (2015). The embodied turn in research on language and social interaction. *Research on Language and Social Interaction* 48: 121–151.

Ortega, L. (2014). Ways forward for a bi/multilingual turn in SLA. In *The multilingual turn: Implications for SLA, TESOL and bilingual education*, S. May (ed.), 32–53. New York: Routledge.

Östman, J.-O. (1981). *You Know. A Discourse-Functional Approach*. Amsterdam: John Benjamins.

Pallotti, G., & Wagner, J. (eds.). (2011). *L2 Learning as Social Practice: Conversation-Analytic Perspectives*. Honolulu, HI: University of Hawai'i, National Foreign Language Resource Center.

Pease, A. & Pease, B., (2006). *The Definitive Book of Body Language*. New York: Bantam Books

Pedersen, H. F. (2014). Om konstruktionen *sån en N* i danske samtaler. S.O.S. Skrifter om samtalegrammatik 1 (1): 1–23. [On the construction *a kind of N* in Danish conversations. S.O.S. Notes on the grammar of conversation 1 (1): 1–23]

Pekarek Doehler, S., & Pochon-Berger, E. (2015). The development of L2 interactional competence: evidence from turn-taking organization, sequence organization, repair organization and preference organization. In *Usage-based Perspectives on Second Language Learning*, T. Cadierno & S. W. Eskildsen (eds.), 233–268. Berlin: Mouton de Gruyter.

Reder, S. (2005). The "Lab School." *Focus on Basics*, 8(A). Available at http://www.ncsall.net/fileadmin/resources/fob/2005/fob_8a.pdf

Robbins, P. & Aydede, M. (2009). A short primer on situated cognition. In *The Cambridge Handbook of Situated Cognition*, P. Robbins & M. Aydede (eds.), 3–10. Cambridge: Cambridge University Press.

Roehr-Brackin, K. (2015). Long-term development in an instructed adult L2 learner: Usage-based and complexity theory applied. In *Usage-based Perspectives on Second Language Learning*, T. Cadierno, & S. W. Eskildsen (eds.), 75–104. Berlin: Mouton de Gruyter.

Rupert, R. D. (2011). Cognitive systems and the supersized mind. *Philosophical Studies* 152: 427– 436.

Sacks, H., Schegloff, E. A., & Jefferson, G. (1974). A simplest systematics for the organization of turntaking for conversation. *Language* 50: 696–735.

Schegloff, E. A. (1972). Notes on a conversational practice: Formulating place. In *Studies in Social Interaction*, D. Sudbow (ed.), Glencoe, IL: Free Press.

Schegloff, E. A. (1979). The relevance of repair to syntax-for-conversation. In *Syntax and Semantics*, vol. 12., Givon, T. (ed.), 261–286. New York: Academic Press.

Schegloff, E. A. (1987). Between macro and micro: contexts and other connections. In *The Micro-Macro Link*, J. Alexander, B. Giesen, R. Munch & N. Smelser (eds.), 207–234. Berkeley, CA: University of California Press.

Schegloff, E. A. (1992). Repair after next turn: The last structurally provided defense of intersubjectivity in conversation. *The American Journal of Sociology* 97 (5): 1295–1345.

Schegloff, E. A. (2007). *Sequence Organization in Interaction. A Primer in Conversation Analysis. Volume 1*. Cambridge, UK: Cambridge University Press.

Schegloff, E. A., Jefferson, G., & Sacks, H. (1977). The preference for self-correction in the organization of repair in conversation. *Language* 53: 361–382.

Schegloff, E. A., Koshik, I., Olsher, D. & Jacoby, S. (2002). Conversation analysis and applied linguistics. *ARAL* 22: 3–31.

Seedhouse, P. (2004). *The Interactional Architecture of the Language Classroom: A Conversation Analysis Perspective*. Oxford: Blackwell's

Seo. M.-S. & Koshik, I. (2012). A conversation analytic study of gestures that engender repair in ESL conversational tutoring. *Journal of Pragmatics* 42: 2219–2239

Stam, G. (2015). Changes in thinking-for-speaking: A longitudinal case study. *The Modern Language Journal* 99 (Supplement): 83–99.

Stivers, T. (2010). An overview of the question-response system in American English conversation. *Journal of Pragmatics* 42: 2772–2781.

Stivers, T., Mondada, L., & Steensig, J. (2011). Knowledge, morality and affiliation in social interaction. In *The Morality of Knowledge in Conversation*, T. Stivers, L. Mondada, & J. Steensig (eds.), 3–26. Cambridge, UK: Cambridge University Press.

Swain, M., & Deters, P. (2007). "New" mainstream SLA theory: Expanded and enriched. *The Modern Language Journal* 91: 820–836.

ten Have, Paul. (2004). *Understanding Qualitative Research and Ethnomethodology*. London: Sage.

ten Have, Paul. (2007). *Doing Conversation Analysis: A Practical Guide* (2nd edition). London: Sage

Theodórsdóttir, G. & Eskildsen, S. W. (2011). Achieving intersubjectivity and doing learning: The use of English as a lingua franca in Icelandic L2. *Nordand* 6 (2), 59–85.

Thorne, S. L. & Hellermann, J. (2015). Sociocultural approaches to expert-novice relationships in second language interaction. In *The handbook of classroom discourse and interaction*, N. Markee (ed.), 281–298. Chichester, UK: Wiley Blackwell.

van Compernolle, R. A. (2015). The emergence of sociolingusitic competence in L2 classroom interaction. In *The Handbook of Classroom Discourse and Interaction*, N. Markee (ed.), 265–280. Chichester, UK: Wiley Blackwell.

van Compernolle, R. A. & McGregor, J. (eds.). (2016). *Authenticity, Language, and Interaction in Second Language Contexts*. Bristol, UK: Multilingual Matters.

Wagner, J. (2015). Designing for language learning in the wild. Creating social infrastructures for second language learning. In *Usage-based Perspectives on Second Language Learning*, T. Cadierno & S. W. Eskildsen (eds.), 75–104. Berlin: Mouton de Gruyter.

Watson-Gegeo, K.. (2004). Mind, language and epistemology: Towards a language socialization paradigm for SLA. *Modern Language Journal* 88 (3): 331–350.

Zuengler, J. & Cole, KM. (2005). Language socialization and second language learning. In *Handbook of Research in Second Language Teaching and Learning*, E. Hinkel (ed.), 301–316. Mahwah, NJ: Lawrence Erlbaum

## Glossary

*Transcription conventions*

| | |
|---|---|
| CAR: TEA: | Participants |
| Wei⌐rd wo⌐rd | Beginning and end of overlapping talk |
| ⌊yeah ⌋ | |
| */#/%/¤ | Beginning of gesture in turn-at-talk |
| */#/%/¤Word | Description of corresponding gesture. In cases with no */#/%/¤, the gesture follows preceding word. |
| (1.0) | Pause/gap in seconds and tenth of seconds |
| (.) | Micro pause (< 0.2 seconds) |
| word= | |
| =word | Continuous turn |
| word | Prosodic emphasis |

| wo:rd | Prolongation of preceding sound |
| word↗,↘ | Falling, rising intonation |
| ↑,↓word | Shift to high/low pitch |
| WORD | Loud volume |
| W<u>o</u>rd | Stressed syllable |
| °word° | Softer than surrounding talk |
| <-word-> | slower than surrounding talk |
| ->word<- | faster than surrounding talk |
| £word£ | distinct prosody, sing-song |
| wo- | Cut-off (e.g., glottal stop) |
| ☺word ☺ | Smiley voice |
| w/o/rd | Phonetic transcription |
| ( ) | Non-audible speech |
| (word) | Uncertain transcription |
| [word word] | Undisclosed information (e.g., dates of birth, addresses) |
| .hh | Hearable in-breath |
| hh | Out-breath |
| H | Possible laughter syllable |
| ((word)) | Transcriber's comment |

CHAPTER 5

# The acquisition of L2 speaking
## A dynamic perspective

Wander Lowie, Marjolijn Verspoor & Marijn van Dijk
University of Groningen

The complex dynamic systems theory approach to second language development has great explanatory power in accounting for the development of
speaking as an emergent process. CDST approaches focus on the process
of development, rather than on the products of learning, and often include
the learner's variability over time as an important source of information.
In this chapter a CDST perspective is given of speaking in a second language. The individually owned and variable process of speaking development is illustrated with longitudinal speaking data of identical twins as
they learn English as a second language in Taiwan. Our observations
emphasize the individual nature of the development of speaking in a second language, which has important implications for effective language
teaching for L2 speaking.

## Introduction

The focus on speaking skills in a second language is inherently challenging, as it
concerns one of the skills within second language data that is most difficult to
capture. Compared to receptive skills, but also compared to written production,
it is possibly the most difficult skill to teach, the most difficult skill to assess and
the most difficult skill to investigate. The reason is that speaking is highly variable and there are many aspects related to speaking that could be the focus of
attention. In addition to accuracy and complexity, fluency is the most pertinent
focus for speaking. Yet speaking is also the skill that is most distinctly representative of what language really is. Speaking is adaptive, communicative, and complex. Effective speaking requires simultaneous control over, among other things,
the changing interaction with the environment and the speaking partners, implicit
linguistic knowledge, articulatory planning, and language-specific motor skills.
In addition, speaking typically occurs under time pressure compared to other
productive skills. The acquisition of speaking skills in the first language (L1) is

https://doi.org/10.1075/aals.17.05low
© John Benjamins Publishing Company

a gradual process in which articulatory skills, categorization of linguistic input, interpersonal interaction and cognitive development go hand in hand, with certain periods of focus on one aspect. In spite of several differences between first and second languages, the process of development consists of essentially similar characteristics. Within the complex dynamic systems theory (CDST) line of thinking, the ability to speak in a second language is not likely to be the direct result of innate language specific abilities, but emerges over time, based on the complex interaction of noticing, interaction, and self-reflection (Macwhinney, 2005). And while some second language skills may to some extent benefit from the consciousness of explicit knowledge about grammatical structures, constraints of time and attention will lead to spoken language production being strongly dependent on unconscious and implicit knowledge (Biber, Gray, & Poonpon, 2011; Dykstra-Pruim, 2003). Due to its complex and emergent nature, speaking skills are highly variable between learners. But also within the same learner the development of speaking over time is highly variable, and the level of attainment is therefore very difficult to predict.

The variable nature and the complexity of the acquisition and use of second language speaking is difficult to account for in one theoretical framework. However, the framework of CDST approaches to second language development has significant explanatory power to account for emergent characteristics of the acquisition of second language (L2) speaking. The starting points of CDST, the iterative nature of language development, the nonlinear relationships of embedded and embodied subsystems, and the emergence of attractor states over time at all time scales are manifested in a highly individual process that is characterized by meaningful patterns of intra-individual variability. Although global changes at the group level may indicate the grand sweep of development, attempts to generalize findings at the group level to the individual language learner are bound to fail (Lowie, Van Dijk, Chan, & Verspoor, n.d.). The individual development of speaking skills over time may depend on the time scale, from the lifespan to the microsecond level. In this contribution, we will elaborate on the development of L2 speaking from a CDST perspective, with a special focus on intra-learner variability. Assumptions of the CDST framework will be illustrated for speaking, and will form the basis for an exploration of the data of two Chinese learners of English. The learners in this study are identical twins that grow up in identical environments, go to the same school, are exposed to the same amount of English, and have similar characteristics like personality and motivation. These learners form the ideal basis of comparison for the individual nature of second language development. The main expectation of speaking development in a CDST framework is that due to the dynamic interactions of all factors in the time domain, the development will show a variable pattern that is unique to each and every individual, leading to the expectation that even between extremely similar learners in identical contexts significant differences in their L2 development can be found.

We will start by describing the complex dynamics of language development, with a focus on speaking in a second language and the relevant measures of dynamic change and will elaborate on the most appropriate dimensions of analysis for these data. We will then describe the process of speaking development of the two participants and evaluate the explanatory power of the CDST approach for these data.

## A complex dynamic systems theory account of L2 speaking

Complex Dynamic Systems Theory is a widely used theory of change. The theory and its associated frameworks like *complexity theory* have extensively been used in many disciplines of science, like physics, meteorology and biology. Complex Dynamic Systems Theory is an application of mathematics to describe nonlinear change. CDST has therefore provided powerful explanations for the behaviour of natural phenomena that are hard to predict in the long run due to nonlinear dynamics of the factors involved. Applications to describe the dynamic characteristics in the physical world provide clear and appealing illustrations of the power of CDST. The weather conditions in temperate climates nicely illustrate the dynamics of nonlinear interactions among the embedded subsystems involved, like the temperature at different localizations and different layers of the sphere, the changing magnitude of the differences between areas of low pressure and high pressure, and the changing humidity. Even if all individual factors that contribute to the connected operations referred to as a "system" are known, the complex and the stochastic nature of the relationships among these factors leads to increasing short term variability and ultimate unpredictability on longer time scales. Another powerful example is the complex and unpredictable behaviour of a flock of birds. Each bird functions as a subsystem in the flock. Each bird has its goals, like avoiding collision, finding shelter from birds of prey, and roosting at a suitable location. The interactions among the birds and their changing environment due to the wind, the temperature, and the presence of other animals lead to spectacular patterns of variability and typical shapes of the flock that result from the emerging attractors of the complex system.

As from the 1990s, CDST has been applied to human cognition (Port & van Gelder, 1995; Thelen & Smith, 1994), developmental psychology (Van Geert, 1998) and first language development (Elman, 1995). Since the late 1990s, the theory has also been applied to second language acquisition (De Bot, Lowie & Verspoor, 2007; Herdina & Jessner, 2002; Larsen-Freeman, 1997). Since then, these and other authors have argued that language development is an iterative, nonlinear, and therefore highly variable individual process that cannot adequately be described in terms of linear relationships and linear systems. Their arguments are based on the most typical properties of complex dynamic systems, like the occurrence of embedded and embodied subsystems that are characterized by non-linear relationships and that lead to the iterative and non-deterministic nature of development, the emergence of self-organization that is manifested in typical patterns of variability, and the fact that complex dynamic systems are open systems. The combination of these properties leads to the expectation that language development is a highly individually owned process and predicts that generalizations at the group level are not warranted in the time domain. In this contribution we will focus on those characteristics that are particularly relevant for the development of speaking abilities in the second language. We will briefly work out the dynamic properties of the use and development of second language speaking and we will subsequently focus on the variable nature of the development of second language speaking.

## Complex dynamic subsystems

The many subsystems involved in language production and language development are embedded at all levels. The components of the L2 speaker's language system, like the vocabulary, the grammar, the phonological system, but also the articulation are all interrelated and contain integrated aspects of the L1 and the L2 linguistic systems (Larsen-Freeman & Cameron, 2008). In addition to the embedded components of the language system, that system itself is embedded in the cognitive system, the body, the environment including the speaking partners, the language community and the embedded levels of society. The integration of the bilingual's systems is corroborated by the observation that bilingualism is a "dynamic process in which new situations, new interlocuters and new language functions involve new linguistic needs" (Grosjean, 2010, p. 89). This leads to the observation that bilingual children possess a unique linguistic profile that cannot be reduced to a combination of two monolinguals in the same mind (Yip & Matthews, 2007). From a CDST perspective it should be added that due to the open nature of the system, each and every (embedded) subsystem tends to change over time, and each subsystem may change at its own timescale or time scales. The level of speaking skills is therefore related to the speaking situation. A second language learner's speaking abilities for spoken production in the form of a monologue will be related to, yet different from those of spoken interaction. This observation has for instance led to a different set of descriptors for the different skills in the Common European Framework of Reference (Europe, 2001). The description of the proficiency levels for speaking focuses on the vocabulary size and lexical sophistication, grammatical accuracy, fluency, coherence, pronunciation, matching of the language level to the target and the speaking partners, interaction, and the use of communicative abilities. Due to the embeddedness of the subsystems, all subsystems are dynamically related. Spoken interaction has been convincingly related to language development, and interaction has been argued to be a leading principle in the acquisition of vocabulary and other components of language development (Long, 1996; Mackey, 1999). In the current study we will concentrate on the development of the interrelated subsystems of syntax and vocabulary, which is characterized as a nonlinear relationship that is highly variable.

Many models of second language acquisition are based on the implicit assumption of a linear process of development, with a starting point (minimal L2 knowledge) and an end-point (a full command of the second language) (see for instance, Pienemann, 1998). Not all learners will reach the ultimate goal, a full command of the L2, as many are assumed to stop developing somewhere along the line. Research has mostly focused on the individual factors contributing to achieving, or failing to achieve, the ultimate goal. However, according to the CDST perspective language is a fully integrated embedded and embodied system. This implies that the isolation of single factors affecting the process of language acquisition is not a feasible goal, as the developing system is more than the sum of all factors involved. All factors are strongly interacting and change as a function of the system's previous point of development. And since the context in which the system operates is again a system in itself, any change of the language system will also change its context. In principle, a complex dynamic system can produce linear development, but in reality development tends to be nonlinear, as it emerges from the interaction of the components of the system and the context in which they develop (Van Geert, 2003). Nonlinear relationships are not proportional and therefore long term development is unpredictable. In other words, the emerging development is non-deterministic and stochastic. This "unruly" behaviour of the system is commonly referred to as *chaos*. Chaos in CDST should not be equated with random behaviour, as the dynamic interaction of systems leads to shaping the self-organization of the system in a certain direction. In the CDST literature, the point that the system tends towards is commonly referred to as an "attractor". Chaos in this context implies that the development of these attractors emerges from the interaction of subsystems and is non-deterministic.

## Variability

The nonlinear, iterative developmental patterns are normally manifested in variability in learner data. Longitudinal studies have demonstrated the non-deterministic nature of second language development and have emphasized the relevance of variability. In dense longitudinal analyses Verspoor, Lowie, and Van Dijk (2008) show that the amount of variability fluctuates between progress and decay. Their analyses show that increased variability tends to coincide with a subsequent increase in development. As Larsen-Freeman (2006) puts it, "there are no discrete stages in which learners' performance is invariant, although there are periods in which certain forms are dominant (…). There appears to be a need for the necessary building blocks to be in place in sufficient critical mass to move to a period where a different form dominates" (Larsen-Freeman, 2006, p. 592). And as Verspoor and Van Dijk (2013) point out, variability is especially large during periods of rapid development because at that time the learner explores and tries out new strategies or modes of behavior that are not always successful and may therefore alternate with old strategies or modes of behavior (Thelen & Smith, 1994). From a more formal perspective, systems have to become "unstable" before they can change (Hosenfeld, Van der Maas, & Van den Boom, 1997). For instance, high intra-individual variability implies that qualitative developmental changes may be taking place (Lee & Karmiloff-Smith, 2002). The cause and effect relationship between variability and development is considered to be reciprocal. On the one hand, variability permits flexible and adaptive behavior and is a prerequisite to development –just as in evolution theory, there is no selection of new forms if there is no variation. On the other hand, free exploration of performance generates variability. The processing of new tasks leads to instability of the system, and consequently leads to an increase in variability. Therefore, the general claim is that stability and variability are indispensable aspects of human development. There is no reason to assume that language development forms an exception to the variable nature of human development. Especially speaking can be expected to show high degrees of variability due to the complex and time-restrained nature of the task.

Not only does a person's linguistic behavior continually change and reorganize, but also his or her other experiences change over time. According to Heraclites (c. 535–c. 475 BCE), one can never step in the same river twice. This refers to the continuous change of everything in the universe. In the context of the present volume, it may be asked to what extent Heraclites's phrase also applies to speaking tasks in language learning. In a way the answer is straightforward: two tasks are never exactly the same over time. The very fact of doing a task changes the system and the second time a task has to be done it is essentially different from the first time. Both the learner who performs these tasks and the environment in which the task is carried out have changed. Changes that do occur cannot be directly attributed to the task repetition itself. As has been shown by several single-case studies tracing linguistic development, the highly dynamic processes are manifested by variability over time. As different linguistic sub-systems relevant for language develop over time, they have different relations. For example, some sub-systems (e.g. the lexicon) have to be in place before others (e.g. longer constructions) can develop. At subsequent moments in the process, these two sub-systems may very well compete for attention and one may develop at the expense of the other. After a while, these sub-systems may become coordinated and develop rather synchronously. An illustration of this is given by Caspi (2010). In a 36-week CDST study on writing using L2-English subjects with differing L1 backgrounds, Caspi found learners to develop in several lexical complexity measures before their lexis became more accurate, and the lexis seemed to develop before syntax and syntactic accuracy. A second finding is that some sub-systems may show sudden spurts accompanied with a great deal of variability (e.g. a particular type of verb phrase construction) (Van Dijk, Verspoor, & Lowie, 2011), whereas others develop more gradually (e.g. the use of more academic words) (Spoelman & Verspoor, 2010). A third finding is that some subsystems show a period of increased variability that may indicate a major shift in the whole linguistic system; for example, a period of overuse or overgeneralisation is often followed by a more stable phase with less variability (Van Dijk, Verspoor, and Lowie, 2011). In other words, learners will change their linguistic behaviour over time in many different ways as their language reorganizes and changes cannot always clearly be attributed to single external causes.

Several longitudinal group studies tracing linguistic development inspired by a CDST approach have revealed that no single measure adequately represents linguistic development over time and that no two learners are exactly alike (Bulté, 2013; Vyatkina, 2012). For example, in Larsen-Freeman's (2006) study of five Chinese learners retelling a narrative in English at intervals of approximately six weeks over a four-month period, there was considerable variability and variation. Moreover, in a cross-sectional study on written texts, Verspoor, Schmid, and Xu (2012) explored the differences in the use of 64 linguistic measures among 5 different levels of proficiency (as determined by raters, from beginner to high intermediate). The data showed that only a few very general developmental indices increased significantly between most levels: the decline of simple sentences (or the increase in complex sentences), the decline of the use of the present tense (or the increase in other tenses), the decline in total errors (or the increase in accuracy), the increase in type-token ratio, and the increase in the use of formulaic sequences. However, there were also significant increases between two consecutive levels, suggesting that some sub-systems develop at different phases of proficiency. Between level 1 and 2, there were significant differences mainly with respect to lexical measures, suggesting that developmental changes are more obvious in the lexicon early on (in line with Caspi, 2010). Between levels 2 and 3, relatively more changes occurred in syntactic measures, suggesting that once there are enough words, learners have room for sentences to become more complex. Between levels 3 and 4, changes occurred in both lexical and syntactic measures, but between levels 4 and 5, change was again mainly observed in lexical measures, specifically in formulaic sequences, which suggests that the lexical subsystem was focused on. Another important finding was that there was generally more variation in all the measures among beginners than among the more proficient writers, probably because the system is still unstable. Finally, Penris and Verspoor (2017) clearly showed in their 13-year longitudinal study of writing that the learner developed in different linguistic subsystems at different stages.

To summarize, research taking a CDST perspective has pointed to the fact that language itself is variable (there are many different linguistic ways to express the same notion), that learners in different phases will be focusing on different linguistic subsystems, causing variability in those particular subsystems, and that different subsystems may be changing at different stages of development. Most of the studies of second language development carried out within the CDST framework have focused on written data, with most attention being given to syntactic complexity and lexical sophistication. Although some longitudinal studies have been conducted with dense data to make observations about children's speech development (Pine, Lufkin, Kirk, & Messer, 2007), no studies to date have focused on variability over time in second language speech development. To illustrate the observation that variability and variation are the norm, we will zoom in on the speech data collected on identical twins.

## A twin study in speaking development[1]

The goal of the study described here was to explore intra-learner variability and inter-learner variation in development and to see to what extent we can observe common developmental patterns in two very similar learners living in a similar environment, performing 100 similar tasks over a period of 8 months. We will focus on dense measurements of syntactic complexity and lexical sophistication as they evolve over time.

---

1.    The data we use as example in this section was discussed previously in Chan, Verspoor, and Vahtrick (2015) and Lowie et al. (2017)

Whenever our studies show high levels of variability and variation in development among single learners or small groups of learners, reviewers bring up questions about control variables such as whether the learners were similar to begin with, had exactly the same experiences, had similar amounts of exposure, and so on. To illustrate the individual nature of second language development while limiting variation in as many control variables as possible, we will focus on the L2 development of identical twins, two highly similar learners with highly similar experiences who performed 100 simple speaking tasks (albeit not exactly the same) over a period of 8 months. Chan, Verspoor, and Vahtrick (2015) have already shown that these learners have individual learning paths, and Lowie et al. (2017) provide evidence that there are significant differences in their patterns of variability.

The reason we focus on identical twins is relatively simple. These twins live in the same home and have attended the same school in the same class, and weekly assignments involving extra English exposure were kept similar for the learners. The majority of twin studies focusing on linguistics have found identical twins to perform more similarly than fraternal twins (Stromswold, 2006). We assume that twins who share 100% of their genes and who have been raised in an identical environment are more likely than any other pair of learners to exhibit similar developmental patterns (Hayiou-Thomas, 2008). There is a rich literature on the development of cognitive skills in identical twins, typically related to the role of nature/nurture and heritability. There is also some work on the development of language skills in very young children, but longitudinal studies on bilingual development in adolescents are not available to our knowledge, other than the data set reported on here (Chan, 2015). If, like for the twins in our study, the linguistic environment is also highly similar, then two main sources of variation are more or less eliminated, and other factors, thus far not considered as being relevant, like the repetition of tasks, can be included in the study. Stromswold (2006) provides an extensive overview of cognitive and linguistic development of monozygotic and dizygotic twins. The outcomes of the analysis suggest that heritable factors account for a little more than two-thirds of variance for both written and spoken language impairments. In an earlier meta-analysis of some 100 twin studies Stromswold (2001) found that depending on what aspect of language is assessed, heritable factors account for between half to two thirds of the variance in language-impaired twins' linguistic abilities and much less of the variance in non-impaired twins' linguistic abilities. Genetic factors appeared to play a greater role for phonological and syntactic abilities than for lexical abilities. For example, heritable factors accounted for about a third of the variance in normal twins' lexical abilities and about a half of the variance in their phonological and syntactic skills.

One of the few studies on this topic is Dale et al. (2010). They studied 604 14-year old twins on their language proficiency. They found substantial heritability (.67) and low influence of shared environment (.13) on this measure of second-language acquisition. The levels of proficiency of the pupils were assessed by their teachers based on rubrics for the national curriculum. Females scored significantly higher than males, and males showed significantly greater variance than females. Multivariate behavior genetic analyses suggest very high, but not complete, overlap of genetic influences on first- and second-language acquisition, and less overlap between shared environmental influences. So on the basis of these results substantial overlap in scores was expected, while the impact of the linguistic environment is limited.

In the current study, we investigated the development over time in dense longitudinal data of twins' speech in English as a second language. We investigated the global improvement of these participants, their individual trajectory and the variability in their development. The following research questions were addressed:

1. Do our data show differences between the twin girls in our study across the entire trajectory?
2. Do the data show a significant global increase (or decrease) in the scores over time?
3. Do the data show a difference in variability between the twin girls in our study across the entire trajectory?
4. Did the observed patterns of variability change over the time course of the data collected?

## Participants

Gloria and Grace (not their real names) are two female identical twins, aged 15 at the time of the study. For ten years, they attended school in Taiwan in the same English class with the same English teacher, where English classes were taught in Mandarin Chinese with a focus on grammar. In other words, until the current study began, they had mainly received written input in English. At the beginning of the study, they had a very similar English proficiency level (see Table 1) as measured by the General English Proficiency Test (GEPT) (Wu, 2012).

## Materials

During the time of the data collection, spanning 8 months, the participants produced spoken texts approximately three times a week, which was usually on

**Table 1.**  English proficiency scores for the twins

GEPT scores

|  | Grace | Gloria |
|---|---|---|
| Listening (120) | 112 | 112 |
| Speaking (100) | 80 | 80 |
| Reading (120) | 108 | 105 |
| Writing (100) | 88 | 82 |

Friday, Saturday, and Sunday. For each participant, 100 spoken texts were gathered. The topics were selected from the list of standard TOEFL tests and of the same genre, such as the following:

> **Example of a speaking topic**
>
> Which of the following statements do you agree with? Some believe that TV programs have a positive influence on modern society. Others, however, think that the influence of TV programs is negative. What TV programs have a positive influence? Why? What TV programs have a negative influence? Why?

The data were digitally recorded in a Facebook group created for the purpose of the study. To keep the participants motivated, the researcher reacted to the content of what they said on Facebook to show she was really interested in what they had to say.

## Measures

Bulté (2013), who studied the development of a great number of linguistic complexity measures over time in a group of Dutch high school learners of English, suggests that hybrid and aggregate measures are more robust and may be better indicators of general progress over time than specific ones such as number of adverbial clauses. In order to keep variability and variation due to the measurement instruments to a minimum, two very general, robust complexity measures were used to trace development in the current study. The effect of T-unit length is one of the most robust fluency measures (Wolfe-Quintero, Hae-Young, & Inagaki, 1998, pp. 97–98). A T-unit is defined as "one main clause plus any subordinate clause or non-clausal structure that is attached to or embedded in it" (Hunt, 1970, p. 4). A subordinate clause is defined as a finite adjective, adverbial, or nominal clause, while non-finite verb phrases are excluded in the definition of clauses (eg. Bardovi-Harlig & Bofman, 1989). As a general lexical measure of lexical sophistication we chose lexical diversity, VocD (Malvern, Richards, Chipere, & Durán, 2004). According to Lu (2012), lexical variation rather than other lexical measures correlated most strongly with the raters' judgments of the quality of Chinese ESL learners' oral narratives. VocD is an adjusted metric for TTR, which is standardized for text length.

### Data analysis

The data analysis and results are based on Lowie, van Dijk, Chan, and Verspoor (2017), briefly summarized here. First, the scores of each data series (MLT and VocD) were averaged to see if there was a difference between the girls across the entire trajectory (research question 1). Secondly, for each girl tests were run to see whether there was a significant increase (or decrease) in the score over time (research question 2). Then the degree of variability in the data was explored to discover whether there was a difference in variability between the two girls across the entire trajectory (research question 3). Finally, tests were run to see if patterns of variability changed over time (research question 4). To test the significance of the observed differences between the girls and increases or decreases within each time series, Monte Carlo permutation analyses were performed (Van Dijk, Verspoor, & Lowie, 2011). Monte Carlo analyses are based on the comparison of iterations in the original data series compared to the same data that are randomized in order. In this way, a Monte Carlo calculates the probability of obtaining the data by chance. All analyses were performed in Excel in combination with Poptools (Hood, 2004).

### Results

#### MLT/spoken

Visual inspection of the MLT in spoken texts suggests that the trajectories of the girls largely overlap (see Figure 1). At the beginning we see relatively higher levels of MLT and high degrees of variability. However, it seems that the variability is more concentrated in the first half of the measurement period and decreases over time.

The results of the Monte Carlo analyses show a small, but significant ($p = .01$) difference in MLT between the girls (for Gloria 13.1 and for Grace 14.2). Also their respective slopes of development, that is the overall progress or decay over time, are different. Grace's slope was significantly negative ($-.31$, $p < .01$), while

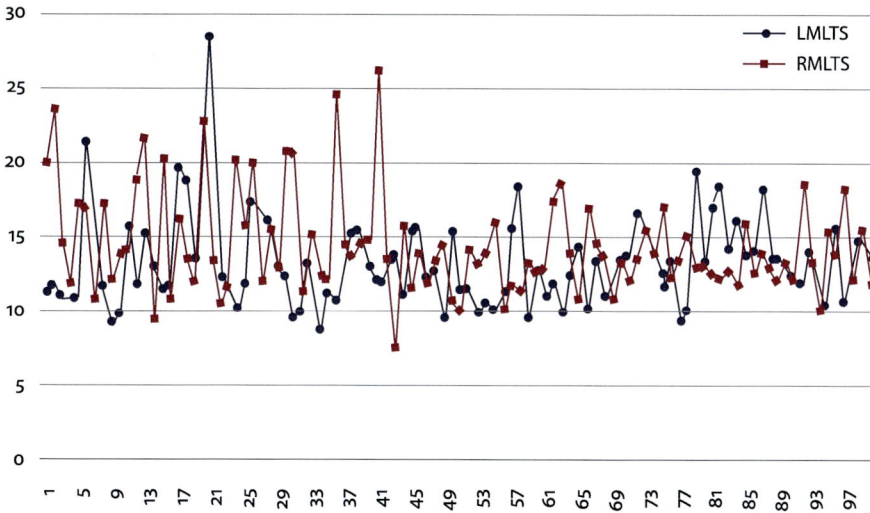

**Figure 1.**  Spoken MLT as the representation of syntactic complexity for both Gloria (grey) and Grace (black)

Gloria's was not (.18; $p=.43$). This implies that Gloria's spoken system is relatively stable over time and that there is a slight but significant decrease for Grace. As far as the amount of variability is concerned, Grace shows generally more variability over the whole time period (Gloria has an average local range of 6.6 and Grace of 7.9, $p<.01$), and that the amount of variability decreases over time for both. The slopes of the local ranges are negative and significant for both girls (−.4 for Gloria and −.8 for Grace; $p<.01$ in both cases).

Combined, this shows that there is no general increase in proficiency in spoken syntactical development, but instead that both girls seem to stabilize. Grace's performance is somewhat more variable from moment to moment.

## VocD/spoken

As far as lexical development is concerned, Gloria seems to be slightly more proficient than Grace, especially at the beginning of the trajectory (see Figure 2). Visual inspection suggests that Grace is "catching up" with her sister over time. As far as variability is concerned, there does not seem to be a clear trend for VocD/spoken.

The Monte Carlo analyses show that Gloria's average VocD is indeed higher than her sister's (Gloria's is 42.626 and Grace's is 38.580; $p<.01$). As far as development is concerned over time, Grace shows a significant positive slope (0.090, $p<.01$), but Gloria does not (−0,018, $p=.711$). As far as the average amount of variability is concerned, the girls are the same (Gloria's is 19.158 and Grace's is

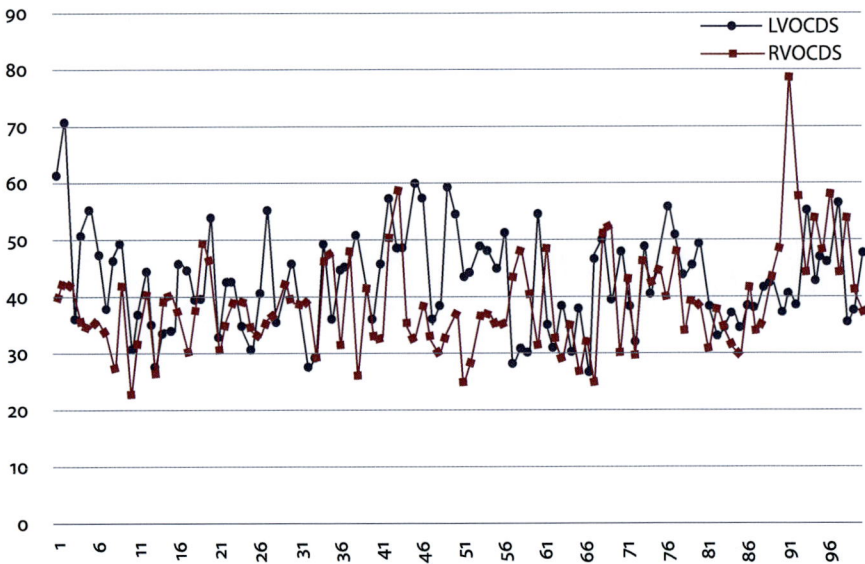

**Figure 2.** Lexical sophistication in Spoken VocD for both Gloria (grey) and Grace (black)

17.578, $p = 0.067$). However, the slopes of variability are different: Gloria's variability is decreasing across time ($-0.081, p < .001$) whereas Grace's is increasing (0.078, $p = .003$).

These results show clear differences between the two girls: Grace is the one who is showing signs of development (increase in level and increase of variability), whereas Gloria, who has an initial higher level, only seems to stabilize over time.

**Table 2.** Summary of the findings of the analyses for spoken language

|  | MLT | | VocD | |
|---|---|---|---|---|
|  | Gloria | Grace | Gloria | Grace |
| Higher average scores |  |  | X |  |
| Significant increase or decrease in score over time |  | X neg |  | X pos |
| More variability in scores |  |  | X |  |
| Significant increase or decrease in degree of variability over time | X neg | X neg | X neg | X pos |

## Discussion and conclusion

In this study we illustrated the spoken language development of two identical twins, who started off with similar levels of proficiency, with similar experiences and similar tasks over the course of eight months on two very robust measures that are assumed to be less prone to variability, one reflecting syntactic development (length of T-units) and one reflecting lexical development (VocD). Although as many variables as possible were identical for the twins in our data, the data show that the two girls show clear individual differences in the development of their spoken language.

These data show that that linguistic behaviour is highly variable, even if it concerns rather robust, general linguistic variables such as average T-unit length or lexical diversity. Apparently, it is difficult to predict linguistic behaviour from one moment to the next. The data also show that when all possible variables are controlled for as much as we can, the behaviour among individuals is not exactly the same. Even if we look at only ten tasks in a row, over about four weeks or so, we can see big differences within and among learners.

The scores shown in Figures 1 and 2 go up and down rather unpredictably. Much of the variability seems to be rather random and may be considered "noise" in traditional statistics. This variability would be filtered out in a statistical group analysis (for example in the first five measures of VocD in Figure 2). However, some of the variability may be developmental as the system is trying to reorganize and may become less stable (for example in the last five measures of VocD in Figure 2). Of course, in group studies, multi-level analyses with several measures may alleviate the problem of variability and variation to some extent, but findings will still have to be interpreted very cautiously. The high variability and variation in spoken language production found in the current study suggests that many immediate effects may only be very transitory as learners tend to change continuously, even in measures that are as general and robust as MLT and VocD.

Studies that have applied CDST principles to second language development have argued that it is crucial to acknowledge the dynamic nature of the developmental process. Due to the dynamic interaction of embedded and embodied subsystems involved, language development will have to be regarded as a nonlinear system that is changing in multiple dimensions leading to dynamically emerging attractor states. As would be predicted in the CDST approach, these multiple changes are manifested by a high degree of variability that constitutes a meaningful indication of self-organization. Like the increased amount of variability is associated with an increase in development, the lack of variability tends to signal a relative lack of change. The current study has shown that these characteristics also hold for the development of second language speech. The striking difference in variability in the speaking data in the comparison of two highly similar learners has confirmed the general CDST premise that (second) language development is an individually owned process. The current study has demonstrated that a CDST description of speaking as one of the most complex modalities of language learning is helpful and can importantly add a longitudinal dimension of speaking research. The study has also demonstrated the value of considering variability as a relevant source of behavioral data.

These observations lead to several important implications for the teaching context. First, the observed variability in speech production is not a sign of the learner's limitation but is a positive sign of an actively developing system. This implies that we should be careful with the assessment of spoken language production at one moment in time. From a CDST perspective, continuous assessment as it is advocated in the CEFR using language portfolios (North, 2007) is to be preferred over single oral exams (Lowie, 2013). Second, since all of the learner's subsystems are essentially unique, the dynamic interactions of these subsystems over time emphasize the individual nature of this process. Consequently, teaching should ideally cater for the individual's needs and challenges and customize instruction to optimize the effect. This implies that individual "language coaching" is bound to be more effective than traditional language teaching in groups. It can also be inferred from this that the larger the group in the classroom context is, the less efficient the language coaching is bound to be. Finally, an important implication of the CDST approach to second language development is that language instruction should not be taken literally. The emergent and self-organizing nature of second language speech development implies that language cannot be taught, but can only be acquired. This requires a type of language coaching that optimizes the learner's opportunities to learn. Explicit instruction is simply less likely to lead to successful perturbations of the language system than meaningful communicative interaction. The relative success of immersion settings and language learning situations in which the target language is also the main language of communication confirms this observation for the development of speaking. Organizing personalized opportunities of communicative interaction may be challenging for language instructors, especially when confronted with large groups of learners, but is a requirement that needs to be taken seriously.

From this study we may conclude that all measures show a large degree of variability, and no two learners will do it the same way. Therefore, we need to accept the limitations of short-term interventions: we may see short-term effects, but they can predict little about future performance. Language development is not predetermined and is an individually owned process as demonstrated in the speaking data in the current study that show striking differences in the variability patterns of identical twins as they learn English as a second language in Taiwan. The individual and variable nature of speaking has important implications for effective language teaching for speaking.

## References

Bardovi-Harlig, K., & Bofman, T. (1989). Attainment of syntactic and morphological accuracy by advanced language learners. *Studies in Second Language Acquisition*, 11(1), 17–34.

Biber, D., Gray, B., & Poonpon, K. (2011). Should we use characteristics of conversation to measure grammatical complexity in L2 writing development? *TESOL Quarterly*, 45(1), 5–35. <https://doi.org/10.5054/tq.2011.244483>

Bulté, B. (2013). *The development of complexity in second language acquisition: A dynamic systems approach*. Unpublished PhD dissertation. University of Brussels.

Caspi, T. (2010). *A dynamic perspective on second language development*. Groningen: University of Groningen.

Chan, H. (2015). *A dynamic approach to the development of lexicon and syntax in a second language*. Groningen: University of Groningen.

Chan, H., Verspoor, M., & Vahtrick, L. (2015). Dynamic development in speaking versus writing in identical twins. *Language Learning*, 65(2), 298–325. https://doi.org/10.1111/lang.12107

Council of Europe. (2001). *Common European Framework of Reference for Languages: Learning, teaching, assessment*. Cambridge: Cambridge University Press.

Dale, P.S., Harlaar, N., Haworth, C.M., & Plomin, R. (2010). Two by two: A twin study of second-language acquisition. *Psychological Science*, 21(5), 635–640.

De Bot, K., Lowie, W., & Verspoor, M. (2007). A dynamic systems theory approach to second language acquisition. *Bilingualism: Language and Cognition*, 10(1), 7–21. https://doi.org/10.1017/S1366728906002732

Dykstra-Pruim, P. (2003). Speaking, writing, and explicit-rule knowledge: Toward an understanding of how they interrelate. *TT –Foreign Language Annals TA -*, 36(1), 66–76.

Elman, J. (1995). Language as a dynamical system. In T. van Gelder (Ed.), *Mind in motion: Explorations of the dynamics of cognition* (pp. 195–225). Cambridge, MA: The MIT Press.

Grosjean, F. (2010). *Bilingual life and reality*. Cambridge, MA: Harvard University Press.

Hayiou-Thomas, M.E. (2008). Genetic and environmental influences on early speech, language and literacy development. *Journal of Communication Disorders*, 41, 397–408.

Herdina, P., & Jessner, U. (2002). *A dynamic model of multilingualism. Perspective of change in psycholinguistics*. Clevedon: Multilingual Matters.

Hood. (2004). *PopTools Version 2.6.2*. Canberra, Australia: CSIRO. Retrieved from <http://www.cse.csiro.au/poptools>

Hosenfeld, B., Van der Maas, H.L.J., & Van den Boom, D.C. (1997). Indicators of discontinuous change in the development of analogical reasoning. *Journal of Experimental Child Psychology*, 64, 367–395.

Hunt, K.W. (1970). Do sentences in the second language grow like those in the first? *TESOL Quarterly*, 4, 195–202.

Larsen-Freeman, D. (1997). Chaos/complexity science and second language acquisition,. *Applied Linguistics*, 18(2), 141–165. Retrieved from <http://www.scopus.com/inward/record.url?eid=2-s2.0-0040151244&partnerID=40&md5=68465fc5cd8f0bc3db4bf803ce3ce4ce>

Larsen-Freeman, D. (2006). The emergence of complexity, fluency and accuracy in the oral and written production of five Chinese learners of English. *Applied Linguistics*, 27, 590–619.

Larsen-Freeman, D., & Cameron, L. (2008). *Complex systems and applied linguistics*. Oxford: Oxford University Press.

Lee, K., & Karmiloff-Smith, A. (2002). Macro- and microdevelopmental research: assumptions, research strategies, constraints, and utilities. In N. Granott & J. Parziale (Eds.), *Microdevelopment: Transition processes in development and learning* (pp. 243–268). Cambridge: Cambridge University Press.

Long, M. H. (1996). The role of the linguistic environment in second language acquisition. In W. C. Ritchie & T. K. Bhatia (Eds.), *Handbook of language acquisition, Vol. 2: Second language acquisition* (pp. 413–468). New York, NY: Academic Press.

Lowie, W. (2013). The CEFR and the dynamics of second language learning: Trends and challenges. *Language Learning in Higher Education*, 2(1), 17–34.

Lowie, W., Van Dijk, M., Chan, H. P., & Verspoor, M. H. (2017). Finding the key to successful L2 learning in groups and individuals. *Studies in Second Language Learning and Teaching*.7(1), 127–148.

Lowie, W., Van Dijk, M., Chan, H., & Verspoor, M. (2017b). Finding the key to successful L2 learning in groups and individuals. *Studies in Second Language Learning and Teaching*, 771(7), 127–148. https://doi.org/10.14746/ssllt.2017.7.1.7

Lu, X. (2012). The relationship of lexical richness to the quality of ESL learners' oral narratives. *Modern Language Journal*, 96(2), 190–208.

Mackey, A. (1999). Input, interaction and second language development: An empirical study of question formation in ESL. *Studies in Second Language Acquisition*, 21(4), 557–587.

Macwhinney, B. (2005). The emergence of linguistic form in time. *Connection Science*, 17, 191–211.

Malvern, D., Richards, B., Chipere, N., & Durán, P. (2004). *Lexical diversity and language development*. New York, NY: Palgrave Macmillan.

North, B. (2007). The CEFR illustrative descriptor scales. *Modern Language Journal*, 91, 656–659.

Penris, W., & Verspoor, M. (2017). Academic writing development: A complex, dynamic process. In S. E. Pfenninger & J. Navracsics (Eds.), *Future research directions for applied linguistics* (pp. 215–242). Bristol: Multilingual Matters.

Pienemann, M. (1998). *Language processing and second language development. Processability Theory*. Amsterdam: John Benjamins.

Pine, K. J., Lufkin, N., Kirk, E., & Messer, D. (2007). A microgenetic analysis of the relationship between speech and gesture in children: Evidence for semantic and temporal asynchrony. *Language and Cognitive Processes*, 22(2), 234–246. https://doi.org/10.1080/01690960600630881

Port, R., & van Gelder, T. (1995). *Mind as motion: Exploration in the dynamics of cognition*. Cambridge, MA: The MIT Press, Bradford Books.

Spoelman, M., & Verspoor, M. (2010). Dynamic patterns in the development of accuracy and complexity: A longitudinal case study on the acquisition of Finnish. *Applied Linguistics*, 31(4), 532–553.

Stromswold, K. (2001). The heritability of language: A review and metaanalysis of twin, adoption, and linkage studies. *Language*, 77(4), 674–723.

Stromswold, K. (2006). Why aren't identical twins identical? Genetic, prenatal and postnatal factors. *Cognition*, 101, 333–384.

Thelen, E., & Smith, L. B. (1994). *A dynamic systems approach to the development of cognition and action*. Cambridge, MA: The MIT Press.

Van Dijk, M., Verspoor, M. H., & Lowie, W. (2011). Variability and DST. In M. Verspoor, K. De Bot, & W. Lowie (Eds.), *A dynamic approach to second language development: Methods and techniques* (pp. 55–84). Amsterdam: John Benjamins.

Van Geert, P. (1998). A dynamic systems model of basic developmental mechanisms: Piaget, Vygotsky and beyond. *Psychological Review*, 5, 634–677.

Van Geert, P. (2003). Dynamic systems approaches and modeling of developmental processes. In J. Valsiner & K. J. Conolly (Eds.), *Handbook of developmental Psychology* (pp. 640–672). London: Sage.

Verspoor, M., Lowie, W., & Van Dijk, M. (2008). Variability in second language development from a dynamic systems perspective. *Modern Language Journal*, 92(2), 214–232. https://doi.org/10.1111/j.1540-4781.2008.00715.x

Verspoor, M., Schmid, M. S., & Xu, X. (2012). A dynamic usage based perspective on L2 writing. *Journal of Second Language Writing*, 21(3), 239–263. https://doi.org/10.1016/j.jslw.2012.03.007

Verspoor, M., & Van Dijk, M. (2013). Variability in a dynamic systems approach. In C. A. Chapelle, *The encyclopedia of applied linguistics* (pp. 2051–6059). Malden, MA: Wiley-Blackwell.

Vyatkina, N. (2012). The development of second language writing complexity in groups and individuals: A longitudinal learner corpus study. *The Modern Language Journal*, 96(4), 576–598. https://doi.org/10.1111/j.1540-4781.2012.01401.x

Wolfe-Quintero, K., Hae-Young, K., & Inagaki, S. (1998). *Second language development in writing: Measures of fluency, accuracy, and complexity*. Honolulu, HI: University of Hawaii Press.

Wu, J. R. W. (2012). GEPT and English language teaching and testing in Taiwan. *Language Assessment Quarterly*, 9(1), 11–25. https://doi.org/10.1080/15434303.2011.553251

Yip, V., & Matthews, S. (2007). *The bilingual child: Early development and language contact*. Cambridge: Cambridge University Press. Retrieved from <http://www.cambridge.org/catalogue/catalogue.asp?isbn=9780521544764>

# Appendix

The texts are the first and last samples collected. They are coded for formulaic sequences with words in the sequences highlighted, the beginning of a chunk marked with an * and the end of a single chunk or a series of connected chunks marked with **. The coding was done according to definitions and procedures used in Verspoor, Schmid, and Xu (2012).

## Gloria 1 (257 words)

* Attending a university** means you can have *more opportunities *to choose your carrier**. I also *want to *attend the university**. If I *want to *have a good job**, I should learn more knowledge, and I can *make more friends *in the university**. We can *make good use of the time *in the college**. I really except for the *guitar club** *in the college**. Everyone can *sing and dance** and *play the guitar** together. I *want to *join a band** and I can enjoy in the wonderful *music world**! *It sounds nice**, doesn't it ? *The time in college** may be *really free**. I like the class *in the college** because I don't *have to *get up *early**. It is *hard *for me *to wake up *too early**. *Truly speaking**, I am a little *lazy girl**. If I *have more time** maybe I can *have *a part-time job**. I am *looking forward to *have a party** *when I grow up to** a college student. The parties on the movie *look really fun**. Everyone can *talk and sing and dance together**. *That way**, everyone can *be good friends**. Studying is also *important to** me. *Most of the parents** *want their children to *study hard** and *so do my parents**. But my *math teacher** said it *didn't matter *whether you *go to courses* or not**. So I just *want to *choose the subjects** which I like. And I *won't go to** classes I am not* interested in**. I hope I can *enjoy my life in the college**.

## Gloria 101 (309 words)

*To begin with**, *the population of *cell phone users** is intensifying because *smart phones** are *going from strength to strength**. Second, I am *startled by** the rank because I consider that Taiwan *ranks behind** Singapore. Third, I believe that this phenomenon will *make everyone *drift apart**. *Many people *use *cell phones** *in a bid *to kill time**, so they make *using phone** as *a daily routine**. *A good illustration** is that *most of the people** will *use their phones** when *taking the MRT**, and they will *distract from** looking to their environment. There was *a piece of extremely bad news** *happened recently**. *A college student** killing 4 people *on the MRT** *at random**, 21 *people were injured with** a flash insight. *According to** the accurate analysis, *many people** *ignored their own safety** *because of** being *immersed in *their cell phones**. *In my point of view**, 99 being *a mature person**, you must *keep thing in perspective**.

　　Why *cell phones** are *so attracting to** Taiwanese? *From my point of view**, there are *too many kinds of *video games *for us to download**, and *cell phones** include many functions. *To name a few**, you can *use *cell phones** *to chat with *intimate friends**, *play with *complimentary apps**, and *take pictures**. My dad is *a very good example**. He can *lie on the sofa** *with his phone** *almost 10 hours every day** *without saying a word**, and he is *indulged in** *those boring games**. Some people *see technology as** *a runaway force** that we humans can *no longer control**, and *it is hard to believe that** some people even *have *more than one cell phone *with them**. *Using phones** wherever you are has been *a popular trend**, and it seems that *no one** can *get rid of ** this phenomenon. *In a nutshell**, *the rate of** *using phones** *in Taiwan** will *keep stepping up**.

## Grace 1 (176 words)

I think everyone *wants to** *improve themselves**, so they *study harder** and they can have a better job. But I think getting more knowledge *in university** is *the most important thing**. Getting more knowledge is an important work. If you just *graduate from the senior high school**, your experience and knowledge are so little .And If you are a boss, you want to have a new employee, you will choose a person who *graduated from senior high school** or university? Everyone is nobody before they get knowledge, but when you *keep learning and studying**, *you will be somebody**. And if you learn more, you will *get a good job** .If you *get a good job** ,you will have *a better life**. You can buy the *things you like**, you also can *travel around the world**. So I think that why we *have to** study in university? Because there are still *a lot of** things we have to know. Because we have to get *a good job**. Because we *want to make our dream come true**!

## Grace 101 (266 words)

People are *inclined to** *own *at least one *cell phone** *in Taiwan**. *From the elder to** the youth, people are *used to having** a *cell phone** even it's not indispensable *at all**. *Take my grandma for an instance**, she's *not busy at all** but she also own two *smart phones**. *Chatting with** friends and *hanging around on** Facebook seem to be *her daily routine**. *Not only** my grandma, I am not excluded. Line and Facebook seem to *play a vital role in my *dreary life**.

*The ratio of** using *cell phones** is *increasing rapidly** *because of** the *habit of** Taiwanese. People *in Taiwan** are *getting more and more indifferent**, we just *absorbed in** the *virtual life** *all day long**. 72 We *get used to** *talk on** the net *instead of** *chatting with each others** *face to face**. *Hanging out with** friends and *attending outdoor activities** seem to be *less and less attractive to us**. *Thanks to** the convenient wi-fi, people can *talk to** others *through the internet** easily, so it makes the *popularity of** *using cell phones** rise *much more** exceedingly. Although *it's handier to *connect with friends** *on the net**, I still *prefer *chatting with others *face to face* to gossiping on the internet**. It's *better to *convey our real emotions *face to face *to others *than typing words**. *Facial expressions** and *the manner of speaking** can help you not to *misunderstand others' words**. I think it's *better not to be *indulged in *the virtual life *all day long**. The time you use the phone *less, the more** real things you can *get in touch with**.

CHAPTER 6

# Exploring the spoken learner English constructicon
## A corpus-driven approach

Gaëtanelle Gilquin
Université catholique de Louvain

This study, which is set in the field of Applied Construction Grammar, seeks to identify the constructions that are typical of higher intermediate to advanced spoken learner English. It does so by relying on the recurrent sequences of part-of-speech (POS) tags extracted from the Louvain International Database of Spoken English Interlanguage (LINDSEI) and its native counterpart. This corpus-driven approach reveals that learner speech mainly consists of basic constructions like [NP] or [Subj V], although longer and more complex constructions can be found among the less frequent sequences. The chapter also discusses methodological issues (such as the link between POS tag sequences and constructions), as well as theoretical matters (including the place of speech in Construction Grammar).

## 1. Introduction: Construction Grammar and learner speech

Construction Grammar (CxG), as developed among others by Goldberg (1995, 2006), is a family of approaches that argue that constructions, defined as "conventionalized pairings of form and function" (Goldberg, 2006: 3), are the fundamental units of language. What is traditionally referred to as the 'mental lexicon', that is, the repertoire of words and information about these words stored in the mind, therefore takes the form, in construction grammarians' view, of a 'constructicon', a network of constructions that represent speakers' knowledge of a language. In CxG, constructions cover a wide range of phenomena, not only syntactic structures (like the ditransitive construction), but also morphemes, words or idioms, with various degrees of specification (idioms, for instance, can be fully specified, as in *kick the bucket*, or partly specified, as in *kick <someone> when PRONOUN BE down*). Empirical studies, based on corpus data and/or experiments, have demonstrated the existence of speakers' mental representations of constructions (e.g.

https://doi.org/10.1075/aals.17.06gil

Bencini & Goldberg, 2000) and have provided very detailed information about the use of some constructions in naturally-occurring language (see Boas, 2003 on resultative constructions or Hilpert, 2008 on future constructions, among many other examples).

While constructions have been studied in English and, increasingly, in other languages as well (Hilpert's 2008 study, for example, investigates future constructions in English, German, Dutch, Danish and Swedish, and some publications have focused on constructions in other languages, e.g. French in Bouveret & Legallois, 2012), non-native language varieties have hardly been dealt with from a CxG perspective, although it was demonstrated over ten years ago that learners of a language do have constructions too (cf. Gries & Wulff, 2005). In fact, the field of 'Applied Construction Grammar' (De Knop & Gilquin, 2016), which adopts a CxG perspective to examine second/foreign language teaching and learning, is a very recent development within constructionist approaches. In a literature review on the subject, Gilquin & De Knop (2016) have identified ten studies or so that apply the theory of CxG to the study of learner language, and the volume edited by De Knop & Gilquin (2016) includes another eleven studies representing Applied Construction Grammar. What is typical of these studies – and, one could add, of many studies in CxG – is that they rely on written data. De Knop & Mollica (2016), for example, apply among learners of German an experimental design (sorting task) that has often been used to test the existence of constructions in native speakers' mental representations: on the basis of a written questionnaire listing a number of sentences, the subjects are required to write down the sentences in different boxes according to their overall meaning. As for Valenzuela Manzanares & Rojo López (2008), they rely on the International Corpus of Learner English (ICLE; Granger et al., 2002), a corpus of argumentative essays written by learners of English, to investigate the use of the ditransitive construction by Spanish learners of English.[1]

As a result of this bias towards written learner language, we have very little information about the use of constructions in learner speech, at least from a purely CxG perspective.[2] In an attempt to fill this gap in Applied Construction Grammar, the present chapter explores the spoken constructicon typical of Eng-

---

1. Studies in Applied Construction Grammar that have dealt with speech include Ellis & Ferreira-Junior (2009), Eskildsen (2014) and Roehr-Brackin (2014). What is characteristic of these studies, however, is that they investigate a small number of learners, from only one (in Eskildsen, 2014 and Roehr-Brackin, 2014) to seven (in Ellis & Ferreira-Junior, 2009).

2. We do have information about the use of linguistic phenomena in learner language that could be said to correspond to constructions in the CxG sense (e.g. clausal complementation in Tizón-Couto, 2014, epistemic adverbial markers in Gablasova & Brezina, 2015, or formulaic language in Wood, 2010), but these studies are not theoretically embedded within CxG. More-

lish as a foreign language (EFL), by examining the spoken production of a large number of higher intermediate to advanced EFL learners.[3] Its aim is to identify the constructions that are likely to be entrenched in the spoken EFL constructicon. The methodology adopted is corpus-driven and relies on the extraction of part-of-speech tag sequences from the Louvain International Database of Spoken English Interlanguage (LINDSEI; Gilquin et al., 2010) and its native counterpart, the Louvain Corpus of Native English Conversation (LOCNEC; De Cock, 2004). In this respect, too, the study can be said to be exploratory, since it tests a recent proposal by Cappelle & Grabar (2016) to use part-of-speech tag sequences as an approximation to constructions. In the next section, it will be explained how a part-of-speech tagged corpus can provide information about the constructicon, while in Section 3 the corpora and methodology used in this study will be described. The results of the analysis can be found in Section 4, followed by some methodological afterthoughts in Section 5 and concluding remarks in Section 6.

## 2. Part-of-speech tagging to explore a constructicon

Part-of-speech (POS) tagged corpora are annotated in such a way that each token in the corpus is accompanied by a tag indicating the part of speech of the word. These tags are useful to disambiguate forms that can correspond to different word classes (e.g. *promise* as a noun or as a verb), but also to retrieve all items that belong to a specific word class (e.g. all adjectives). Interestingly, in the same way as one can extract clusters of words from a corpus (see, e.g., Conrad & Biber, 2004 or Chen & Baker, 2010), it is also possible, on the basis of a POS tagged corpus, to extract clusters of POS tags, that is, sequences of POS tags that are recurrent in a corpus (e.g. a sequence of an adjective followed by a noun). Such sequences are interesting because, as pointed out by Kennedy (1996:225), they represent

---

over, they are limited to the investigation of one or a small set of similar constructions and do not seek to adopt the kind of global approach that is aimed at here.

3. In that, it differs from Eskildsen (2014), a bottom-up constructionist study of the spoken production of one ESL (English as a second language) learner. While Eskildsen (2014) provides a qualitative analysis of an individual constructicon, showing for example how the emergence of a construction relates to previous utterances produced by the learner, the constructicon that will be described here is an abstraction based on the production of a large number of learners. This abstracted constructicon may not correspond to the actual constructicon of any of the individuals, but because it relies on many individual constructicons, it may be said to present a higher degree of representativeness than Eskildsen's (2014) description of a single constructicon.

"expressions of syntactic patterning" and can form "the basis for quantitative studies of the use of syntactic structures and processes".

The first corpus-based study that used POS tag sequences to investigate (written) learner language was Aarts & Granger (1998). They borrowed this technique from stylometry, in which POS tag sequences are used as a possible marker of authorship (cf. Spassova & Turell, 2007 or Bel et al., 2012). Applying this technique to three components of ICLE (the Dutch, French and Finnish components) as well as a comparable native corpus, they sought to "uncover EFL learners' fingerprints" (Aarts & Granger, 1998: 132). They thus discovered that, in comparison with the native writers, the three learner populations overused patterns starting with a connective and underused patterns involving prepositions. They also showed that patterns specific to a certain mother tongue (L1) population were quite common, with French-speaking learners, for example, overusing sentence-initial *to*-infinitive clauses of purpose. This study was followed by a few others which sought either to find out more about the structure of interlanguage (cf. Tono, 2000 on interlanguage development or Borin & Prütz, 2004 on L1 transfer) or to automatically identify learners' L1, in the spirit of the earlier studies in authorship attribution (cf. Golcher & Reznicek, 2011).

Recently, it was suggested by Cappelle & Grabar (2016) that POS tag sequences, or 'POS n-grams', can be used to approximate constructions in a CxG sense.[4] More precisely, the authors claim that "common (…) grammatical n-grams are constructions, in a Construction Grammar sense: they are form-function pairings which native speakers have memorized (and which learners of a language should acquire) as a result of their high frequency". While in Goldberg (1995) non-compositionality was seen as the necessary condition for a construction to exist, later on, in Goldberg (2006), it is frequency that became the main criterion for a pattern to be recognized as a construction. It therefore makes sense, as Cappelle & Grabar (2016) do, to consider that frequent POS tag sequences can correspond to constructions – although not all POS tag sequences are necessarily constructions, as we will see below. Relying on this assumption and using the Corpus of Contemporary American English as a basis for the extraction of the 100 most frequent POS 5-grams,[5] Cappelle & Grabar propose

---

4. See also Wible & Tsao (2010) and Forsberg et al. (2014) for an automatic extraction of constructions partly based on POS n-grams.

5. It should be pointed out that Cappelle & Grabar (2016) define frequency in terms of types. For them, the most frequent POS tag sequences are those that correspond to the highest number of *different* lexical sequences. Here, frequency will be defined in terms of tokens, rather than types, since it is high token frequency that is said to promote entrenchment (see Bybee & Thompson, 1997; Ellis, 2013).

constructing an "n-grammar" of English, a repertoire of POS n-grams that can serve as a useful resource for the teaching of the English language. More generally, and more importantly for our purposes, they establish a convincing link between frequent POS tag sequences and the constructicon of a language or language variety (although they do not use the term 'constructicon' as such). Building on this principle, the present study will consider POS tag sequences in a corpus of spoken learner English as a way of approaching the constructicon that is typical of EFL speech.

The reliance on POS n-grams has the obvious advantage that the extraction can be done fully automatically. The technique can thus be applied to large corpora including the production of many individuals, which ensures a high degree of representativeness and generalizability of the results (see also footnote 3). In addition, it allows for a global approach to constructions, with no a priori (and presumably subjective) selection of certain constructions for investigation, as would for example be the case for a technique like collostructional analysis, whose starting point has to be a (set of) specific construction(s). Here, all the POS tag sequences are considered to be of potential relevance. It should be underlined, however, that POS tag sequences only make it possible to approach, or approximate, a constructicon. For one thing, not all POS tag sequences are "units of language" (Goldberg, 1995:4). Cappelle & Grabar (2016:281) recognize this too when they write that "n-grams are 'blind' to constituent structure. Sometimes, an n-gram does not contain enough (or one might say, it may contain too much) to make up what we would intuitively consider an ordinary linguistic sequence". In order to overcome this problem, Cappelle & Grabar 'complete' the POS n-grams when necessary, turning for example the sequence "*to* verb *the* X$_{noun}$ *of*" into "*to* verb *the* X$_{noun}$ *of* (Y$_{NP}$)" (as illustrated by *to improve the quality of* / *to improve the quality of life*). Here, the POS n-grams will not be completed, but the lexical sequences underlying them will be examined, as recommended by Aarts & Granger (1998:135), so as to check the status of these POS n-grams. The second reason why POS tag sequences only paint an incomplete picture of what the constructicon looks like is that, as mentioned in Section 1, constructions in a CxG sense cover a variety of phenomena. By looking at POS n-grams, we mainly focus on the more syntactic types of constructions and neglect word-based constructions (like individual words or idioms). While this could be viewed as a limitation of the study, it can also simply be seen as a reflection of construction grammarians' closer attention to syntactic constructions (cf. the so-called 'argument structure constructions') to the detriment of more word-based constructions.[6] It can also be

---

6.  Morphemes, for instance, are considered as an extension of the category of constructions by Goldberg (1995:4): "*expanding the pretheoretical notion of construction somewhat,* morphemes

said that this predominantly syntactic approach is in fact an ideal complement to the corpus linguistic perspective on learner language, which is more often centred on word-based phenomena (cf., for example, Nesselhauf, 2005 or Ädel, 2006), and a good starting point for a first exploration of the constructicon of learner speech.

## 3.    Corpora and methodology

The POS-based exploration of the spoken EFL constructicon is based on LIND-SEI, the Louvain International Database of Spoken English Interlanguage, whose first version was released in 2010. LINDSEI is made up of the transcription of informal interviews of higher intermediate to advanced learners of English representing different L1 backgrounds. All the components of LINDSEI in its published version have been exploited in this study, namely eleven components corresponding to eleven L1 backgrounds (Bulgarian, Chinese, Dutch, French, German, Greek, Italian, Japanese, Polish, Spanish and Swedish) and a total of almost 800,000 words produced by 554 different learners (the interviewers' turns have been disregarded).[7] To serve as a point of reference, LINDSEI has been used in combination with LOCNEC (Louvain Corpus of Native English Conversation), the (British) native counterpart of LINDSEI, corresponding to some 125,000 words for the interviewees' turns. All the components of LINDSEI and LOCNEC were compiled according to the same design criteria, which makes them perfectly comparable with each other. Thus, each of the interviews lasts about 15 minutes and includes three tasks: a warming-up activity, in which the interviewees had to talk about one of three set topics for a few minutes, a free informal discussion about topics of concern to young people, and a picture description, based on the same cartoon. The interviewees all have a similar profile, being students in their third or fourth year at university, with English as their main subject. The interviews were also transcribed with the same guidelines and were linked up with metadata about the interviewer, the interviewee and the context of the interview.

The released versions of LINDSEI and LOCNEC consist in raw text, with no annotation other than the tags that are part of the transcription conventions,[8] e.g. the use of the tags <B> and </B> to open and close, respectively, the interviewees'

---

are clear instances of constructions in that they are pairings of meaning and form that are not predictable from anything else" (emphasis added).

7.  A second version of LINDSEI is currently in preparation and should include twenty sub-corpora.

8.  The transcription conventions can be found at <https://uclouvain.be/en/research-institutes/ilc/cecl/transcription-guidelines.html>.

turns, or the use of the equals sign to indicate word truncation (like *esp=*). Thanks to the help of the *Centre de Traitement Automatique du Langage* of the University of Louvain, however, all the data were POS tagged and it is these POS tagged versions of LINDSEI and LOCNEC that were used here.[9] One of the problems with automatic POS taggers is that, with some rare exceptions, they have been designed to process standard written language (Gilquin & De Cock, 2011: 149). Running them on spoken and/or learner corpus data, therefore, is not necessarily a straightforward matter. Yet, attempts to POS tag LINDSEI by means of CLAWS (the Constituent Likelihood Automatic Word-tagging System; Garside & Smith, 1997) turned out to be relatively successful, with an accuracy rate of about 92% (see Gilquin, 2016).[10] In the process of POS tagging LINDSEI for this study, a simplified version of the CLAWS tagset was used that reduced the number of different tags, from 137 separate POS tags in the original tagset to 27 POS tags in the simplified version (the list of simplified tags and their meanings can be found in the Appendix).[11] In addition, the settings of CLAWS had to be adapted to take into account the specificities of the LINDSEI and LOCNEC transcription conventions.

Once LINDSEI and LOCNEC were POS tagged, recurrent sequences of POS tags were extracted from the interviewees' turns. Sequences of two to ten POS tags were retrieved, together with the raw frequency of these sequences in the corpus and the lexical sequences corresponding to these POS tag sequences. It should be noted that filled pauses were excluded from the analysis. Theoretically, they could easily be accommodated by a constructionist approach. Like any other construction, they consist in a pairing of form and function, the form being something like *er* or *erm*, and the function being, for example, stalling for time or segmenting discourse (see Clark & Fox Tree, 2002 for an overview of some of the functions of filled pauses). However, from a practical point of view, the occurrence of filled pauses within sequences of POS tags prevents the automatic detection of the types of constructions that have traditionally been recognized in CxG. In (1), for instance, the NP construction cannot be identified due to the filled pause found between the determiner and the noun. While I believe that, ultimately, such

---

9.  I am deeply indebted to Hubert Naets, from the *Centre de Traitement Automatique du Langage*, both for POS tagging the two corpora and for extracting the POS n-grams that served as a basis for the analysis presented in this chapter.

10.  The latest version of the POS tagger, CLAWS4, was used in conjunction with the C7 tagset. I thank Paul Rayson for providing access to CLAWS locally.

11.  For example, "CC" (coordinating conjunction) and "CCB" (adversative coordinating conjunction) in the original tagset were combined into the tag "CCO" (coordinating conjunction). A tag for truncation ("TR") was added to account for incomplete words. Foreign words were tagged as "unclassified words" ("FU"). See <http://ucrel.lancs.ac.uk/claws7tags.html> for the original C7 tagset.

phenomena should be taken into account in a CxG of speech, for a first CxG-based exploration of spoken interlanguage it might be safer to rely on constructions that are close enough to the classic repertoire of constructions in CxG. This does not mean that features typical of spontaneous speech are totally excluded. Thus, truncations, which represent parts of words in the traditional sense, have been retained, as have repetitions of POS tags, which can correspond to disfluent sequences but also to standard constructions (compare *exam exams* and *bus station* for the combination of two nouns). Unfilled pauses, corresponding to blanks in the recording, are not assigned any POS tags and are therefore not included in the analysis.

(1)   she shows off before <u>her er friends</u>                               (LINDSEI-PL017)[12]

The approach adopted here can be described as 'corpus-driven' or bottom-up, in that it starts from the free exploration of the corpus data to make generalizations about language, and more particularly about the spoken EFL constructicon. This approach can be contrasted with a 'corpus-based' or top-down approach, which looks at the corpus data through the prism of a specific idea or hypothesis. The difference between corpus-based and corpus-driven should be seen as a continuum, though, with studies being more or less corpus-based or corpus-driven. Purely corpus-driven studies, in particular, are difficult to set up as researchers often have some sort of (even vague) idea before embarking on an analysis. The corpus-driven approach, in fact, has been characterized as an "idealized extreme" along the continuum by McEnery et al. (2006:8). In the present case, POS tagging could be said to limit the corpus-driven scope of the analysis. Relying on a pre-existing POS tagset means that one starts from a definition of word classes that, to a certain extent, will guide the analysis and the interpretation of the results, while, as pointed out by Biber (2010:201), "[i]n its most extreme form, the corpus-driven approach assumes only the existence of word forms; grammatical classes and syntactic structures have no a priori status in the analysis". However, Biber (2010) himself classifies as "corpus-driven research" (though of a hybrid type) the studies in 'pattern grammar' which "assume the existence of some grammatical classes (e.g., verb, noun) and basic syntactic structures" (Biber, 2010:202). In the present case, the fact that, on the basis of pre-existing POS tags, patterns are made

---

12.  In the examples, the relevant part corresponding to the POS tag (sequence) being discussed is underlined. Dots represent unfilled pauses (of various lengths), and the equals sign marks truncated words. The code between brackets after each example provides information about the corpus from which the sentence is taken (LINDSEI or LOCNEC) as well as the number of the interview. In the case of LINDSEI, the code also indicates the interviewee's mother tongue background (BG = Bulgarian, CH = Chinese, DU = Dutch, FR = French, GE = German, GR = Greek, IT = Italian, JP = Japanese, PL = Polish, SP = Spanish, SW = Swedish).

to emerge automatically from the data, with no human control over what should be kept and what should be left out, suggests that the initial stages of the analysis are sufficiently atheoretical to qualify as a corpus-driven study. In addition, we will focus on the most frequent sequences of POS tags, which also contributes to the more 'corpus-driven' orientation of the study, since "recurrent patterns" and "frequency distributions" are the two elements cited by Tognini-Bonelli (2001: 87) as constituting the foundation of a corpus-driven approach. Such a corpus-driven approach is rare in CxG, which has tended to start from hypotheses about specific constructions that are tested by examining instances of these constructions in corpora. Yet, it is ideally suited for the purposes of the present study, which seeks to explore a language variety that has hardly been dealt with in CxG.

## 4.  A corpus-driven analysis of LINDSEI's constructicon

### 4.1  Single POS tags

As a first overview of the constructicon emerging from LINDSEI, we can consider Table 1, which provides a list of the POS tags found in the corpus, in decreasing order of (raw) frequency. A similar list is provided for LOCNEC by way of comparison. What we see is that the three most frequent POS tags in LINDSEI are word classes that compose noun phrases: personal pronouns ("PRONpers"), common nouns ("N") and determiners ("DET"). They are followed by lexical verbs ("Vlex"), which come in fourth position in LINDSEI. This top four seems to point to a rather basic structure in learner language, made up of noun phrases and verbs.

If we compare the list of POS tags for LINDSEI with that for LOCNEC, we notice that, aside from the obvious differences in frequency, which are essentially due to the differing sizes of the two corpora, there is quite some overlap in the ranks occupied by the POS tags. Most of them are ranked similarly in the two corpora, either having exactly the same rank or being just one rank apart. The POS tags that present a difference of two ranks or more are in bold in the table. Among these, we can mention adverbs and determiners. While, as mentioned above, determiners round out the top three in LINDSEI, in LOCNEC it is adverbs ("ADV") that occupy this position. This suggests that adverbs are more important in the native spoken constructicon than they are in the learner spoken constructicon. The verb *have* ("Vhave") and existential *there* ("EX") are ranked higher in native than in non-native speech, whereas for the infinitive marker *to* ("TO"), proper nouns ("Nprop") and truncated words ("TR"), it is the opposite. That "TR" is ranked higher in LINDSEI than in LOCNEC seems to indicate that disfluency

**Table 1.** Single POS tags and their frequency in LINDSEI and LOCNEC

| | LINDSEI | | | LOCNEC | | |
|---|---|---|---|---|---|---|
| Rank | POS | Meaning | Freq. | POS | Meaning | Freq. |
| 1 | PRONpers | Pers. pron. | 102454 | PRONpers | Pers. pron. | 16869 |
| 2 | N | Common noun | 90727 | N | Common noun | 14132 |
| 3 | DET | Determiner | 84590 | ADV | Adverb | 13921 |
| 4 | Vlex | Lexical verb | 77605 | Vlex | Lexical verb | 13265 |
| 5 | ADV | Adverb | 76653 | DET | Determiner | 12066 |
| 6 | PREP | Preposition | 55376 | PREP | Preposition | 8975 |
| 7 | Vbe | Verb *be* | 45582 | Vbe | Verb *be* | 7816 |
| 8 | CCO | Coord. conj. | 42826 | CCO | Coord. conj. | 6442 |
| 9 | ADJ | Adjective | 36038 | ADJ | Adjective | 5267 |
| 10 | CSU | Subord. conj. | 24022 | UH | Interjection | 3769 |
| 11 | UH | Interjection | 18076 | CSU | Subord. conj. | 3287 |
| 12 | NEG | Negation | 15417 | Vhave | Verb *have* | 2219 |
| 13 | TO | Inf. marker *to* | 13675 | NEG | Negation | 2202 |
| 14 | Vhave | Verb *have* | 11165 | Vdo | Verb *do* | 2059 |
| 15 | Vdo | Verb *do* | 11104 | TO | Inf. marker *to* | 1926 |
| 16 | Nprop | Proper noun | 10684 | NUM | Numeral | 1674 |
| 17 | NUM | Numeral | 10473 | Vmod | Modal verb | 1640 |
| 18 | Vmod | Modal verb | 9926 | Nprop | Proper noun | 1554 |
| 19 | TR | Truncation | 9525 | PRONindef | Indef. pron. | 928 |
| 20 | PRONindef | Indef. pron. | 5353 | EX | Exist. *there* | 484 |
| 21 | ZZ | Letter | 3961 | TR | Truncation | 381 |
| 22 | EX | Exist. *there* | 2513 | ZZ | Letter | 346 |
| 23 | PRONwh | *wh*-pronoun | 1549 | PRONwh | *wh*-pronoun | 199 |
| 24 | GE | Gen. marker | 530 | GE | Gen. marker | 109 |
| 25 | FU | Unclassified | 340 | FU | Unclassified | 22 |

as expressed through truncation is a comparatively more typical phenomenon in learner English than in native English.

## 4.2   Top POS n-grams

In this section, we examine the top thirty POS n-grams, that is, the most frequent sequences of POS tags, whatever their length. The list for LINDSEI and LOCNEC can be found in Table 2, which also includes the absolute frequency of the POS tag sequences as well as a concrete example of a lexical instantiation for each sequence.[13]

As can be expected, bigrams represent the bulk of the sequences, with longer n-grams being much less frequent. In a similar way to lexical bundles (cf. Altenberg, 1991: 127), the longer the POS tag sequence, the less likely it is to occur frequently in a corpus. In fact, only bigrams and trigrams (in bold in the table) can be found among the top thirty POS tag sequences. The first 4-gram is ranked 54th in LINDSEI and 66th in LOCNEC. A comparison of the top thirty POS n-grams in LINDSEI and LOCNEC shows that, while the first trigram is ranked higher in LINDSEI (5th rank) than in LOCNEC (8th rank), there is a smaller number of distinct POS n-grams (types) in the former (three types) than in the latter (five types). Native speakers thus appear to have assimilated a higher number of longer, and hence presumably more complex, constructions than non-native speakers, but among the latter such constructions might be more entrenched, since they are ranked higher than in native speech.

When considering the actual POS tag sequences, one important element to underline is that they do not necessarily correspond to constructions in the sense of complete structural units (see Section 2). The POS bigram "PREP DET" (preposition and determiner, ranked 4th in LINDSEI and LOCNEC), for example, is incomplete, in that it normally requires a noun to form a prepositional phrase. The POS trigram "PREP DET N", ranked 5th in LINDSEI and 8th in LOCNEC, is one way in which the sequence can be completed (with a common noun),[14] but there are others, which can be found among the longer POS tag sequences, cf. "PREP DET ADJ N", a sequence illustrated by *for the whole year*, but which, because of its length and structural complexity, only appears much later in the list of POS tag sequences (rank 151 in LINDSEI and 140 in LOCNEC). Some of these POS n-grams are also incomplete due to the spontaneous and unrehearsed nature of speech. Thus, in the lexical sequence <u>*in my*</u> *in my hometown*, taken from LINDSEI-BG012, the first "PREP DET" sequence is left incomplete, and it is only when the sequence is repeated that it is completed by a noun. In other cases, the sequence is simply interrupted and never taken up again, cf. the "PREP DET" sequence in *the sands <u>on the</u> . and the sands is very soft* (LINDSEI-CH001).

---

**13.**  For the meaning of the POS tags, see Appendix.

**14.**  It must be emphasized that a POS tag sequence that is structurally complete could still have other elements added to it, cf. "PREP DET N PREP N", an extension of the "PREP DET N" sequence which, like the former, can correspond to a [PP] construction (see below on the [PP] construction), e.g. *from my point of view*.

**Table 2.**  Top thirty POS n-grams and their frequency in LINDSEI and LOCNEC

| Rank | LINDSEI | | | LOCNEC | | |
|------|---------|------|---------|--------|------|---------|
| | POS n-gram | Freq. | Example | POS n-gram | Freq. | Example |
| 1 | DET N | 46177 | a bird | DET N | 6380 | my sister |
| 2 | PRONpers Vlex | 30008 | I agree | PRONpers Vlex | 4754 | he plays |
| 3 | PRONpers Vbe | 25320 | he is | PRONpers Vbe | 4605 | they are |
| 4 | PREP DET | 24276 | on the | PREP DET | 3690 | from a |
| 5 | **PREP DET N** | 15220 | after our exam | N PREP | 2677 | group of |
| 6 | N PREP | 15180 | essay about | ADV ADV | 2601 | quite early |
| 7 | N CCO | 14560 | sheet and | Vlex PRONpers | 2580 | call them |
| 8 | ADJ N | 14414 | clean city | **PREP DET N** | 2361 | for a day |
| 9 | Vlex PRONpers | 14091 | dislike it | Vlex ADV | 2246 | came up |
| 10 | Vlex DET | 13856 | chose my | ADJ N | 2233 | bad guy |
| 11 | CCO PRONpers | 13626 | and they | CCO PRONpers | 2201 | but she |
| 12 | CSU PRONpers | 13578 | that we | Vbe ADV | 2132 | are still |
| 13 | ADV PRONpers | 12517 | maybe it | CSU PRONpers | 2115 | because we |
| 14 | ADV ADV | 12397 | only then | Vlex PREP | 2111 | known as |
| 15 | Vlex PREP | 12158 | come to | N CCO | 2086 | day or |
| 16 | Vbe ADV | 11164 | was very | ADV PRONpers | 2053 | sometimes we |
| 17 | ADV ADJ | 10383 | just nice | Vlex DET | 1973 | heard the |
| 18 | Vlex ADV | 10216 | eat well | ADV ADJ | 1592 | quite big |
| 19 | TO Vlex | 9885 | to speak | PREP N | 1585 | on holiday |
| 20 | DET ADJ | 9294 | a fine | ADV Vlex | 1566 | never heard |
| 21 | N PRONpers | 9253 | books we | PRONpers Vhave | 1460 | they had |
| 22 | **DET N PREP** | 8585 | the list of | DET ADJ | 1437 | a real |
| 23 | **Vlex DET N** | 8306 | buy a house | PRONpers Vmod | 1392 | he can |
| 24 | PREP N | 8005 | for lunch | **PRONpers Vbe ADV** | 1362 | it is really |
| 25 | NEG Vlex | 7610 | not say | TO Vlex | 1334 | to see |
| 26 | PRONpers Vmod | 7563 | I should | **DET N PREP** | 1320 | the head of |

| Rank | LINDSEI | | | LOCNEC | | |
|------|---------|------|---------|---------|------|---------|
| | POS n-gram | Freq. | Example | POS n-gram | Freq. | Example |
| 27 | Vbe DET | 7527 | is the | N PRONpers | 1318 | country I |
| 28 | PRONpers Vdo | 7488 | she does | **PRONpers Vlex PRONpers** | 1212 | we saw him |
| 29 | PRONpers Vhave | 7468 | we have | **DET ADJ N** | 1195 | a good sign |
| 30 | DET DET | 7426 | its own | PRONpers ADV | 1179 | I hardly |

Table 2 also reveals that, quite interestingly, the top four POS n-grams are identical across native and non-native speech, with the combination of a determiner and a common noun ("DET N") being the most frequent sequence, followed by the combination of a personal pronoun and a lexical verb ("PRONpers Vlex"), and that of a personal pronoun and the verb BE ("PRONpers Vbe"), and finally the (incomplete) "PREP DET" sequence mentioned above. This suggests that both native and non-native speakers' constructicons rely, in the first place, on short and simple constructions of the type [NP], [Subj V] and [PP],[15] whose internal structure seems relatively basic: among the complete sequences, the NP is made up of a determiner and a noun, the Subject consists in a personal pronoun, and the Verb is either a lexical verb or the verb BE. Examples from LINDSEI illustrating each of these constructions are provided in (2) to (4).

(2)  and this was just it was just <u>a guesthouse</u>                    (LINDSEI-SW042)

(3)  <u>she was</u> . in a coma for .. a year .. and then <u>she awoke</u>      (LINDSEI-GR039)

(4)  I read the story <u>before the</u> representation but er it was eh very touching to see it                                                          (LINDSEI-IT035)

Variants of each of these three constructions can be found further down the list, both in LINDSEI and LOCNEC. In the case of [NP], there are two other n-grams in Table 2 that can correspond to complete constructions, namely "ADJ N", which occurs in both corpora and is illustrated in (5), and "DET ADJ N", found only in the top thirty of LOCNEC and exemplified in (6). However, full [NP] constructions can also take the form of a single word, either a noun or a pronoun, and as such their presence in Table 2 can be detected whenever a personal

---

**15.**  Throughout this chapter, constructions will be enclosed in square brackets. The abbreviations used in these constructions are as follows: N = noun; NP = noun phrase; Obj = object; Obl = oblique; PP = prepositional phrase; Prt = particle; S = sentence/clause; Subj = subject; V = verb; VP = verb phrase; Xcomp = predicative complement.

pronoun ("PRONpers") or a common noun ("N") is part of an n-gram, e.g. "N PREP" or "CCO PRONpers". It should also be underlined that nouns and personal pronouns need not be part of a recurrent sequence to function as an [NP] construction, which means that Table 2, which lists n-grams only, underestimates the predominance of the [NP] construction in native and non-native speech. It will be reminded from Table 1, which lists single POS tags, that "PRONpers" and "N" are the two most frequent POS tags in LINDSEI and LOCNEC, and all of these personal pronouns and common nouns are potential [NP] constructions, whether they are part of highly recurrent POS n-grams like those in Table 2 or not. As for the incomplete sequences that belong (and are common) to the top thirty of LINDSEI and LOCNEC, some seem to point to the presence of longer and more complex [NP] constructions, involving post-modification introduced by, e.g., prepositions or (zero) relative pronouns. The former is illustrated by the bigram "N PREP" and the trigram "DET N PREP", whose (possible) status as an [NP] construction is confirmed by examples (7) and (8). As for the latter, it is suggested by the presence of a POS tag sequence that, at first sight, might be difficult to parse, namely "N PRONpers" (common noun and personal pronoun, ranked 21st in LINDSEI and 27th in LOCNEC). When examining in context the lexical sequences that underlie this POS bigram, it appears that in a number of cases they correspond to nouns followed by a bare relative clause, as shown in example (9).

(5)   yes of course we have <u>beautiful landscapes</u>                    (LINDSEI-IT027)

(6)   but erm that was that was definitely <u>a new experience</u>         (LOCNEC-E030)

(7)   I think if . one director is really good em . he can talk about women and make <u>films about</u> them                                                   (LINDSEI-BG025)

(8)   it cannot work because <u>the rest of</u> the people doesn't do it      (LINDSEI-SP024)

(9)   that's . one <u>thing I</u> have to do of course                       (LINDSEI-DU021)

The [Subj V] construction is also very prominent in the list through its several variants. Next to the "PRONpers Vlex" and "PRONpers Vbe" sequences that belong to the top three, Table 2 includes the combinations of a personal pronoun with the verb *HAVE* ("PRONpers Vhave") and with a modal auxiliary ("PRONpers Vmod") – two sequences that are ranked higher in native speech than in non-native speech – and the combination of a personal pronoun with the verb *DO* ("PRONpers Vdo"), a sequence that is only part of the top thirty of LINDSEI. In addition, the list for LOCNEC includes two trigrams which can both involve a [Subj V] construction: "PRONpers Vbe ADV", with the addition of an adverb, and "PRONpers Vlex PRONpers", which can correspond to a [Subj V Obj] construction, as illustrated in (10).

(10)   I don't really want to go back to do that .. <u>I enjoyed it</u> but I don't want I want to
do something different now                                            (LOCNEC-E013)

Among the four most frequent POS tag sequences shared by native and non-native speakers, we also noticed an incomplete sequence that could correspond to a [PP] construction, since it is made up of a preposition followed by a determiner ("PREP DET", see example (4)). Next to this incomplete sequence, Table 2 includes two POS n-grams that have the structure of full [PP] constructions, combining, respectively, a preposition and a noun ("PREP N", example (11)), and a preposition followed by a determiner and a noun ("PREP DET N", example (12)). The latter, in fact, is the first POS trigram of the list and it happens to be ranked higher in LINDSEI than in LOCNEC. This suggests that the [PP] construction is relatively well entrenched in the spoken constructicon of EFL learners, allowing them to produce with a certain degree of automaticity sequences of three words that, in certain cases, will function as post-modifiers of another phrase, thus making the sequence even longer and more complex. Compare, in this respect, (12), where the "PREP DET N" sequence functions independently as an adverbial, with (13), where the underlined "PREP DET N" sequence post-modifies another similar sequence (*at the end*) and is thus part of a longer [PP] construction.

(11)   there w= there was more . er friendship that could be felt <u>among students</u>
                                                                     (LINDSEI-PL018)

(12)   first everyone had to become quiet and <u>at that moment</u> . you saw how he got
more nervous actually                                               (LINDSEI-DU022)

(13)   eventually at the end <u>of the book</u> the two women . erm come together again
                                                                     (LINDSEI-FR033)

It was suggested earlier that the [Subj V] construction occupies a prominent position in the constructicon as it emerges from LINDSEI and LOCNEC. Among the top thirty POS tag sequences, we also find some that seem to point to the prominence (though to a lesser extent) of the [V Obj] construction. The "Vlex PRONpers" sequence, illustrated in (14), is a case in point. The sequence is shared by native and non-native speakers, but is ranked slightly higher among the former (7th rank in LOCNEC and 9th rank in LINDSEI). In addition, LINDSEI and LOCNEC each have a POS trigram which potentially involves a [V Obj] construction and which is not found in the top thirty list of the other corpus: a sequence made up of a lexical verb followed by a determiner and a noun ("Vlex DET N") in LINDSEI (rank 23), and the "PRONpers Vlex PRONpers" sequence referred to above in LOCNEC, which combines with the [Subj V] construction to form a [Subj V Obj] construction. The trigrams are exemplified in (15) and (16), respectively.

(14)    since it's not compulsory attending I . try to <u>avoid it</u>        (LINDSEI-GR020)

(15)    that's what I realised cos a friend of mine he <u>bought a car</u> there

(LINDSEI-GE015)

(16)    I went travelling in Israel for a week and <u>it impressed me</u> cos it was so different
to England                                                                 (LOCNEC-E032)

In Section 4.1 it was pointed out that the POS tag for adverbs is ranked higher
in LOCNEC than in LINDSEI. This predominance of adverbs in native speech
is also visible in the list of POS tag sequences. As appears from Table 2, quite
a few sequences include an adverb ("ADV"), but there are more such sequences
in LOCNEC (8 sequences) than in LINDSEI (5 sequences), and the first one is
ranked higher in LOCNEC (rank 6) than in LINDSEI (rank 13). Adverbs being
often optional elements in the sentence, they are rarely included in the type of
constructions that are typically described in CxG. However, some interesting findings emerge from the top thirty POS tag sequences including an adverb, especially
when we compare the native and non-native sequences. I would like to focus on
two sequences in particular, namely "ADV PRONpers" and "Vlex ADV", where
the adverb precedes a personal pronoun and follows a lexical verb, respectively.
While the former is ranked higher in LINDSEI than in LOCNEC, the latter presents the reverse profile. The prominence of the "ADV PRONpers" sequence in
LINDSEI could be related to the tendency of learners, documented for written
English (e.g. Granger & Tyson, 1996, see also Aarts & Granger, 1998: 137), to
overuse connectors like *however* or *therefore* (which are tagged as adverbs by
CLAWS) in initial position, that is, before the subject. This feature is exemplified
in (17), which illustrates the "ADV PRONpers" sequence. Interestingly, LOCNEC,
unlike LINDSEI, includes in its top thirty list of POS n-grams the combinations
of an adverb followed by a lexical verb ("ADV Vlex") and a personal pronoun followed by an adverb ("PRONpers ADV"), which both correspond to an alternative
positioning of the adverb within the sentence, cf. (18) and (19). As for the "Vlex
ADV" sequence, which is more characteristic of LOCNEC than of LINDSEI, it
could partly be explained by the underuse of the phrasal verb construction [V Prt
(Obj)] by learners of English, which characterizes both speech and writing but is
particularly striking in speech (see Gilquin, 2015). (20) provides an example of
this construction in LOCNEC.

(17)    <u>actually he</u> played a trick on everybody                         (LINDSEI-BG039)

(18)    we <u>actually ended</u> up in a s = very tiny village on the coast not far from
Dubrovnik                                                                  (LOCNEC-E039)

(19)    and <u>I suddenly</u> thought well I'm enjoying teaching              (LOCNEC-E022)

(20)   through rehearsing it you <u>find out</u> more about .. what . the the different layers
     of meaning are                                           (LOCNEC-E004)

Finally, Table 2 provides some insight into the use of coordination and subordination in native and non-native speech. Given the fact that subordination is usually considered to be syntactically more complex than coordination (cf. Beaman,
1984: 45; Pallotti, 2015: 124), we might expect coordinate constructions to be more
typical of learner speech and subordinate constructions to be more typical of
native speech. This expectation seems to be confirmed by the much higher rank of
the "N CCO" sequence (noun followed by coordinating conjunction) in LINDSEI
(7th rank) as compared to LOCNEC (15th rank). This sequence can be used to
coordinate two nouns ([N *and* N], cf. (21)) or two clauses ([S *and* S], cf. (22)), but
in both cases the structure is relatively simple. However, the "CCO PRONpers"
sequence (coordinating conjunction followed by a personal pronoun), exemplified in (23), does not show any difference in ranking between LINDSEI and LOC-
NEC (both are ranked in 11th position). As for the only top thirty POS n-gram
including a subordinating conjunction, "CSU PRONpers", contrary to expectations it is ranked slightly higher in LINDSEI (rank 12) than in LOCNEC (rank
13). This result and the example in (24) demonstrate that learners are capable of
syntactic complexity in speech, just like (and sometimes even more than) native
speakers, and that these complex constructions can be well entrenched in the
learner constructicon.

(21)   I could see the <u>advantages and</u> disadvantages of both systems really
                                                   (LINDSEI-GE011)

(22)   we just met at the university <u>centre and</u> we . had lunch all together
                                                   (LINDSEI-FR021)

(23)   I'm not so professional in in these these fields <u>but I</u> like it very much
                                                   (LINDSEI-CH007)

(24)   she looks at it and she's not very happy with the result <u>although it</u> does look
     like her                                      (LINDSEI-SW047)

What this analysis reveals about the spoken EFL constructicon is first of all that
it is not necessarily so different from its native equivalent. Among the thirty
most frequent POS tag sequences, twenty-five are shared by native and non-native
speakers – despite having different ranks, for the most part. And while the more
complex nature of native speech transpires for example from the proportion of
POS trigrams in the top thirty, it appears that learners can deal with the complexity of certain structures at least as well as native speakers do. The differences that

emerge mainly concern individual sequences, like the phrasal verb construction or the positioning of adverbs within a construction.

A second finding is that the constructions that are most highly entrenched in the native and non-native spoken constructicons are relatively basic constructions of the phrase type (NP, PP, etc. or a combination thereof). The top thirty list of POS tag sequences includes very few constructions that could form a complete clause (which, of course, is related to the length of the n-grams). If we exclude cases of ellipsis (which could result in a clause status for, e.g., "PRONpers Vbe" as in *I am* or "PRONpers Vmod" as in *He should*) and imperatives (with which POS n-grams like "Vlex PRONpers" or "Vlex DET N" could be complete clauses, cf. *Check it!* or *Answer this question!*), we find possible instances of the intransitive construction [Subj V] in LINDSEI and LOCNEC through the POS n-gram "PRONpers Vlex" (e.g. *I sympathise*), as well as the [Subj V Obj] construction through the POS n-gram "PRONpers Vlex PRONpers" (e.g. *I like it*), which however is only found in the top thirty of LOCNEC. The sorts of constructions that are typically discussed in CxG, like the ditransitive construction, the caused motion construction or the resultative construction, do not seem to rank among the most commonly produced constructions in (native or non-native) speech. If we examine longer and less frequent POS n-grams, however, we discover sequences that can correspond to some of these constructions, e.g.

(25)  "PRONpers Vlex PRONpers DET N" ~ ditransitive double object construction [Subj V Obj$_1$ Obj$_2$]
I just er <u>I gave her some yogurt</u> . and eh she was so happy she was like smiling all the time                                (LINDSEI-PL011)

(26)  "PRONpers Vlex DET N PREP DET N" ~ caused motion construction [Subj V Obj Obl]
<u>she takes the picture . to her home</u> . and . all her . friends or or family look at the picture and . admire it                (LINDSEI-GE045)

(27)  "PRONpers Vlex PRONpers ADJ" ~ resultative construction [Subj V Obj Xcomp] because it's horrible you know <u>they drive you crazy</u>  (LINDSEI-SP017)

A third element worth underlining, which is perhaps not so apparent from the results outlined above but which has been constantly observed during the analysis, is that one and the same POS tag sequence hides a great variety of linguistic instantiations (especially, as can be expected, for open word classes). Some of these are lexically unique, in that the exact words of the sequence are not repeated elsewhere in the corpus, but they share a syntactic pattern which is brought to light thanks to the POS tagging. Without this syntactic level of abstraction, it would have been impossible to group these sequences together and take them as evidence that some construction might be entrenched in a constructicon of spoken (learner) English. This does not mean, of course, that the lexical sequences are irrelevant for a CxG-based analysis. For one thing, it is only through the careful examination of these sequences that we can interpret the constructions (see also Section 5). For another, it would be useful to combine the analysis of POS n-grams with an analysis of lexical n-grams in order to try and distinguish cases where it is the fully abstract construction that seems to be entrenched from cases where, arguably, it is lexically specified constructions with the same syntactic structure that are entrenched.

## 5. Methodological afterthoughts

Since one of the aims of this chapter was to test the use of POS n-grams as a way of identifying entrenched constructions, a few methodological afterthoughts are in order. The first element to emphasize is that, as demonstrated in the preceding section, POS n-grams do provide valuable insights into the constructicon by highlighting recurrent patterns that, in some cases, correspond to self-contained constructions as defined in CxG. That this is only true *in some cases*, however, already points to one of the limitations of the methodology, namely that some of the POS tag sequences extracted from the corpora do not qualify as constructions as they have traditionally been recognized in CxG, since they are not structurally complete. The remaining sequences are *potential* constructions in the CxG sense. Sometimes, however, this potential status is not confirmed when we look at (some of) the lexical instantiations of the POS n-gram. For example, it was noted above that the "PRONpers Vlex PRONpers" can correspond to a [Subj V Obj] construction. But next to actual [Subj V Obj] constructions such as *I called her* or *he invited us*, the list of lexical sequences underlying this POS n-gram includes examples like *I believe she*, which in fact introduces a subordinate clause with an ellipted *that*. We also have to take account of the possible embedding of constructions. A "DET N" sequence can be a complete [NP] construction, but it can also be an NP that is embedded in a [PP] construction (cf. *a boy* in *about a boy*). And finally, a POS n-gram could correspond to several distinct constructions depending on the lexical items that are used in the concrete realizations. The "PRONpers Vlex DET ADJ N" sequence, for instance, points to the presence of a transitive construction of the type [Subj V Obj], as illustrated by *she cooked a nice meal*. However, provided a certain kind of verb is used, the sequence can also correspond to a "copular construction" (Goldberg, 2006: 8), as in *it became a major success*. What this suggests is that POS n-grams are only an approximation to constructions. Since constructions in CxG are usually expressed in the form of phrases and/or functions, parsing would probably be a more reliable basis than POS tagging for the identification of constructions. The problem is that parsing of learner language is still in its infancy. Schneider & Gilquin (2016) propose an analysis of a parsed learner corpus, but this is a corpus of written English, and we may assume that parsing a corpus of learner speech would be even more challenging.

Related to this last point is the fact that trying to describe the constructicon of spoken production brings its own share of difficulties. Filled pauses have been mentioned earlier as one type of element that, by interrupting structural units, makes it impossible to extract certain constructions automatically – at least if we take the position, implicit in CxG, that constructions should not include disfluency features. Truncated words, though less common, can have the same effect. While such phenomena can easily be disregarded in the identification of POS n-grams, as has been done here for filled pauses, other disfluent phenomena are more difficult to detect, and thus remove from the data, as they present the same pattern as standard, fluent phenomena. Compare, for example, *a card every day* and *a country a country*, which are both linguistic instantiations of the "DET N DET N" sequence, but only the second of which presumably corresponds to a disfluent repetition. False starts are another example of a typically spoken phenomenon that could not easily be distinguished from fluent sequences with the same succession of POS tags (unless such phenomena have been annotated beforehand in a special way, probably manually). Solving this problem would involve developing more sophisticated techniques for the automatic treatment of disfluency in corpora, or perhaps simply recognizing the specificity of speech in CxG and admitting that filled pauses or false starts, for example, should have their place, not only as constructions, but also within constructions.[16]

Another feature of this study is that it has adopted an essentially corpus-driven approach. While such an approach comes with a commitment to "the integrity of the data as a whole" (Tognini-Bonelli, 2001:84), since it does not start with (possibly biased) assumptions, hypotheses or theories which could cast light on certain data only, in practice the analyst may be overwhelmed by the "wealth of data" (Aarts & Granger, 1998:135). The extraction of the POS n-grams from LINDSEI and LOCNEC provided a huge quantity of data, which could all be examined at different levels of analysis: the level of the POS n-grams (e.g. "DET ADJ N"), their realizations in the form of different lexical sequences (e.g. *the best way*), and the use of these lexical sequences by a certain speaker in a specific con-

---

16. The recognition of typically spoken phenomena is of course not totally absent from CxG or CxG-inspired works (see, e.g., Fried & Östman, 2005; Fischer, 2010; Fischer & Alm, 2013). However, the "bias away from spoken language" that Fried & Östman (2005:1753) referred to over ten years ago is still very much a feature of most constructionist approaches.

text (e.g. *perhaps it's not the best . erm it's not the best way to put it* (LINDSEI-PL033)). In this chapter, only a tiny proportion of these data could be examined, and for the top thirty POS n-grams that were analyzed more thoroughly it was not possible to look at all the lexical instantiations of these POS n-grams in context. This also means that manual disambiguation of all the data is not feasible and that the frequencies that have been provided in this study are raw, not only in the sense of being absolute rather than relative frequencies, but also in the sense of being unedited. This is the reason why, in this chapter, it was decided not to place too much emphasis on frequencies, and on quantitative results in general. While we were not able to consider the top 100 POS n-grams that Cappelle & Grabar (2016) suggest should be included in an "n-grammar" of English and that represent, in their own words, less than "the tip of the tip of the tip of the iceberg" (Cappelle & Grabar, 2016:287), this exploratory study has made it possible to draw a first sketch of the constructicon as it emerges from the spoken production of EFL learners.

## 6.    Concluding remarks

In this chapter, a methodology recommended some 20 years ago for the analysis of learner grammar, and recently applied to the identification of constructions in a CxG sense, has been tested on spoken learner English with a view to exploring the constructicon of this language variety, whose study has so far largely been neglected in CxG. Despite its limitations, the methodology has offered some new insights into the structure of learner speech. To those readers who are familiar with constructionist approaches, the results may seem disappointing because they do not reveal the presence, among the top-ranking POS n-grams, of the type of constructions that are typically dealt with in CxG. However, the results are a reflection of the fact that learner speech – and, to a large extent, native speech too – mainly relies on relatively basic constructions of the type [NP], [PP] or [Subj V]. Note that this does not necessarily say anything about the quality of the speech produced. A basic construction may be instantiated by more or less sophisticated sequences, lexically speaking, depending on the choice of words. Compare, for example, *a really nice place* and *this wonderfully accurate picture*, which are both examples of the "DET ADV ADJ N" POS n-gram but which differ in their degree of lexical sophistication. In addition, POS n-grams do not normally provide information about the correct or idiomatic nature of a sequence. Thus, the "DET ADJ N" POS n-gram includes, next to perfectly appropriate sequences such as *a bright future* or *a famous singer*, less acceptable or idiomatic lexical sequences like *a academical world*, *a beautiful hair* or *a big amount* (5 occurrences of *big amount(s)* in the British National Corpus, as opposed to 714 occurrences of *large amount(s)*). Claiming that learner speech mostly relies on basic constructions, therefore, does not imply any judgment about this language variety. Besides, the list of the top twenty POS trigrams provided in Aarts & Granger (1998: 141) for native and non-native (argumentative) writing suggests that, even in native writing, which arguably represents the kind of default language variety that is (implicitly or explicitly) relied on to make theoretical claims in CxG, syntactically elaborate constructions might not make up the largest proportion of the constructicon.

As can be expected from an exploratory study such as this one, there are many avenues of research that open up in order to refine the preliminary results that have been obtained. Next to the analysis of more and longer POS n-grams in LINDSEI and LOCNEC, we could compare the findings for speech with similar ones for writing, in order to determine what the specificities of each constructicon are. A more targeted approach to the data could also be adopted. While LINDSEI has been treated as an aggregate here, in an attempt to access 'the' spoken learner English constructicon, an obvious next step would be to consider certain L1 components of LINDSEI individually in order to pinpoint constructions that are specific to these L1 populations (cf. Aarts & Granger, 1998) and discover possible traces of L1 transfer in the use of these constructions (cf. Borin & Prütz, 2004). The constructicons thus identified would still be 'collective' constructicons, however, emerging from the combined use of language by several learners. Only by analyzing each LINDSEI interview separately would it be possible to identify individual constructicons. Finally, it has been assumed in this chapter that learners' constructicon is reflected in their language production, and that the corpus frequency of constructions provides information about their degree of entrenchment. However, a constructicon is a mental repertoire of constructions and it might be, for example, that a construction is found in a person's constructicon but is not instantiated in their language production, especially within the specific context of a 15-minute interview, or that the frequency of a construction in a corpus does not serve as the most accurate indication of how strongly entrenched the construction is in mental representations. It has also been assumed that there is a distinct spoken constructicon, but again, even if the constructions typical of speech and of writing differ from each other, it might not be the case that such a distinction actually exists in people's minds. In order to answer questions of this type, a more experimental kind of approach should be adopted. Because so little research has been conducted on spoken interlanguage within constructionist approaches, the range of issues that can be investigated is wide. It is to be hoped that the exploration started here can be taken further and provide fresh insights into both learner language and the nature of speech.

# References

Aarts, J., & Granger, S. (1998). Tag sequences in learner corpora: A key to interlanguage grammar and discourse. In S. Granger (ed.), *Learner English on computer* (pp. 132–141). London: Addison Wesley Longman.

Ädel, A. (2006). *Metadiscourse in L1 and L2 English*. Amsterdam: John Benjamins.

Altenberg, B. (1991). Amplifier collocations in spoken English. In S. Johansson & A.-B. Stenström (Eds.), *English computer corpora: Selected papers and research guide* (pp. 127–147). Berlin: Mouton de Gruyter.

Beaman, K. (1984). Coordination and subordination revisited: Syntactic complexity in spoken and written narrative discourse. In D. Tannen (Ed.), *Coherence in spoken and written discourse* (pp. 45–80). Norwood, NJ: Ablex.

Bel, N., Queralt, S., Spassova, M., & Turell, M. T. (2012). The use of sequences of linguistic categories in forensic written text comparison revisited. In *Proceedings of the International Association of Forensic Linguists' Tenth Biennial Conference* (pp. 192–209). Birmingham: Centre for Forensic Linguistics, Aston University.

Bencini, G. M. L., & Goldberg, A. E. (2000). The contribution of argument structure constructions to sentence meaning. *Journal of Memory and Language*, 43(4), 640–651.

Biber, D. (2010). Corpus-based and corpus-driven analyses of language variation and use. In B. Heine & H. Narrog (Eds.), *The Oxford handbook of linguistic analysis* (pp. 193–223). Oxford: Oxford University Press.

Boas, H. C. (2003). *A constructional approach to resultatives*. Stanford, CA: CSLI.

Borin, L., & Prütz, K. (2004). New wine in old skins? A corpus investigation of L1 syntactic transfer in learner language. In G. Aston, S. Bernardini, & D. Stewart (Eds.), *Corpora and language learners* (pp. 67–87). Amsterdam: John Benjamins.

Bouveret, M., & Legallois, D. (Eds.). (2012). *Constructions in French*. Amsterdam: John Benjamins.

Bybee, J. L., & Thompson, S. (1997). Three frequency effects in syntax. In *Proceedings of the Twenty-Third Annual Meeting of the Berkeley Linguistics Society: General Session and Parasession on Pragmatics and Grammatical Structure* (pp. 378–388). Berkeley, CA: Berkeley Linguistics Society.

Cappelle, B., & Grabar, N. (2016). Towards an n-grammar of English. In S. De Knop & G. Gilquin (Eds.), *Applied construction grammar* (pp. 271–302). Berlin: De Gruyter.

Chen, Y.-H., & Baker, P. (2010). Lexical bundles in L1 and L2 academic writing. *Language Learning & Technology*, 14(2), 30–49.

Clark, H. H., & Fox Tree, J. E. (2002). Using *uh* and *um* in spontaneous speaking. *Cognition*, 84, 73–111.

Conrad, S. M., & Biber, D. (2004). The frequency and use of lexical bundles in conversation and academic prose. *Lexicographica*, 20, 56–71.

De Cock, S. (2004). Preferred sequences of words in NS and NNS speech. *Belgian Journal of English Language and Literatures (BELL), New Series*, 2, 225–246.

De Knop, S., & Gilquin, G. (Eds.). (2016). *Applied construction grammar*. Berlin: De Gruyter.

De Knop, S., & Mollica, F. (2016). A construction-based analysis of German ditransitive phraseologisms for language pedagogy. In S.De Knop & G. Gilquin (Eds.), *Applied construction grammar* (pp. 53–87). Berlin: De Gruyter.

Ellis, R. (2009). Task-based language teaching: sorting out the misunderstandings. *International Review of Applied Linguistics*. 19(3): 221–246.

Ellis, N. (2013). Construction grammar and second language acquisition. In T. Hoffmann & G. Trousdale (eds), *The Oxford handbook of construction grammar* (pp. 365–378). Oxford: Oxford University Press.

Ellis, N. C., & Ferreira-Junior, F. (2009). Constructions and their acquisition. Islands and the distinctiveness of their occupancy. *Annual Review of Cognitive Linguistics*, 7, 187–220.

Eskildsen, S. W. (2014). What's new? A usage-based classroom study of linguistic routines and creativity in L2 learning. *International Review of Applied Linguistics*, 52(1), 1–30.

Eskildsen, S. W. (2015). What counts as a developmental sequence? Exemplar-based L2 learning of English questions. *Language Learning*. 65(1): 33–62.

Fischer, K. (2010). Beyond the sentence. Constructions, frames and spoken interaction. *Constructions and Frames*, 2(2), 185–207.

Fischer, K., & Alm, M. (2013). A radical construction grammar perspective on the modal particle-discourse particle distinction. In L. Degand, B. Cornillie, & P. Pietrandrea (Eds.), *Discourse markers and modal particles: Categorization and description* (pp. 47–87). Amsterdam: John Benjamins.

Forsberg, M., Johansson, R., Bäckström, L., Borin, L., Lyngfelt, B., Olofsson, J., & Prentice, J. (2014). From construction candidates to constructicon entries: An experiment using semi-automatic methods for identifying constructions in corpora. *Constructions and Frames*, 6(1), 114–135.

Fried, M., & Östman, J.-O. (2005). Construction grammar and spoken language: The case of pragmatic particles. *Journal of Pragmatics*, 37(11), 1752–1778.

Gablasova, D., & Brezina, V. (2015). Does speaker role affect the choice of epistemic adverbials in L2 speech? Evidence from the Trinity Lancaster Corpus. In J. Romero-Trillo (Ed.), *Yearbook of Corpus Linguistics and Pragmatics 2015: Current approaches to discourse and translation studies*, 117–136. Dordrecht: Springer.

Garside, R., & Smith, N. (1997). A hybrid grammatical tagger: CLAWS4. In R. Garside, G. Leech, & A. McEnery (Eds.), *Corpus annotation: Linguistic information from computer text corpora* (pp. 102–121). London: Longman.

Gilquin, G. (2015). The use of phrasal verbs by French-speaking EFL learners. A constructional and collostructional corpus-based approach. *Corpus Linguistics and Linguistic Theory*, 11(1), 51–88.

Gilquin, G. (2016). POS-tagging LINDSEI: An experiment. Presentation at the *LINDSEI workshop on the POS-tagging of spoken interlanguage*, Louvain-la-Neuve, 15 October.

Gilquin, G., & De Cock, S. (2011). Errors and disfluencies in spoken corpora: Setting the scene. *International Journal of Corpus Linguistics*, 16(2), 141–172.

Gilquin, G., De Cock, S., & Granger, S. (2010). *Louvain International Database of Spoken English Interlanguage. Handbook and CD-ROM*. Louvain-la-Neuve: Presses universitaires de Louvain.

Gilquin, G., & De Knop, S. (2016). Exploring L2 constructionist approaches. In S. De Knop & G. Gilquin (Eds.), *Applied construction grammar* (pp. 3–17). Berlin: De Gruyter.

Golcher, F., & Reznicek, M. (2011). Stylometry and the interplay of topic and L1 in the different annotation layers in the FALKO corpus. In *Proceedings of Quantitative Investigations in Theoretical Linguistics 4 (QITL-4)* (pp. 29–34). Berlin.

Goldberg, A. E. (1995). *Constructions. A construction grammar approach to argument structure*. Chicago, IL: The University of Chicago Press.

Goldberg, A. E. (2006). *Constructions at work. The nature of generalization in language*. Oxford: Oxford University Press.

Granger, S., Dagneaux, E., & Meunier, F. (2002). *The International Corpus of Learner English. Handbook and CD-ROM*. Louvain-la-Neuve: Presses Universitaires de Louvain.

Granger, S., & Petch-Tyson, S. (1996). Connector usage in the English essay writing of native and non-native EFL speakers of English. *World Englishes*, 15(1), 17–27.

Gries, S. T., & Wulff, S. (2005). Do foreign language learners also have constructions? Evidence from priming, sorting, and corpora. *Annual Review of Cognitive Linguistics*, 3, 182–200.

Hilpert, M. (2008). *Germanic future constructions. A usage-based approach to language change*. Amsterdam: John Benjamins.

Kennedy, G. (1996). The corpus as a research domain. In S. Greenbaum (Ed.), *Comparing English worldwide: The International Corpus of English* (pp. 217–226). Oxford: Clarendon Press.

McEnery, T., Xiao, R., & Tono, Y. (2006). *Corpus-based language studies. An advanced resource book*. New York, NY: Routledge.

Nesselhauf, N. (2005). *Collocations in a learner corpus*. Amsterdam: John Benjamins.

Pallotti, G. (2015). A simple view of linguistic complexity. *Second Language Research*, 31(1), 117–134.

Roehr-Brackin, K. (2014). Explicit knowledge and processes from a usage-based perspective: The developmental trajectory of an instructed L2 learner. *Language Learning*, 64(4), 771–808.

Schneider, G., & Gilquin, G. (2016). Detecting innovations in a parsed corpus of learner English. *International Journal of Learner Corpus Research*, 2(2), 177–204.

Spassova, M., & Turell, M. T. (2007). The use of morpho-syntactically annotated tag sequences as markers of authorship. In *Proceedings of the Second European IAFL Conference on Forensic Linguistics, Language and the Law* (pp. 229–237). Institut Universitari de Lingüística Aplicada, Universitat Pompeu Fabra, Barcelona.

Tizón-Couto, B. (2014). *Clausal complements in native and learner spoken English. A corpus-based study with LINDSEI and VICOLSE*. Bern: Peter Lang.

Tognini-Bonelli, E. (2001). *Corpus linguistics at work*. Amsterdam: John Benjamins.

Tono, Y. (2000). A corpus-based analysis of interlanguage development: Analysing part-of-speech sequences of EFL learner corpora. In B. Lewandowska-Tomaszczyk & P. J. Melia (Eds.), *PALC'99: Practical Applications in Language Corpora. Papers from the International Conference at the University of Łódź, 15–18 April 1999*, 323–340. Frankfurt: Peter Lang.

Valenzuela Manzanares, J., & Rojo López, A. M. (2008). What can language learners tell us about constructions? In S. De Knop & T. De Rycker (Eds.), *Cognitive approaches to pedagogical grammar: A volume in honour of René Dirven* (pp. 197–230). Berlin: Mouton de Gruyter.

Wible, D., & Tsao, N.-L. (2010). StringNet as a computational resource for discovering and investigating linguistic constructions. In *Proceedings of the NAACL HLT Workshop on Extracting and Using Constructions in Computational Linguistics* (pp. 25–31). Los Angeles, CA: Association for Computational Linguistics.

Wood, D. (2010). *Formulaic language and second language speech fluency: Background, evidence and classroom applications*. London: Continuum.

# Appendix    Simplified version of the C7 tagset

| POS tag | Meaning |
|---------|---------|
| ADJ | adjective |
| ADV | adverb |
| CCO | coordinating conjunction |
| CSU | subordinating conjunction |
| DET | determiner |
| EX | existential *there* |
| FO | formula |
| FU | unclassified word |
| GE | genitive marker |
| N | common noun |
| Nprop | proper noun |
| NEG | negation *not* or *n't* |
| NUM | numeral |
| PREP | preposition |
| PRONindef | indefinite pronoun |
| PRONpers | personal pronoun |
| PRONwh | *wh*-pronoun |
| PUNC | punctuation |
| TO | infinitive marker *to* |
| TR | truncated word |
| UH | interjection |
| Vbe | verb *be* |
| Vdo | verb *do* |
| Vhave | verb *have* |
| Vlex | lexical verb |
| Vmod | modal verb |
| ZZ | alphabetical symbol (letter) |

CHAPTER 7

# Creating and using the space for speaking within the foreign language classroom
## What, why and how?

Martin Bygate
Lancaster University

Oral and written language differ in terms of the processing they involve, and the patterns of spoken and written discourse. These in turn imply differences in the challenges each presents to learners. I will consider how these can be distinctive to speaking, and suggest some implications for language teaching and research. I suggest that these characteristics imply a need to create 'pedagogic spaces' for the teaching of speaking, and that for these tasks are a crucial tool. Using examples I identify two particular ways in which tasks can contribute. Firstly the design of tasks can influence the kinds of oral discourse students engage in. Secondly tasks can be used to structure and motivate whole class talk through and across lessons.

## Introduction

Language teaching is of course concerned with developing learners' all round language abilities. However it has been recognised for decades now that oral and written language differ, both in terms of the processing skills that they require, and in terms of the differing patterns of spoken and written discourse. This implies differences in the learning aims in the different parts of the curriculum, as well as differences in the challenges each domain offers to learners. This is not to suggest that speaking can or should be taught separately from the other skills. As Norris et al. (2017: 86) point out, while

'much of language teaching and learning will be concerned with complex, skills-integrated communication tasks rather than teaching towards the disarticulated parts of a holistic language competence one at a time [....n]evertheless, theory and research on the teaching and learning of the four language skills does have much to offer by way of implications for instructional design, even where asso-

https://doi.org/10.1075/aals.17.07byg
© John Benjamins Publishing Company

ciated techniques are embedded within an overall approach to language learning that is fundamentally skills-integrated in orientation'.

Similarly, Gilabert, Manchon, and Vaylets (2016) emphasise the different processes implicated in oral versus written mode tasks. Thus in this chapter I would like to rehearse some of the particular aspects of speaking which deserve our attention, and suggest some key implications for language teaching, and for research. My title reflects the belief that an essential part of teaching (of all kinds) involves creating space in the classroom for learners to engage the target skills, and then using that space in ways that stimulate and support learning. As the classroom is typically (though not necessarily) already an 'oral' space, a central concern for teachers therefore is how that space can be structured and exploited effectively to develop learners' speaking. My main concern in this chapter then is the design and use of tasks for oral language.

## Background to the problem

Since the 1970s, it is perhaps a paradox that focusing on the spoken language has not always been straightforward. Although from the early 1970s SLA has consistently focused on the ability to use language as distinct from knowing about language, nonetheless SLA research and language teaching methodology have tended not to focus explicitly or specifically on the teaching and learning of speaking. Instead most attention has been paid to the ways in which second language capacities develop in general, and to how teaching and communication processes can influence that development.

Since the 1970s few research monographs or edited collections have appeared specifically on the learning or development of oral second language abilities – Hughes, 2002; and Segalowitz, 2010 are notable exceptions. Oral interaction has attracted more attention as a *medium* for language acquisition rather than as a curricular objective, whether through the lens of the interaction hypothesis (e.g. Mackey (Ed.), 2007), in the context of broader approaches to the study of interaction (such as the majority of the papers in McDonough & Mackey, 2013), or from the perspective of socio-cultural theory (e.g. Lantolf & Poehner, 2014). These perspectives tend to have in common the assumption that the spoken medium is a site for important processes for the acquisition of new language –processes such as 'negotiation for meaning', 'recasts', 'co-construction', and 'vertical constructions' (though an exception in the McDonough & Mackey, 2013 volume is the paper by Ziegler et al. on conversational style). It is of course true that in investigating the impact of interaction (such as negotiation for meaning) on learning, many of these studies have concentrated on the impact of interactive talk on changes in the accuracy of learners' speech, and that this is an element of oral language development. Nonetheless, the kind of impact being attributed to interactive processes has less to do with the development of oral discourse capacities and more to do with the growth of learners' lexico-grammatical resources. From this perspective, oral language is handled more as an enabling context than as the focus or object of teaching and learning.

In contrast, another group of SLA researchers has concentrated more closely on the nature of second language performance: the Complexity-Accuracy-Fluency (CAF) group (Housen & Kuiken, 2009) or more recently with the addition of lexical measures (Skehan, 2015), the CALF group. This approach has concentrated on analysing quality of performance and how aspects of task design or implementation can affect it, in terms of fluency, complexity, its accuracy, and its lexical patterning. This work has broadly contributed to understanding quality of oral second language performance – in terms of the incidence of fluency/disfluency markers, of different types of complexity, of different degrees of accuracy. The primary concern has been to attempt to track down the ways in which particular task types and task conditions can differentially affect levels of fluency, accuracy or complexity, and how the level of performance on one measure correlates, or not, to that of another measure. Partly in order to generate differential performances, this research explored ways of varying task designs and the conditions of task performance, thus relating quality of performance to conditions such as the structured or unstructured nature of the task, the presence or absence of pre-task or on-task planning time, the presence or absence of an interactive dimension to the task, and the expectation of some outcome from the task, such as a follow-on activity, or teacher feedback. Development per se has generally not been in focus, and thus longitudinal studies have been relatively rare. Thus the major concern here so far has been to improve understanding of the nature of the phenomena in question than their development. As a result, although this is certainly a simplification, it is broadly true that to date relatively little progress has been made in understanding changes in learners' second language speech over time. Furthermore, it is also the case that the overwhelming majority of studies have been sited in laboratory-type contexts or at best within host classrooms, rather than in the context of classroom practice within ongoing language programmes. The connection between research and the classroom needs to be reinforced.

Neglect of the classroom teaching and learning of speaking is not limited however to the SLA community: something similar can be said of those concerned with the teaching of speaking. Few publications have appeared on the teaching of speaking (exceptions being Bailey & Savage, 1994; Burns & Joyce, 1997; Hughes, 2002; Fulcher, 2003; Pavlenko, 2011; Thornbury, 2005; Folse, 2006;

Thornbury & Slade, 2006; and Weissberg, 2007 (on connecting writing and speaking), even including publications on testing). A search of google scholar brings up only five monographs in the first 12 pages which focus explicitly on speaking, all others being devoted to general issues of second language teaching and learning, or second language acquisition. This contrasts strikingly with the immense output on the teaching of second language reading (demonstrated by the existence of the journal entitled *Reading in a Second Language*) and of second language writing (illustrated by the *Journal of Second Language Writing*) since the 1970s. This may well be due to the default assumption that second language acquisition is primarily concerned with speech. However SLA is also centrally concerned with interlanguage development, which is a quite distinct focus.

Finally, a survey of language teaching course books shows relatively little emphasis on the oral element of the language curriculum, or of putting specifically *oral* language use and development centre stage (e.g. Redstone & Cunningham, 2013). As an example take the following activity from Redstone and Cunningham which is clearly designed to be done orally:

> Activity 8 (in a section on a topic entitled 'The coffee shop')
>
> a.   Work in pairs. Imagine you are going to open a coffee shop, café or restaurant together. Decide on these things:
>    - Name
>    - Location
>    - Theme
>    - The menu
>    - Your own ideas
>    - Interior decoration
>    - Opening hours
>    - Entertainment/music
>    - Number of employees
>
> b.   Work in groups. Tell each other about your new business. Which of the areas in **8a** will be the most difficult to get right? Which will cost the most money?
>
> (Redstone & Cunningham, 2013:93)

The focus in this activity is language forms that are generalizable across modes of communication rather than practices that are particular to oral discourse. The activity is self-contained with no indication in the book that the students' oral work will feed into some further oral activity. So the questions I want to ask are 'What spoken language are we teaching?' and 'What is its place in the lesson?' In what follows I want to consider the specific 'shape' of spoken language; the nature of speaking as a process or skill; some aspects of the learning of speaking; some aspects of specifically oral tasks; and finally the potential impact of the use of oral tasks on classroom discourse and more broadly, the lessons in which they occur.

## Attempting to address the problem

### The shape of spoken language

Carter and McCarthy, 1997 provide transcripts of a range of authentic speech samples, such as the following:

–  'I was going, I was quite young then and she said er get a, get a, we had a a bag it was a, quite a strong bag'

(1997: 37)

The speaker is recounting a childhood memory of his mother. We can assume that the memory is extremely familiar, and has been verbalised and edited many times, so we might expect the discourse to be perfectly fluent. Yet in the short extract we recognise several common features of speech. For instance there are three false starts ('I was going', 'she said er get a, get a', and the indefinite article in '[it was] a'); two repetitions ('get a, get a', and 'a a bag'), and a filled pause ('er'). There is reference to the speaker (the two 'I's). There are four pro-forms ('then', 'she', 'we', 'it'). There are three instances of mitigation or vague language (the two uses of the word 'quite', and the verb 'get'), and also typical, repetition of the same lexical item ('quite') at short intervals. In addition, the vocabulary is high frequency. All these features occur within the short space of 28 running words (including the filled pause 'er').

One of the implications of such extracts is that they remind us how spoken language can often be shaped, and that this shaping is something that learners will need to learn both as speakers and listeners. Although there is clearly variation in the patterning of both speech and writing, it is also clear that what Chafe referred to as 'fragmentation' in speech needs to be incorporated into programmes, in the same way that learners need to learn to manage the density, linearity and structuring that can be found typically (though not exclusively) in written text. That is, the shape of the discourse is an important focus for learning. Reflection around samples of transcribed discourse shows a significant number of features that characterise speech. Compared with written discourse, some of them, such as pauses, false starts and interruptions, are clearly unique to speech. Others are simply statistically more likely in speech, such as reference to speaker and addressee, deictic reference including reference to here-and-now or there-and-then, vague language and mitigation, frequent lexis and formulaic expressions, phrasal or lexical repetition. Typical features of speech (see for example Carter & McCarthy, 1997, 2017; Chafe, 1982, 1985, 2006) can be grouped into four types which reflect the typical participation of an interlocutor, and the shared context of time and space, as shown in the table below. My purpose here is not to suggest that these features are all unique to speech, but simply that they are essential for anyone learning to speak in a second language. These features then give speech a distinctive shape, and set learners a particular challenge, suggesting that a specific oral language curriculum could be useful.

**Table 1.** Aspects of the shape of spoken language

|  | Sharing of meanings | Flow/fluency management |
|---|---|---|
|  | *Collaborative management of content* | *Collaborative turn management* |
| Joint work | – convergence e.g. 'speech accommodation', other repetition<br>– mitigators/amplifiers (adjectives, disjuncts) and vague words<br>– face-to-face pragmatics | – turn-taking<br>– interruptions<br>– initiations & responses<br>– collaborative utterances<br>– collaborative repair |
|  |  | *Easing/compensating for the load* |
| Individual work | *Exploitation of shared context*<br>– deictic reference ('here/there' addressee)<br>– tense & aspect ('now/then')<br>– initiations & responses<br>– ellipsis (shared knowledge) | – fragmentation/simple syntax, ellipsis<br>– front/end focus<br>– use of core features, formulaic language & routines<br>– re-use<br>– pausing, hesitation & fillers<br>– self-repairs: false starts, self-corrections |

A second implication of such extracts is that they hint at the constant work that speakers are doing even when speaking on familiar topics in their first language. This leads to my second point.

## Speaking as process

The shape of spoken language reflects aspects of the processes that speakers have to manage. The 'flow/fluency management' column is evidence of the time pressures on speakers to find, assemble and articulate stretches of talk. This pressure results in lack of time to search for language and monitor formulations. This is widely seen (cf. Chafe) as underlying the relative fragmentation, syntactic simplicity and ellipsis of speech; the use of core (i.e. more frequent) features of the language, including formulaic sequences and routines; the tendency to re-use words and phrases within the same stretch of discourse (which when occurring between speakers can of course contribute to acquisition (Bygate, 1988; Eskildsen, 2015));

and the need to pause, hesitate, and self-repair. Similar phenomena such as pausing and self-repair arise in writing of course, but the time available for search and monitoring is greater than in speech, and the traces (such as pauses and self-corrections) are mainly cleaned away in writing. In speech they are part of the product, as scholars such as Markee (2000) and Seedhouse (2004) have shown (see also Bygate, 1987).

The fact that speech is typically enacted in face to face contexts, enables interlocutors to jointly participate in formulation and repair as the discourse is being produced, so that speech is a privileged site for collaborative turn management. Similarly the sharing of meanings can be invoked and ratified (or not) by both interlocutors during speech, something that is not normally possible in written discourse. Hence the common tendency to adjust speech styles and expression to those of the interlocutor (referred to in the table as "speech accommodation"); to moderate (mitigating or augmenting) expressions of judgement or attitude in order to promote maximum convergence between speakers; and to ensure appropriate interpersonal relations (the pragmatics of face). Finally speakers monitor each others' understandings of context so as to align deictic and tense/aspect reference on each others' knowledge.

These features of spoken language are related to processing models of speech, such as Levelt's (1989). Levelt's model highlights the overlapping (or 'parallel') processing of different parts of the speech production process, notably conceptualisation, incorporating mutual understandings, and the selection of relevant message content; formulation, involving selection and organisation of appropriate words, phrases and morpho-syntactic resources; and articulation, in which the prepared formulations are turned into sound. All the various processes are monitored, and if necessary changed, to ensure the speaker is being appropriate, relevant and accurate throughout. This entails an interactive approach to language use. Indeed Levelt makes clear (1989, Chapter 3) that the processes of conceptualisation and formulation of speech are guided and monitored by the speaker's perception of the listener's point of view, whether in terms of focus, deixis, modality or lexical interpretation. Language use is thus seen as a matter of active decision-making from the speaker's initial choice of intention through to its articulation.

No one can ultimately 'teach' learners to 'learn' this process, or the patterns of speech that it produces. What is needed is for spaces to be opened up in classrooms for learners to engage the processes, with opportunities for formative feedback, both during and after speech. For example, during speech formative feedback might take the form of recasts, meaning negotiation, or co-constructed utterances. After speech it might be mediated through teacher or peer feedback based on notes taken during the talk, self-transcription, teacher transcription, peer or teacher correction of transcription (see Lynch, forthcoming). The task then is the site for language use and language incorporation. It is worth considering some of the implications of this account for teaching and learning.

## Tasks for learning speaking

A basic implication of the discussion so far is that learners must practice oral language use: for one thing, as many others have said, to develop the ability to speak requires engaging in oral communication. This could be seen as ensuring the necessary conditions for the development of the relevant psychomotor skills – the element of Levelt's model of conceptualisation, formulation, articulation, monitoring, including processes such as self-correction and reformulation. Associated with this is that what we say and how we say it has to be negotiated, implying that interlocutors check and help adjust each other's formulations and understandings. Part of this is learning to adjust our meanings and expressions to the understanding of our interlocutors – we need to learn to 'accommodate' to other speakers, and develop the ability in the second language to mutually track each other's understandings. Among other things, this involves negotiating and sharing deictic reference, attitude and linguistic formulation. But there is more to it than this: learners also need to have the opportunity to use spoken language for the typical purposes of speech – such as for relating to others, for explaining, for seeking information, for checking and cross-checking, for exploring, for planning, for telling stories, for disagreeing and agreeing, for arguing and making up. Finally, speech involves creating discourse, and we know that developing the use of familiar discourse patterns (Carter & McCarthy, 1997) is essential to effective communication. This implies developing familiarity of content, and familiarity with types of talk. The ability to use oral language, in other words, involves the ability to handle discourse patterns dynamically and collaboratively.

It seems to me however that there is one key learning problem associated with the oral medium, namely, the here-and–now transitory nature of speech. The fact that speech is generated on the spot in real time typically creates two difficulties. One concerns the pressures associated with real-time on-line engagement. As Skehan has consistently argued, at the moment of speech, the learner is likely to have difficulty in managing and monitoring all aspects of the activity. In particular, any one of fluency, accuracy, complexity or lexical range might be prioritised, while others of the aspects suffer. Thus a pressure on fluency might lead to a deterioration in accuracy, or alternatively increased attention to accuracy could accompany a drop in fluency. A further problem is that actual speech is rapidly overtaken by events and hard to recall. Thus learners' on-the-spot perceptions during speech events of interesting language problems or of their potential solutions are likely to be quickly forgotten as other subsequent speech events brush them aside. On their own, then, one-off performances of activities are not likely to bring about improvement. Something is needed to compensate for the transitory 'here-and-now' nature of talk. In particular the classroom needs to provide opportunities for the re-iteration of discourses. It is likely also to be valuable if group discourses can be carried into whole class interaction, providing the opportunity not only for the public recycling of talk, but of sharing it and commenting on it with the teacher.

This suggests then two key pedagogic principles for the teaching of oral abilities – firstly that of creating spaces in the classroom for learners to handle the processes, shapes and conditions of oral language; and secondly the principle of using iteration to compensate for the learning problems associated with the spoken medium. These principles could help to inform the teaching of speaking in the classroom, and more generally through the oral language curriculum. Doing so might help to give importance publicly to that space and to the way students use it.

To achieve these aims oral tasks are needed which are able to do the following:

- Provide a representative range of typical purposes for students to jointly improvise meaningful use of oral language
- Ensure meaningful iterative phases through the activity and between enactments of the activity, to compensate for the difficulties of learning under the real-time pressure of speech
- Enable a meaningful functional link between the more private mode of pair and group work, and the more public mode of whole class discourse.

The rest of this paper explores how these three aims can be put into action through the design and use of oral tasks.

## Constructing a task

To narrow our focus to task design, let us consider for a moment how we might use the following picture of a museum reconstruction of Frederic Chopin's drawing room as a basis for an oral task.

(source of image <http://chopin.museum/en/museum/chopin_family_drawing_room/id/217>)

From the designer's perspective, the simplest task design would be to provide the instruction to learners: 'Speak!' It is immediately obvious that such an instruction provides no particular interlocutor, no interactive purpose and no constructed context. Potential designs might include tasks such as the following:

– a simple 'Describe and Draw' task, with the outcome a drawing of the room.
– a 'Describe and Draw' task in which both the drawer and the speaker have to draw the room from memory, subsequently comparing their pictures, comparing their respective pictures with the original, and preparing a new description which would enable a listener to produce a more accurate drawing of the room; the outcome here is a revised description which can be tested out on a new listener/reader.
– students imagine and then prepare a plan and then a description of the part of the room that can't be seen in the picture; the outcome here might be a series of plans and descriptions, for subsequent comparison and evaluation;
– students are asked to prepare an oral and written description of the exhibit for museum visitors; the outcome here is a piece of museum text;
– ask students to devise an estate agent's description of the property to market it for let or sale; the outcome here would be an estate agent style text, that could be compared with similar genuine texts;
– require students to propose a 21st century redecoration of the room;

–   students are tasked with finding ways in which the room could be made usable
    in the present day while keeping its character (for instance offering it for hire
    for private or public events), and devising a proposal for the museum man-
    agement.

These different 'proto-tasks' clearly provide different opportunities for learners to
shape the content and form of their talk. Although they are simply sketches of
potential tasks, in this form they already illustrate how using the same picture
prompt can result in the design of different spaces for learners to interact in, each
design likely resulting in different language, different types of interaction, and different outcomes.

Now, although these putative tasks provide a basis for actual classroom tasks,
there is a crucial element which is missing from many of them, and that is a simulated real life context capable of motivating on-going commitment to the task as
a whole. Here a way forward would be to consider how people could genuinely
be asked to seriously engage with a scene such as this (i.e. a photograph of a
museum reconstruction of Chopin's drawing room). By way of example, one possibility would be if the students were confronted with the (very real) problem for
a museum of how oral language might be used to make accessible to the public an
exhibit of this kind, and ask them to provide solutions. Even for students not spe-
cialised in museum studies, a task such as this can mobilise interest in the topic
and the general issue, with library and internet searches a potentially important
resource.

Before looking at the stages of the task from beginning to end, let us first consider how the topic as a whole could be organised, so that different groups work in
parallel on different subtasks. There are various options. One basic subtask might
be to provide a series of notes for guides to explain the style and the historical ori-
gin and use of the different parts of the display. This would require the students
to prepare information that a guide might usefully present to visitors. The groups
could jointly come up with suggestions about the different types of information
which would be appropriate (some biography, some information about the actual
exhibits, including the piano, some information about Chopin's music, perhaps
some brief selections of recordings, and about how the drawing room might have
been used by Chopin), and divide the topics between them. Each group would
need to decide what information would likely be the most effective, and then how
to present it to the guide so they could turn it into an oral commentary. They
might be asked to model how the guide might present the information orally. A
further task might be for the groups to prepare a recorded commentary.

With these subtasks in mind, how then might the lesson (or series of lessons)
unfold? First of all each of these tasks would require students to research informa-

tion on line prior to preparing the material. Each group would 'trial' their material with the other groups as listeners, to assess their presentations for accessibility and effectiveness. Material could be then further revised. In a subsequent phase the different presentations could be integrated into a single display. Next some or all of the groups could then be asked to adjust the materials for different kinds of visitors – children, or groups with a special interest in Chopin (for whom the more general base-line material would not be appropriate). A final step in the activity could be to ask the students to reflect on the problems of preparing the material, perhaps in new groups so that each one is composed of people who had each had experience of preparing the different materials. As the activity unfolds, there are clear intended outcomes from each phase.

This outline is of course still far from complete, and it could be extended to also include the production of written material for visitors. A further step in the development of the task will require us to consider how the whole activity could be presented to the teacher and to the students as a valuable opportunity for language development – a crucial element without which it would be unreasonable to expect the activity to be used. Among other things, this would likely require us to consider the domains of language that would be activated, and the types of discourse and vocabulary which it could be used to explore. We would also want to consider varieties of language practice activities that could be useful in helping learners exploit the task and its subtasks for language improvement.

This example illustrates some basic principles of the processes of task design, because as we think about the differences between the proto-tasks, we find ourselves starting to engage in some of those processes. In particular, we start anticipating how the students might respond to the various designs. For example, we find ourselves anticipating things like:

- the number of students likely to work together on the task
- the intended outcome of the task
- how the students would attempt to reach the intended outcome, including things like:
  - how they would likely start work
  - what kinds of information content (opinions, description and so on) they would be working with
  - how far they would consult each other, about what, and how
  - what kinds of problems they would likely face, whether these are desirable from the point of view of the designer and teacher, and if not, how the task should be revised to avoid those problems
  - what if any support the groups might need during their work
  - how the task would conclude

- how the task could feed forward into plenary work
- more generally, how the teacher would frame the task to the students in terms of why do it, and what is expected from doing it

Above all, the activity illustrates how the design of the task itself serves to open up 'spaces' for oral language use. The topic of Chopin's drawing room within a museum setting is of course an illustration, and would need to be changed in light of the interests of the students. However, as Ellis (2009) has argued, it is important to distinguish between two types of 'authenticity', 'situational authenticity' and 'interactional authenticity':

> some tasks may achieve situational authenticity [...], but *all* tasks are designed to instigate the same kind of interactional processes (such as the negotiation of meaning, scaffolding, inferencing, and monitoring) that arise in naturally occurring language use. (227)

Thus a task might not meet clearly identifiable contextual needs of a group of students (for example they might not expect to be involved in designing museum displays) but may nonetheless provide very realistic – and very valuable –interactive language use. My main purpose here then has been to highlight the generalizable features of the design, rather than the particular content, and how the design can enable the creation of spaces in the classroom for just such oral interaction.

And the process of designing such tasks requires us to consider our designs in light of what we are planning on our students to do. This sets up the possibility of some internal structure to tasks, which I would now like to turn to.

## Internal task structure

Although tasks such as these are clearly not designed on behaviourist principles– that is they are not activities intended to force students through pre-determined phases and utterances – nevertheless a well-designed task often has some sort of internal structure, which provides options for students to work with, and a basis for focus and predictability in what the students will do. It is worth reflecting on the elements of task structure. Consider the following:

### Oral description task

The optimum school bag
In pairs, each of you describe the things you like and dislike about your school bag, explaining why. Agree on what you think would be the best school bag. Be prepared to report to the class. You will later do a written report which will be circulated around the class.

The reader will have noticed a number of elements that structure this task:

1.  It starts from concrete material that is familiar and moves to the more abstract generalisation, implying some likely internal iteration of language, and some likely changes as the focus changes across these different phases (i.e. description of features, explanation, negotiation of agreement, preparation of oral report, delivery of oral report, and subsequent written report)
2.  Students know they will be expected to report to the class, which:
    –   links pair work to plenary talk, and in the process to teacher talk
    –   provides a further in-built motivation for iteration
3.  Students know that they will be expected to write up a recommendation (providing different groupings and further iteration)

Iteration is one key element, allowing learners to engage progressively with the ideas and the language to express them, and in the process become more and more conversant with both, and more and more effective. The element to be highlighted is the in-built link between the phase of student pair-work, the whole class interaction, and the subsequent written task. The concatenation of these phases is mutually reinforcing – each one is justified by the expectation of the other phases, creating a form of sub-task dependency.

Samuda's 2001 'Things in Pockets' task similarly entailed iterative phases and a connection between group and whole class activity.

> Students had to work out as much as they could about an unknown person purely on the basis of things found in their pockets. This involved them in estimating the probability of a particular personal characteristic on the basis of the things in the person's pockets. E.g. an empty glasses case; a return train ticket; a cigarette lighter; a membership card of a library; a theatre ticket; a restaurant bill for two meals; etc..
>
> After completing the task, they presented posters to the class, and subsequently wrote up their accounts.

–   The purpose of the task engaged them in 'epistemic modality' – the modality concerned with degrees of certainty.

Similar design features can be found here:

–   Creating space
    the task created the space for the students to explore degrees of probability or certainty: *could be; might be; must be; may be;* and words like *probably', 'possibly',* and so on.

- Outcome
  students knew that the activity would end with group reports to whole class and a subsequent written report.
- Iteration arising via cycles of group work, interim plenary reporting and teacher feedback, final class discussion, posters, and subsequent writing.
- Link between group and classwork cycles of group talk led into whole class talk

Without these elements, there are a number of potentially serious problems:

- Without anticipating an overall outcome to the task (the report to the class)
  - learners work without getting feedback on what they have done
  - they work without their work seeming to matter, resulting in less attention to their communication, less attention to their language, less monitoring of their own talk and their partners'

- Without iteration, whatever they say at any point is of little subsequent consequence
- Without the link between group and classwork
  - they finish without knowing what others have done
  - there is no clear relationship between what they do in groups and pairs and the teacher's overall purpose
  - there is less opportunity for post-task exploitation – carrying forward what they do to a further activity
  - there is no connection between their talk on-task and the teacher-class talk

This link between students' on-task talk and the teacher-class talk leads me to my final section, the use of oral tasks in relation to teacher-class discourse.


## The use of oral tasks in relation to teacher-class discourse

In this section I want to explore the idea that establishing a link between pair/group phases of a task and a teacher-class phase can impact productively both on group talk and on teacher-class talk (a distinction that is different from that drawn by Batstone & Philp, 2013 between public classroom talk and private talk which is confidential to the individual concerned). This link also introduces an iterative dimension to the talk. To make the point I would like to consider two examples.

Example 1.  Things in pockets task                                    *(Samuda, 2001)*

In this task, students have been in groups trying to work out plausible predictions of the likely owner of a coat on the basis of things found in the pockets. The teacher interrupts them for an interim progress check, and to share ideas and language. I would first like to focus on the language.

S1:  Habits?
Y:   Well first he smokes
C:   But we think uh 50% we think just 50%
N:   Yes just maybe. We're not sure.
T:   Oh yeah? Only 50%? Why's that?
S2:  Yes, give proof (laughter)
N:   Because here [showing matchbox]. A matchbox
T:   Hmmm. But you're not certain if he smokes, huh? (looking at matchbox)
A:   Look (opens matchbox). Many matches so maybe he just keep for friend, not for him (laughter)
T:   Mmmm I – I guess it's possible he might smoke. It's hard to tell just from this
A:   Yeah, not sure
S2:  You have more proof?                                    (Samuda, 2001: 129)

As with the Chopin museum task, the first thing to note is the intended language focus of the design, rather than the topic in which it is contextualised. Readers may have noticed that the design is intended to create the need amongst the learners to use epistemic modality. That is, the design could be recontextualised in other topics while retaining the focus on the same language domain. In other words, the design itself is generalizable.

The design would also carry with it however a number of features of spoken language, notably in the talk of both the teacher and the students, which we noted earlier when discussing 'the shape of spoken language'. These include things like shared meanings; shared responsibility; colloquialisms; interruptions; deictic and first and second person reference; questions and answers; syntactic fragmentation. However the feature I would like to emphasise particularly is the way teachers and students are interactive *partners* in the discourse, with the students contributing constructively, and the teacher treating the students as genuine interlocutors. The preceding group work gives the students a footing in the ensuing whole-class interaction, which in turn affects the teacher's own talk. The focus is on sharing meanings, with language being mobilised collaboratively by students and teacher to clarify their thinking.

Later in the lesson, there are further examples, such as the following:

S4: We think just 50% so we think she must live in California
T:  Mmm hang on a minute how certain are you?
S4: 50 (looks at chart) yes 50
T:  50%? So you're not VERY certain but you think it is possible?
S4: Not very not very just 50 ahh she might
T:  Yeah she might live in California. With must the grammar is good but the meaning changes
S4: Ahh she might live in California yes                    (ibid:133)

Once again the whole class talk is an extension of the students' group talk, as if the whole-class oral interaction is grounded in the group work. And here too this shapes the language, giving rise to colloquialisms typical of informal collaborative talk, syntactic fragmentation, interruptions, repetition, and collaborative constructions (such as the teacher's 'So you're not VERY certain but you think it is possible?' followed by the student's 'Not very not very just 50 ahh she might', in turn followed by the teacher's 'Yeah she might live in California'). If it is true that the whole class talk amounts to an 'extension' (or perhaps a 'development') of the group talk, then we could conclude that this relationship constitutes a form of iteration: the students are revisiting ideas and expressions explored earlier. Group talk becomes whole class talk.

In addition to what we might call the internal 'validity' in terms of the resulting shape of talk, and the element of iteration, there are also some potentially important pedagogical advantages in extending group talk into classroom talk. One is that it enables the teacher to join in and 'ratify' or 'validate' the students' interaction: they realise that their private group talk is relevant and that it works, that it is not being overlooked or left ignored. It can also enable the interaction to be shared across the whole class: the internal talk of individual groups becomes public across the whole class. This also enables others to cross-check their solutions and their ways of expressing them. More obviously it enables the teacher to appraise learners' oral work, both in terms of content and form. And it provides the opportunity for the teacher to build on what was done for the next phase of work: the teacher is in a better position to mediate the onward flow of the scheme of work.

What I am arguing for then is the use of pair and group work in relation to whole class interaction. A similar logic was proposed some time ago by Douglas Barnes, for the use of task-based work within mother tongue classrooms. This will be my final example.

Example 2.   The L1 science class task                    *(Barnes 1976)*

Douglas Barnes studied the use of group work in L1 classrooms across the curriculum. His purpose was to suggest that skilful use of tasks by the teacher could enable students to engage in the topic, and that this engagement could be carried across into whole-class interaction. An example illustrates how this might work.

In the following case, the theme of the lesson is air pressure. In order to open up the topic and get the students thinking about it, rather than provide an initial exposition of the issues, he gets them to engage in an investigative task. To this end, he has given them a stoppered jar with a straw going through the stopper into water, and asked them to find out and then explain what happens when they blow strongly into the water. In this extract, two young male students are getting involved with the task.

17. S  What about what about this glass of milk though, Glyn?
18. G  Well that's 'cause you make a vacuum in your mouth…
19. S  When you drink the milk you see…you…
20. G  Right!…You you make a vacuum there, right?
21. S  Yes well you make a vacuum in the … er…transparent straw…
22. G  Yes.
23. S  Carry on.
24. G  And the er air pressure outside forces it down, there's no pressure inside to force it
     back up again so….
25. S  OK.

(Barnes 1976: 40)

This extract shows once again a number of features of oral language which illustrate the spontaneous but focused co-construction of talk, features such as: shared meanings; shared responsibility; colloquialisms; interruptions; deictic and first/second person reference; completions of each other's utterances; repetitions; pauses; questions and answers; syntactic fragmentation.

Barnes doesn't show transcripts of the teacher interacting with these two students, but in another extract we are able to see the teacher engaging with a group who have been attempting to solve the science problem.

*Teacher:  Come on, describe this one to me … I can't do it because there's no water left in*
*here, is there; you've used it all up [girls' laughter] but you can describe it to me,*
*can't you?*
24.  B    Em…well…Theresa blew down it and it bubbled and then she took em … her
        mouth away, and it all came up because of the air pressure.
Teacher: Which air pressure?
25.  B    The …er…inside the bottle.….Inside the bottle.
Teacher: Alright! Now why didn't it come up before then? …Before we blew the air in
        why didn't it come up?

27. C= Sir, 'cos…em…'cos there wasn't enough air…air pressure
28. T= [Clash of voices – words not transcribed]
28. T There wasn't enough air in, but when you blew into it… there was more air in and it came up.
Teacher: And it forced it…Why did it stop? …At what point did it stop?…It's not going now…why isn't it going now?
29. T 'Cos there's no air left in.
Teacher: Well there's still the air left in; but what can you tell me about the air out here and the air in there?
30. C Sir, the air outside is stronger than the air in the bottle.

(Barnes, D., 1976: 72–73)

Here too we can note all the features of talk which we discussed earlier. And once again we can see how involvement in the group work provides the students with a footing that enables them to interact with the teacher. And this in turn affects the teacher's own talk.

What I am suggesting then is firstly that this quality of talk likely is enabled by the preceding pair and group work which:

- provides information for them to interact with the teacher, giving the learners a positive role and footing in the talk
- makes what the teacher says more relevant for the groups
- enables the teacher's discourse to become more collaborative, enabling more student involvement and more two-way negotiation for meaning

In addition I am arguing that this play between group work and teacher-class interaction helps recycle language and extend the students' audience.

Oral task work can thus provide a basis for collaborative talk between teacher and students, and not just between students.


## Conclusion


In considering the teaching of spoken language, we should come to grips with the fact that spoken language has its own shape and is used under different conditions from written language, and that it is the nature of instruction to set up pedagogically desirable conditions. This should be the starting point for determining the nature of the oral syllabus, in terms of what is to be learnt and how it should be taught, and how it can fit into the overall curriculum. As with other types of learning, the challenge of teaching the spoken language can be usefully conceptualised in terms of typical conditions of use which should be enabled and engaged through appropriately designed tasks. What is and is not an appropriate design is an empirical question which is ultimately only answerable through trial and error in the classroom. Effective tasks will provide some kind of structure and target outcome which together create spaces for speaking, which would otherwise be absent from the classroom. The intended task outcome additionally provides a potentially crucial bridge between initial pair or group work and subsequent plenary teacher-class talk. This can enable normal informal group talk to extend into plenary discourse; it can enable the teacher to join the discourse – both during group work and in subsequent whole-class interaction as a collaborative participant; and it can enable recycling of in-group language into the plenary context. Without this link between the space of the task and the plenary discourse, tasks become cut off from the lesson and from the other people in the classroom, and at a stroke lose their potential importance and motivation. Review of recent research and contemporary course books suggests there is still plenty for research to do in exploring the creation and use of the space for learners' classroom talk.

## References

Bailey, K. M., & Savage, L. Eds.. (1994). *New ways in teaching speaking*. Alexandria, VA: TESOL.

Barnes, D. (1976). *From communication to currriculum*. Harmondsworth: Penguin.

Batstone, R., & Philp, J. (2013). Classroom interaction and learning opportunities across time and space. In K. McDonough & A. Mackey (Eds.), pp. 109–125.

Boxer, D., & Cohen, A. D. (Eds.). (2004). *Studying speaking to inform second language learning*. Clevedon: Multilingual Matters.

Brown, G., & Yule, G. (1983). *Teaching the spoken language*. Cambridge: CUP.

Burns, A., & Joyce, H. (1997). *Focus on speaking*. Sydney: Macquarie University, NCELTR.

Bygate, M. (1987). *Speaking*. Oxford: Oxford University Press.

Bygate, M. (1988). *Linguistic and strategic features of the language of learners working in oral communication exercises*. Unpublished PhD dissertation. University of London Institute of Education.

Bygate, M. (2009).Teaching and testing speaking. In C. Doughty & M. H. Long (Eds.), *Handbook of second and foreign language teaching* (pp. 412–440). Malden, MA: Blackwell.

Bygate, M. (2009). Teaching the spoken foreign language. In K. Knapp & B. Seidlhofer (Eds.), *Handbooks in applied linguistics, Vol. 5: Foreign language communication and learning* (pp. 401–438). Berlin: Mouton De Gruyter.

Byrne, D. (1976). *Teaching oral English*. London: Longman

Byrnes, H. (2015). Linking 'task' and curricular thinking: An affirmation of the TBLT educational agenda. In M. Bygate (Ed.), *Domains and directions in the development of TBLT* (pp. 193–224). Amsterdam: John Benjamins.

Carter, R., & McCarthy, M. (1997). *Exploring spoken English*. Cambridge: Cambridge University Press.

Carter, R., & McCarthy, M. (2017). Spoken grammar: Where are we and where are we going? *Applied Linguistics*, 38(1), 1–20.

Chafe, W. L. (1982). Integration and involvement in speaking, writing and oral literature. In D. Tannen (Ed), *Spoken and written language*. (pp. 35–53) Norwood, NJ: Ablex.

Chafe, W. L. (1985). Linguistic differences produced by differences between speaking and writing. In D.R. Olson, N. Torrance, & A. Hildyard (Eds.), *Literacy, language and learning* (pp. 105–123). Cambridge: Cambridge University Press.

Chafe, W. L. (2006). Reading aloud. In R. Hughes (Ed.), *Spoken English, TESOL and applied linguistics* (pp. 53–71). Houndmills: Palgrave Macmillan

Ellis, R. (2009). Task-based language teaching: sorting out the misunderstandings. *International Review of Applied Linguistics* 19(3): 221–246.

Eskildsen, S. (2016). What counts as a developmental sequence? Exemplar-based L2 learning of English questions. *Language Learning* 65(1): 33–62.

Folse, K. S. (2006). *The art of teaching speaking: Research and pedagogy for the ESL/EFL classroom*. Ann Arbor, MI: University of Michigan Press.

Fulcher, G. (2003). *Testing second language speaking*. Harlow: Pearson Education.

Gass, S. M. (2013). *Input, interaction and the second language learner*. New York, NY: Routledge.

Gilabert, R., Manchon, R., & Vasylets, O. (2017). Mode in theoretical and empirical TBLT research: Advancing research agendas. *Annual Review of Applied Linguistics*, 36(2016), 117–135.

Housen, A., & Kuiken, F. (Eds.). (2009). *Complexity, accuracy and fluency (CAF) in second language acquisition research*. Special issue of Applied Linguistics, 30, 4.

Hughes, R. (2002). *Teaching and research speaking*. Harlow: Pearson Education.

Lantolf, J. P., & Poehner, M. E. (2014). *Sociocultural theory and the pedagogical imperative in L2 education. Vygotskian praxis and the theory/practice divide*. New York, NY: Routledge.

Leech, G. (1983). *Pragmatics*. Harlow: Longman.

Levelt, W. J. M. (1989). *Speaking: From intention to articulation*. Cambridge, MA: The MIT Press

Lynch, A. J. (forthcoming). Perform, reflect, recycle: Enhancing task repetition in second language speaking classes. In M. Bygate (Ed.), *Learning language through task repetition*. Amsterdam: John Benjamins.

Mackey, A. (Ed.). (2007). *Conversational interaction in second language acquisition*. Oxford: Oxford University Press.

Markee, N. (2000). *Conversation analysis*. Mahwah, NJ: Lawrence Erlbaum Associates.

McDonough, K., & Mackey, A. (Eds.). (2013). *Second language interaction in diverse educational contexts*. Amsterdam: John Benjamins

Norris, J., Davis, JMcE., & Timpe-Laughlin, V. (2017). *Second language educational experiences for adult learners*. New York, NY: Routledge.

Oliver, R., & Philp, J. (2014). *Focus on oral interaction*. Oxford: Oxford University Press.

Pavlenko, A. (Ed.). (2011). *Thinking and speaking in two languages*. Bristol: Multilingual Matters.

Redstone, C., & Cunningham, G. (2013). *Face 2 face, Upper intermediate*. Cambridge: Cambridge University Press.

Richards, J. C. (2008). *Teaching listening and speaking*. Cambridge: Cambridge University Press.

Samuda, V. (2001). Guiding relationships between form and meaning during task performance: The role of the teacher. In M. Bygate, P. Skehan & M. Swain (Eds.), *Researching pedagogic tasks: Learning, teaching and assessment*. Harlow: Pearson Education.

Samuda, V. (2005). Expertise in second language pedagogic task design. In K. Johnson (Ed.), *Expertise in language teaching*. Houndmills: Palgrave Macmillan

Seedhouse, P. (2004). *The interactional architecture of the language classroom*. New York, NY: Wiley

Segalowitz, N. (2010). *Cognitive bases of second language fluency*. Abingdon: Routledge

Skehan, P. (2015). Limited attention capacity and cognition: Two hypotheses regarding second language performance on tasks. In M. Bygate (Ed.), *Domains and directions in the development of TBLT* (pp. 123–156). Amsterdam: John Benjamins.

Taylor, L. (2011). *Examining speaking: Research and practice in assessing second language speaking*. Cambridge: Cambridge University Press.

Thornbury, S. (2005). *How to teach speaking*. Harlow: Pearson Education.

Thornbury, S., & Slade, D. (2006). *Conversation: From description to pedagogy*. Cambridge: Cambridge University Press.

Underhill, N. (1987). *Testing spoken language*. Cambridge: Cambridge University Press.

Weissberg, R. (2007). *Connecting speaking and writing in second language writing instruction*. Ann Arbor, MI: University of Michigan Press

Yule, G. (1997). *Referential communication tasks*. Mahwah, NJ: Lawrence Erlbaum Associates.

# CHAPTER 8

# Code-switching in the Spanish heritage language classroom
## Communicative and cognitive functions

Ana Fernández Dobao
University of Washington

Code-switching is a common practice among bilingual speakers, including Spanish heritage language learners. Research on Spanish-English bilinguals in the United States has provided plenty of evidence documenting the use of code-switching in daily conversation with a variety of communicative and social functions. In the Spanish heritage language classroom, however, code switching is generally frowned upon. In this setting, the goal is to minimize the use of English in order to develop the formal academic register, where code switching is not acceptable. However, in this chapter I provide evidence that, in the context of the Spanish heritage language classroom, English can serve important social, communicative, and cognitive functions, and, when used efficiently, mediate Spanish language learning.

## Introduction

This chapter analyzes peer interaction in the Spanish heritage language classroom. It focuses on those moments when heritage language learners switch to English, their dominant language, while interacting with their peers in Spanish. In this setting, the most common practice is to instruct students to avoid any form of language switching in order to maximize the use of the heritage language and the development of a formal academic register. In this chapter, however, I will argue that the use of the dominant language among heritage language learners can have important social, communicative, and cognitive functions, and sometimes serve as a cognitive tool for the development of their Spanish, in particular their academic Spanish language proficiency.

In the United States, the term heritage language learner is used by both teachers and researchers to make reference to "a student who is raised in a home where a non-English language is spoken, who speaks or merely understand the heritage

https://doi.org/10.1075/aals.17.08dob

language, and who is to some degree bilingual in English and the heritage language" (Valdés, 2001:1). This definition, the most commonly cited and widely adopted by educators, emphasizes the heterogeneity of this group of learners. However, it has also been criticized for being too "narrow", since it excludes learners who have a cultural connection with the language but cannot speak it (Fishman, 2001). Furthermore, it is limited to the United States, where English is the societal majority language–for a full discussion of the current debate around the definition of heritage language learners see Montrul (2016) and Potowski (2014). In this chapter, the term Spanish heritage language learner is used to refer to any learner who has been exposed to Spanish since childhood and has acquired the language naturalistically, in the family environment. As indicated in Valdés' definition, the proficiency level of heritage language learners may vary widely. They may be highly fluent in Spanish or fall at the lowest end of the bilingual spectrum and have only limited receptive skills. Although Spanish is their first language (L1) in order of acquisition, their dominant language is the majority language, English (see Silva Corvalán & Treffers-Daller, 2016). In most cases, their grammatical competence differs in important ways from the grammatical competence of other Spanish native speakers who grew up in a predominantly monolingual context (Montrul, 2012, 2016). The work of Carreira and Kagan (2011) and Benmamoun, Montrul and Polinsky (2010) shows that, in the United States, most heritage speakers have received little or no instruction in their heritage language and therefore have weak literacy skills in this language. Writing is usually their least developed skill. Furthermore, since they have learned the language at home, they have been exposed mostly to colloquial speech. They possess a limited range of registers and, in many cases, have not acquired proficiency in standard academic Spanish (see also Beaudrie & Fairclough, 2012; Pascual y Cabo, 2016).

The needs of adult heritage learners seeking to reacquire or expand their knowledge of their home language are therefore very different from those of second language (L2) learners. Recognizing that these learners are better served by separate courses geared towards their specific needs, more and more universities in the United States are now offering separate courses for Spanish heritage language learners (Beaudrie, 2011, 2012). The current study was conducted in one of these courses, in the first of a series of three Spanish heritage language courses offered at a large public university in the northwest of the United States. The students in this course possess both receptive and productive skills. To enroll in the class, they need to pass an oral interview and demonstrate they can speak Spanish fluently. The course builds upon their knowledge of informal colloquial Spanish and aims to develop their reading and writing skills. The goal is to expand learners' linguistic repertoires by incorporating knowledge of formal and academic registers–what scholars have described as second dialect acquisition (Fairclough,

2016; Valdés, 2007). While acknowledging the legitimacy of all learners' linguistic varieties, the program recognizes that command of what is considered standard Spanish is important for students' academic and professional success.

The language of heritage learners exhibits linguistic phenomena characteristic of language contact situations, such as lexical borrowings, calques, and code-switching (Bullock & Toribio, 2009; Montrul, 2016; Toribio, 2002). Code-switching, generally defined as the alternating use of two languages in conversation, is in fact a very common, and extensively documented, practice among English-Spanish bilinguals. However, as mentioned, the heritage language classroom usually operates in a monolingual mode (Carvalho, 2012). The most common policy is a Spanish only policy that inhibits the use of English in order to maximize exposure to and practice of the target language. In this regard, heritage language teaching follows conventional communicative language teaching practice. Furthermore, code-switching is seen as part of the informal, colloquial register, while the goal in the classroom is to develop those features that constitute the standard, which are exclusively Spanish.

The class where I conducted my study was no exception. The teacher spoke entirely in Spanish and students were instructed to use only Spanish during class time. Since all students could speak the heritage language with a relatively high degree of fluency, teacher-learner interaction took place almost exclusively in Spanish. The audio-recordings of learner-learner interaction, however, revealed a very different picture. When working in pairs or small groups, students no longer adhered to the monolingual policy, instead they made full use of their bilingual repertoire. Switches to English were observed regardless of type of activity or goal of the interaction. The present study addresses these uses of English. It explores the functions that English, the learners' dominant language, may serve in the heritage language classroom and its potential impact on the development of heritage language proficiency.

## Background

The study of heritage language learning is a relatively recent area of research, but one that is getting more and more attention as the number of heritage learners, and in particular Spanish heritage learners, continues to grow. Still, to my knowledge, only two studies have specifically analyzed the use of the majority language, English, by adult heritage learners in the context of the Spanish language classroom: Sánchez Muñoz (2007) and Lowther (2010). Sociolinguistic researchers, however, have been analyzing English-Spanish code-switching in informal conversational speech for decades. A vast amount of research has accumulated on this issue (see Bullock & Toribio, 2009; Carvalho, 2012). Another area that has been paying considerable attention to this practice is educational research focused on emergent bilinguals, heritage children with varying levels of proficiency in both the majority and the heritage language (e.g., García, 2009; García & Kleyn, 2016; García & Wei, 2014). Finally, in the field of second language acquisition, a growing interest has developed in recent years on the analysis of the L1 not just as a source of transfer, but as a cognitive tool supporting L2 development (e.g., Antón & DiCamilla, 1998; Storch & Aldosari, 2010; Storch & Wigglesworth, 2003; Swain & Lapkin, 2000). In this section, I review the main contributions from each of these different areas, starting with what has been so far the most common approach to the study of code-switching, the sociolinguistic approach.

Sociolinguistic research has provided plenty of evidence that code-switching is a natural phenomenon and a routine behavior in English-Spanish bilingual conversation. In some settings, even educational settings, code-switching is often stigmatized, misinterpreted as a consequence of lack of linguistic knowledge. However, research has shown that code-switching is systematic and rule-governed (Poplack, 1980, 2004). In fact, intrasentential code-switching requires a sophisticated knowledge of both Spanish and English grammar, and therefore constitutes a hallmark of proficient bilingualism (Carvalho, 2012; Toribio, 2001).

Sociolinguistic studies have also established that code-switching serves a variety of communicative, interactional, and social functions. Bilingual speakers may resort to code-switching to compensate for gaps in vocabulary knowledge, but also as a pragmatic and stylistic strategy. Bilinguals switch languages, for instance, to mitigate or aggravate requests, add emphasis, attract attention, clarify meaning, quote somebody else's words, or indicate a change of topic or tone (Silva-Corvalán, 1983; Valdés, 1981; Zentella, 1997). Furthermore, the use of code-switching is influenced by the setting and the interlocutor. It is an in-group language practice and an identity marker (Cashman, 2005; Lowther, 2010; Potowski, 2009; Toribio, 2002; Zentella, 1997). Through code-switching Hispanic bilinguals assert their bilingual and bicultural identity. In Zentella's words, it's "a way of saying that they belong to both worlds, and should not be forced to give up one for the other" (Zentella, 1997: 114).

Sánchez Muñoz (2007) and Lowther (2010) expanded the study of code-switching to the context of the Spanish language classroom, a formal setting that promotes standard varieties of the language. Sánchez Muñoz (2007) compared Spanish heritage learners' speech in three different social situations, ranging from less to more formal: conversations, interviews, and class oral presentations. Code-switching was frequent in informal conversation outside the classroom, but less frequent in interviews with the researcher, and minimum in classroom oral presentations. Sánchez Muñoz concluded that, in the Spanish language classroom, heritage learners try to avoid code-switching because "switches to English are perceived as not appropriate for academic situations" (Sánchez Muñoz, 2007:133). Lowther (2010) also observed very little use of English in her analysis of interaction in the Spanish heritage language classroom. In less formal and more intimate settings–interviews and focus group discussions, code-switching was frequently used by heritage learners to negotiate language ideologies and construct identity, but not in the class. Like Sánchez Muñoz (2007), Lowther analyzed classroom discourse involving the whole class–teacher and students, no attention was paid to peer interaction. The current study aims to address this gap by focusing specifically on the use of English during pair and small group activities.

Within the educational context, research on emergent bilinguals has analyzed the use of both the heritage and the majority language when children interact not only with their teachers but also with each other. This research, however, rejects the notion of code-switching, which has been replaced with that of translanguaging, defined as "multiple discursive practices in which bilinguals engage in order to make sense of their bilingual worlds" (García, 2009:45) (see also Canagarajah, 2011; Creese & Blackledge, 2010; García & Wei, 2014; Otheguy, García, & Reid, 2015). The concept of translanguaging emphasizes the unitary nature of the bilingual's linguistic system. This perspective rejects the idea that bilingual speakers possess, and switch between, two independent and bounded languages. Instead, it suggests that bilingual speakers perform conversation by drawing on one rich linguistic repertoire that involves features of more than one "socially constructed language" (García & Wei, 2014:3).

Research on translanguaging has largely been conducted in elementary to high school settings where English is the language of instruction. In this context, translanguaging serves as a scaffold. In English-medium math, science, social studies, or English language arts classes, bilingual children translanguage to construct meaning, to engage with content at a deeper level, and to participate in more complex discussions. Translanguaging strategies are also used to explain and clarify vocabulary. In García and Kleyn (2016), abundant examples are offered of children using Spanish to negotiate their understanding of English concepts and words. Some studies have also been carried out in dual immersion settings, documenting the use of translanguaging as a pedagogical tool to enhance children's learning in (and of) the home as well as the majority language (see, for instance, Espinosa & Herrera, 2016; García, 2011; Martín-Beltrán, 2010, 2014). In all these different contexts, the acceptance of translanguaging as a legitimate classroom practice is essential to build a linguistically and culturally inclusive environment. The work I present in this chapter shares this same approach, as it aims to validate the use of the bilingual learner's full linguistic repertoire in the Spanish heritage language classroom. But it draws on the concept of code-switching and previous research in this area to analyze the different functions, communicative and social, that the use of English may have in this context.

In second and foreign language classrooms, the prevalent belief is that the use of the learner's L1, whether by the teacher or by the students, hinders L2 development and should therefore be discouraged. In recent years, however, a number of scholars have also revisited this idea. These scholars have analyzed L1 use in peer interaction from a sociocultural perspective. In sociocultural theory, cognitive development is essentially social. Learning originates in social interaction, in collaboration with more knowledgeable individuals, mediated by semiotic tools–material and cultural artifacts such as language (Vygotsky, 1978). From this perspective, both the L1 and the L2 can be understood as cognitive tools that can be used to regulate mental activity and mediate the co-construction of L2 knowledge. Just like a physical tool, such as for instance a hammer, allows us to carry out physical activities we would not be able to perform without it, language makes it possible to accomplish cognitively demanding tasks we would not be able to accomplish otherwise (Swain, 2000). In the classroom, language enables learners to scaffold each other and to collaborate in the solution of both task- and language-related problems. Through language-mediated activities, such as testing and formulating hypothesis, offering and assessing new input, or correcting themselves or others, learners build their knowledge of the language. This use of language as a psychological tool to make meaning and shape language knowledge is referred to as languaging (Swain, 2006).

One of the first studies to analyze L1 use within a sociocultural framework was Antón and DiCamilla (1998). These authors examined interaction between pairs of English speaking learners of Spanish as a foreign language. They found that learners resorted to their common L1 as a tool to establish a mutual understanding of the task, to provide scaffolded assistance to each other, and to externalize their inner thoughts. These functions of the L1 enabled them to complete challenging tasks more effectively and led Antón and DiCamilla to conclude that "the use of the L1 is beneficial for language learning" (Antón & DiCamilla, 1998:338). Swain and Lapkin (2000) followed this same approach. They analyzed L1 use in a French L2 immersion classroom and identified three main functions: interpersonal interaction, moving the task along, and focusing attention, which involves the use of the L1 to discuss L2 grammar and vocabulary. More specifically, they provided evidence of learners' use of their common L1 to search for L2 vocabulary, to focus each other's attention on form, and to retrieve and share the grammatical information needed to complete their tasks successfully. Other functions of the L1 identified in subsequent studies include task management, discussing and generating ideas, mechanics deliberations, and off-task talk (see Alegría de la Colina & García Mayo, 2009; Azkarai & García Mayo, 2015; Gánem

Gutiérrez, 2008; Lasito, 2013; Storch & Aldosari, 2010; Storch & Wigglesworth, 2003).

The studies just mentioned have analyzed L1 use in L2 learner interaction across a variety of language combinations, task types, and proficiency levels, but they have all reached similar conclusions. They have noticed that, when working in pairs or small groups, most learners use the L1 sparingly. They resort to the L1 when engaged in cognitively demanding activities–such as, for instance, solving grammar problems–as a tool that allows them to "work at a higher level than would be possible were they restricted to sole use of their L2" (Storch & Wigglesworth, 2003:760). This use of the L1 supports L2 learning and therefore should not be banned from the classroom. The argument made is not to encourage L1 use at the expense of the L2, but rather to recognize that "to insist that no use be made of the L1 in carrying out tasks that are both linguistically and cognitively complex is to deny the use of an important cognitive tool" (Swain & Lapkin, 2000:268–269).

In this chapter, I will contend that the same argument can be made for the use of the heritage learner's dominant language, English, in the Spanish heritage language classroom. I analyze peer interaction among heritage learners looking for evidence of switches to English serving not only communicative and social functions–as extensively documented in previous sociolinguistic research, but also as a cognitive tool used by learners to mediate their language learning–see He (2010) for a review of sociocultural research on heritage language learning. More specifically, I address the following two questions:

1. In the Spanish heritage language classroom, does learners' use of English facilitate the co-construction of Spanish language knowledge?
2. What other functions does English have in the context of the Spanish heritage language classroom?

## The study

### Setting

The study was conducted in a Spanish heritage language course offered for credit at a large public university in the United States. The Spanish heritage program in this university consists of a series of three courses. Each course lasts 10 weeks and meets five times per week for 50 minutes. I collected the data in the first of these three courses, which is already considered an advanced level course.

To enroll in this course, students need to pass an oral interview and a multiple choice written test–an adapted version of Potowski, Parada, and Morgan-Short's

(2012) placement test for heritage speakers. Students need to prove oral fluency in Spanish. Written skills are not required. In fact, most students have not received previous instruction in Spanish and are not familiar with Spanish orthography and accentuation. Students who have had extensive schooling in Spanish are placed in a more advanced course.

As discussed in the introduction, the main goal of the course is to develop learners' reading and writing skills, together with their knowledge of standard Spanish. Adding the standard variety to the students' linguistic repertoire is considered essential for them to succeed in advanced Spanish literature and culture courses, as well as in the professional world. The curriculum includes also issues of identity and culture, and activities intended to connect Hispanic students with the Hispanic community in the area.

## Participants

There were 20 learners enrolled in the course. Twelve of them volunteered to participate in the project and five of these to be core participants. Core participants carried a digital voice recorder that audio recorded all the interactions in which they participated, but only those interactions that involved volunteers were analyzed for the purposes of the study.

The ages of the five core participants ranged from 18 to 26. There were four females and one male. One of the females was from Central America and had arrived in the United States before the age of seven. The other four learners were United States-born Mexican Americans. While they could all speak Spanish fluently and had no difficulty carrying out conversation in Spanish, their dominant language was English, the language in which they had been schooled.

## Data collection

Throughout the quarter (10 weeks) a research assistant visited the class an average of twice per week. From week three to week nine, she audio-recorded the speech of the five core participants. Before the class started, she handed a digital voice recorder to each one of them. She made sure the recorders were on and participants carried them during the entire 50 minutes of the class. She also took classroom observation notes, including information about the activities the students were performing and with whom they were working.

The voice recorders recorded everything the core participants said and every interaction in which they participated, including both learner-learner and learner-teacher interaction. For the purposes of the study, only learner interaction during pair and small group activities was considered. But if this interaction involved one of the students who had not volunteered to participate in the project, it was discarded. Therefore, the amount of data collected varies considerably from student to student and from day to day, depending on how much time the teacher devoted to peer interaction activities.

Since the purpose of this study is not to quantify the amount of English used by the learners, but rather to identify whether English was used as a tool to support language learning, a random sample of data collected from each of the core participants was analyzed. This sample includes a total of 15 segments of recordings. Each segment is 10 to 20 minutes long. The pair and small group activities in these recordings are mostly communicative meaning-focused tasks in which students discussed social and cultural issues. Many of them are based on readings completed outside the class, dealing with topics related to the Latino experience in the United States. Vocabulary activities are also frequent, intended to clarify the vocabulary in the readings and, in general, to enrich the learners' lexicon. There are also some orthography and grammar-focused tasks that involve a written component, but these are not very frequent, as writing tasks were usually completed individually and outside the class.

## Data analysis

The audio recordings selected for the purposes of the study were transcribed. Those segments of interaction in which learners switched to English, whether for one single word or for an entire or several turns, were identified and analyzed. Based on previous sociolinguistic and sociocultural research, the following potential functions for the use of English were identified:

1.    Metacognitive function: the learner uses his dominant language, English, to talk about the task. The use of English helps to clarify task goals and procedures, recruit attention, regulate participation, and, in general, solve any task management difficulties (Alegría de la Colina & García Mayo, 2009; Storch & Aldosari, 2010; Storch & Wigglesworth, 2003; Swain & Lapkin, 2000).

2.    Metalinguistic function: the learner uses English to talk about Spanish vocabulary, grammar, or mechanics. Segments of interaction in which English is used with a metalinguistic function constitute language-related episodes (LREs). LREs have been defined as "any part of a dialogue where the students talk about the language they are producing, question their language use, or correct themselves or other" (Swain & Lapkin, 1998: 326). Based on their focus, they can be classified as lexical, grammatical, or mechanical (Storch, 2013; Storch & Aldosari, 2010). In lexical-LREs, learners collaborate to clarify the meaning of words or search for new vocabulary. In grammatical-LREs, they talk about grammar-

related difficulties, and in mechanical-LREs about pronunciation, spelling, or punctuation issues. LREs are instances of languaging, as described in the previous section, and therefore constitute a source of learning. From a sociocultural perspective, in LREs language learning takes place (Swain, 2000).

3.   Conversational function: the learner resorts to English to mark a change of topic or tone, add emphasis, mitigate a request, attract attention, compensate for gaps, etc. This analysis is based on Zentella (1997) who identified "at least 22 conversational strategies" accomplished through code-switching (Zentella, 1997: 92). This framework accounts for the use of code-switching for re-alignment purposes, to control the interlocutor's behavior, to clarify or emphasize meaning, and to compensate for language gaps. It incorporates Gumperz's (1982) discourse strategies and has been used for the analysis of both child and adult bilingual speech (e.g., Reyes, 2004; Vu, Bailey, & Howes, 2010).

## Functions of English in the Spanish heritage language classroom

### Metacognitive function

In the present study, evidence was found of Spanish heritage language learners using English for task organization and management purposes. The data analyzed, however, did not offer many examples illustrating this metacognitive function of the dominant language. Furthermore, this type of switches tended to be relatively short, as illustrated in Examples 1, 2, and 3

(1)   Learner 1:   *cómo la hacemos?*
                         (how do we do it?)
         Learner 2:   **maybe we could just try it**
         Learner 1:   *yo lo puse a: ... aquí*
                         (I put it here)

(2)   Learner 1:   **oh! wait, so: we have to write the whole thing?** *estamos reescribi-*
                         *endo toda la oración?*
                         (are we rewriting the whole sentence?)
         Learner 2:   *la verdad, no sé*
                         (I really don't know)

(3)   Learner 1:   **okay, four question,** *tiene la policía el derecho a entrar a una*
                         *escuela a sacar niños o a un joven indocumentado? quién los pro-*
                         *tege?*
                         (do the police have the right to enter a school to take children or
                         an undocumented young person? who protects them?)

In Example 2, the learner uses English first to attract her peer's attention 'oh! wait', and then to clarify the instructions of the task 'we have to write the whole thing?' She repeats her question in Spanish '*estamos reescribiendo toda la oración?*'(are we rewriting the whole sentence?), which also serves to add emphasis. In other instances, like in Example 3, the use of English helped to move the task along, mark progress, and focus everybody's attention on the same item.

## Metalinguistic function

Spanish heritage learners also resorted to their dominant language, English, to collaborate in the solution of Spanish language-related problems: vocabulary, grammar, and spelling difficulties. In pair and small group activities, heritage learners used English to ask for assistance from their peers – Examples 4 and 5. They switched to English to indicate they were having lexical difficulties and check for confirmation – Example 6. When providing feedback and input, code-switching also served to frame the new input and enhance its salience, as shown in Example 7.

(4) Learner 1: *y necesitamos* … **how do you say space?**
(and we need)
Learner 2: *espacio*
(space)
Learner 1: *más espacio*
(more space)

(5) Learner 1: **how do you say files** *en español?*
(in Spanish?)
Learner 2: *yo no … yo no le … no me gusta decirle* **files**, *porque no es una pal-abra, se llama campos, campos de …*
(I don't, I don't, I don't like saying files, because it is not a word, it is called files, files with)
Learner 1: *donde se cosecha mucha fruta,*
(where lots of fruits are harvested)

(6) Learner 1: *viñedos son a* **vineyard, is that right?**
(vineyards are a vineyard)
Learner 2: *viñedos, sí*
(vineyards, yes)

(7) Learner 1: *y luego acuérdense que iban al, al … cómo se? a la basura?*
(and then remember they were going to, to how do you? to the trash?)

Learner 2:   *a la cabaña,* **they're called** *cabaña*
             (to the cabin, they're called cabin)
Learner 1:   **uhuh**

Example 8 is particularly illustrative. Here one of the learners resorts to English to define the Spanish word '*baldío*'(barren). This learner could just translate '*baldío*' into English, but instead she makes the effort to explain the meaning of the word in Spanish. In the process, she switches to her dominant language, English, when the defining task gets complicated, and switches back to Spanish once the meaning of the word has been established.

(8)   Learner 1:   *baldío es como ... mm, un barrio que no tiene nada, sí? me entien-*
                   *des? que ya, como que* **nothing,** *baldío es* **like kind of like an alley,**
                   **like an alley, like no place, like kind of trashy place,** *algo así, algo*
                   *por el estilo,*
                   (barren is like a neighborhood that has nothing, yes? do you
                   understand me? that no longer, like nothing, barren is like […]
                   something like that, something similar)

The segments of interaction analyzed in Examples 4 to 8 constitute lexical-LREs and provide evidence of learners' use of English to co-construct Spanish knowledge. In these episodes, learners talk about vocabulary and shape their vocabulary knowledge. The use of English helps them to focus their attention, provide scaffolded assistance to each other, and solve the lexical difficulties encountered. It supports the co-construction of knowledge of the Spanish words '*espacio*' (space), '*campos* (fields), '*viñedo*' (vinyard), '*cabaña*' (cabin), and '*baldío*' (barren). From a sociocultural perspective, what we see here is language learning in process, mediated by the heritage learners' use of their dominant language.

It should be noted, however, that not all lexical difficulties triggered a lexical-LRE. Heritage learners also switched to English as a communication strategy, to compensate for lexical gaps without disrupting the flow of the conversation. In Example 9, the pauses and repetitions indicate the learner is having difficulty retrieving the word or expression she wants to use, either she does not know it or she cannot recall it at this moment. She decides to use the English word 'movies' instead. Learners move on with the conversation without making any further attempt to find the Spanish equivalent for this English word.

(9)   Learner 1:   *no te gusta ir a las ... a las ... ir a las* **movies?**
                   (you do not like going to the movies?)
      Learner 2:   *no, no voy mucho*
                   (no, I don't go often)

Sociolinguistic researchers refer to this as compensatory code-switching or crutching (Zentella, 1997). They have noticed that even highly proficient bilinguals use this type of code-switching sporadically in conversation (Lowther, 2010; Zentella, 1997). In everyday communication, the goal is to get the message across, to make oneself understood and keep conversation going. In the heritage language classroom, however, the goal is to build new knowledge, to develop a richer and more sophisticated vocabulary specific to the academic formal register. This goal is achieved when, as observed in Examples 4 to 8, learners switch to English not just as a compensatory strategy, but as a means to get new input and co-construct new knowledge.

Heritage language learners also used English to collaborate in the solution of Spanish spelling and accentuation difficulties. Orthography tends to be a major difficult for these learners. Since most of them have received little or no formal instruction in the heritage language, they have had limited opportunities to develop their writing skills, and usually show deficiencies in their command of orthography and accentuation conventions (Colombi, 1997). What for L2 learners would constitute basic orthographic knowledge, like the accentuation of words ending in *-ión* or the accentuation of verb endings, can represent a challenge for heritage students. In the following examples, heritage learners resort to English as they collaborate to solve accentuation and spelling problems. They switch to English to correct each other's mistakes – Example 10, to ask for help and check for confirmation – Example 11, and to regulate their own mental activity. We see this in Example 12, where the learner manages to figure out the correct spelling of the word '*anchos*' (wide) after repeating it out loud several times. The focus of attention, '*anchos*', is in Spanish, but the language used to regulate the cognitive process through which the learner establishes that '*anchos*' needs to be spelled with an 'h' is in English.

(10)   Learner:   **accent on the** *o, … ión*

(11)   Learner 1:   **this one has an accent in the e? isn't it**
           *cambié? en la e?*
           (I changed? on the e?)
      Learner 2:   *e,* **right**

(12)   Learner:   *y::: … anchos, anchos,* **I don't know if it is with an** *hache, anchos,*
           **yes**
           (and wide, wide […] aitch, wide)

Grammar problems did also elicit the use of English, as previously observed in the L2 classroom where learners often resort to their common L1 to solve L2 grammar difficulties (Alegría de la Colina & García Mayo, 2009; Storch & Aldosari, 2010; Storch & Wigglesworth, 2003; Swain & Lapkin, 2000). Example 13 illustrates the use of English as a cognitive tool to solve a Spanish grammar problem and collaborate in the construction of Spanish grammar knowledge. The problem revolves around the use of 'haiga' and 'haya', two alternative forms for the third person singular present subjunctive of the verb 'haber' (there is/it is). 'Haiga' is the vernacular form for most heritage language learners in this class. It is, however, not acceptable in standard Spanish. In the classroom, learners are instructed to use the standard verb form 'haya', both in written and oral academic speech. In Example 13, the first learner uses 'haiga' in her first turn: 'haiga sol todo el año' (it is sunny all year round), but then she realizes there might be a problem. The rising intonation in her second turn, 'haiga?' and 'haya sol?', is a signal that she is not sure which of the two forms is correct and therefore needs help. The second learner confirms that 'haya' is the form they need to use. 'Haya' is accepted by the first learner in her last turn.

(13)   Learner 1:   *en una ciudad donde haiga sol todo el año*
                    (in a city where it is sunny all year round)
       Learner 2:   mhm
       Learner 1:   *haiga? ... haya sol?*
                    (it is? it is sunny?)
       Learner 2:   *haya, haya porque ella dijo* ... **irregular verb**
                    (it is, it is, because she said)
       Learner 1:   *haya*
                    (it is)
       Learner 2:   **uhuh, it's more correct**

The second learner corrects the first one in Spanish: 'haya, haya', but when it comes to explain why she believes the form 'haya' instead of 'haiga' needs to be used, she switches to English: because it is an 'irregular verb', because 'it's more correct'. The metalinguistic activity is partially performed through English. The use of English, the learners' dominant language, makes it possible for them to analyze the target language as required by the task at hand. To think and talk about language is usually a cognitively demanding task for learners, particular for heritage language learners who have not received grammar instruction and therefore tend to have limited grammatical awareness and metalinguistic vocabulary. The use of English facilitates this activity and allows them to build new linguistic knowledge. Again, English mediates Spanish language learning, in this case, learning of Spanish standard grammar.

## Conversational function

Those uses of English which did not fall under the metacognitive and metalinguistic categories were analyzed for evidence of the conversational functions of code-switching identified in previous sociolinguistic research. Many of these switches were one-item switches, more specifically, discourse markers. Examples 14 and 15 illustrate the use of the English connector 'so', in turns that were otherwise entirely in Spanish. Other English discourse markers used in the Spanish heritage language classroom were 'like' – Example 16, or 'well' – Example 17.

(14)  Learner:  *mi papá era residente,* **so** ... *yo nunca pasé lo que ellos pasaron*
(my father was a resident, so I never had to go through what they went through)

(15)  Learner:  **so:** *sería: ... como se llamaba? Rora?*
(so it would be what was her name? Rora?)

(16)  Learner:  *a mi vecina no más se la llevaron* **like,** *no más porque una señora llamó*
(my neighbor, they just took her, like just because one lady called)

(17)  Learner:  *no?* **well** ... *a mí me encanta ir a ver películas en el cine*
(no? well I love watching movies at the movie theater)

Sociolinguistic research has observed that switches involving discourse markers are the most prevalent type of code-switching among English-Spanish bilinguals (Poplack, 2004). They occur with high frequency and even in contexts where no other type of code-switching is used. It is therefore not surprising that heritage language learners use English discourse markers even in the context of the classroom and while trying to maintain their speech primarily in Spanish.

Code-switching served also as a realignment strategy, a well-documented use in sociolinguistic research (see Carvalho, 2012). Heritage learners switched languages to mark changes in topic, tone, and speaker's voice. In Example 18, two learners are collaborating in a vocabulary task. The second learner switches to English to explain the learning strategies she uses, when working at home, to address new vocabulary. This segment of the conversation takes place mainly in English. As soon as they get back to the task at hand, they switch back to Spanish.

(18)  Learner 1:  *alimaña, un tipo de animal, oh! lo hiciste sin?*
(vermin, a type of animal, oh! did you do it without?)
Learner 2:  *mmm, no* ... **when I was reading the book** *las palabras que yo no sabía,* **uh, I wrote them down, and the page number, so when I did this I can just look, oh!, I don't know what that is and look at the page number, and**
(no [...] the words I did not know)
Learner 1:  **that's smart, I usually just circle them in the book**
Learner 2:  **uhuh**

> Learner 1:  *este:*
>           (so:)
> Learner 2:  *entablar es ...*
>           (to initiate means)

In Example 19, the learner switches languages to quote the teacher's words and in Example 20 to make an aside comment: 'Oh! I love these pens'. In Example 20, the switch to English functions as a conversational strategy to signal the aside, a parenthetical comment unrelated to the task which is the main focus of the conversation.

(19)  Learner 1:  *entonces*
                  (so)
        Learner 2:  **she said** ... *juntas*
                  (together)
        Learner 3:  *o individuales o ... juntas*
                  (individually or together)

(20)  Learner 1:  *mientras, yo busco más palabras que quien sabe si tengas ahí*
                  (meanwhile, I search for more words that maybe you don't have there)
        Learner 2:  o:h, **I love these pens!** ... *leíste? leíste? qué páginas tenemos que leer?*
                  (did you read? what pages do we need to read?)

In Example 20, the switch to English also serves to add emphasis. Examples 21, 22, and 23 illustrate also the use of English to express emotion and add emphasis.

(21)  Learner 1:  *y eran como treinta o más*
                  (and there were like thirty or more)
        Learner 2:  **oh my god!**

(22)  Learner:  **really!?** *algo malo? cómo?*
                (something bad? how?)

(23)  Learner 1:  *cuando yo leo un libro*
                  (when I read a book)
        Learner 2:  **oh yeah!**, *sí, prefiero ver la película*
                  (yes, I prefer to watch the movie)

Examples were also found of learners switching to English to attract and redirect their peers' attention, that is, examples of what Zentella calls control switches (Zentella, 1997: 95). In Examples 24 to 26, learners switch to English to draw their peers' attention and try to regulate their behavior. In the previously analyzed Example 2, the English imperative 'wait' had this same function.

(24)  Learner 1:  *granjeado*
                   (earned)
      Learner 2:  *no sé*
                   (I don't know)
      Learner 1:  *a ver,* **look,** *granjeado*
                   (let's see, look, earned)

(25)  Learner 1:  **yeah, see? look,** *es lo que dice*
                   (this is what it says)

(26)  Learner 1:  *tristemente los estudiantes han sido víctimas erróneas*
                   (sadly, students have been wrong victims)
      Learner 2:  heh
      Learner 1:  heh **take that,** *no no está de acuerdo*
                   (no, he does not agree)

Finally, as discussed in the previous section and illustrated by Example 15, heritage learners also resorted to English as a compensatory strategy. Learners used English to compensate for gaps in their Spanish vocabulary knowledge – Examples 27 and 28, and to make reference to cultural concepts that have no direct equivalent in Spanish – Example 29.

(27)  Learner:  *a lo mejor eso es un … … no sé … un* **clue**
                 (maybe that is … I don't know … a clue)

(28)  Learner:  *hemos terminado, cómo se llama? con unos* **quotes,** *así*
                 (we have finished, how do you say? with quotes, like this)

(29)  Learner:  *el segundo yo puse que el total para* **K-12**
                 (the second one I wrote that the total for K-12)

In most of the examples here analyzed, it is clear that Spanish heritage language learners are not switching to English because of a lack of Spanish vocabulary. In all these examples, the very fact that two languages are used can be considered a mark of identity and intergroup solidarity. But particularly illustrative are examples that involve repetitions in English of what has or is about to be said in Spanish – see Examples 23 and 24, or extremely common words like 'yes', 'yeah', or 'right' – see Examples 11, 12, 23, and 25. These students obviously know how to say 'yes' in Spanish. It is not lack of knowledge that prompts their use of English. Heritage learners are switching languages as a conversational and communicative strategy to convey their message in the most effective possible way. They switch to English because they can, not because they have to, and in doing so, they are constructing and performing their bilingual identity.

## Conclusions and pedagogical implications

To conclude, the data analyzed for the purposes of the current study shows that heritage language learners switch between English and Spanish when working in pairs and small groups in the Spanish language classroom. However, the analysis of this code-switching revealed also that learners did not switch to English due to a lack of knowledge of Spanish or because of laziness, as some detractors of this practice suggest, but rather to perform important social, communicative, and cognitive functions.

First, all the examples of code-switching analyzed in the study come from pair and small group interaction. As mentioned at the beginning of the chapter and also observed in previous research (Sánchez Muñoz, 2007; Lowther, 2010), during whole-class activities teacher-learner interaction took place almost exclusively in Spanish. This means that these heritage learners are able to communicate exclusively in Spanish and also that they can adapt their language to different situations and interlocutors. During whole-class interaction, a more formal type of academic situation, code-switching was perceived as not appropriate and therefore avoided, as suggested by Sánchez Muñoz (2007). But the present study shows that English is used when heritage learners interact with their bilingual peers in pairs and small groups. Code-switching becomes thus a marker of bilingual identity and intergroup solidarity.

Second, this code-switching had a variety of conversational functions, similar to those observed in informal everyday conversations between English and Spanish bilinguals. Language switches served, for instance, to mark a change of topic in the conversation or to add emphasis. In addition, the analysis of code-switching in this study revealed that, in the context of the language classroom, the use of the learners' dominant language can also have a cognitive function. Heritage learners resorted to their dominant language when engaged in collaborative problem-solving activities, that is, when they encountered task or language-related difficulties and collaborated in their solution. The use of English provided cognitive support to discuss Spanish grammar, vocabulary, and orthography: to ask for assistance, to formulate and test hypothesis, to offer and assess new input, and to correct each other. English mediated their problem-solving activity and the co-construction of new language knowledge, knowledge of standard Spanish grammar, vocabulary, and spelling. English, the learners' dominant language, facilitated the learning of Spanish, their heritage language.

The findings of this study suggest that code-switching practices have a role to play in the heritage language classroom, even in advanced level classrooms. A completely monolingual environment creates an unnatural situation for bilingual speakers, who are used to switching between English and Spanish when speaking to other bilinguals. Furthermore, banning the use of English from the Spanish heritage language classroom means denying students the use of a powerful psychological tool that facilitates, rather than hinders, the development of standard academic Spanish.

This does not mean, of course, that the use of English should be encouraged in the classroom or that any use of English can be justified. In the class where the present study was conducted, learners made a judicious use of their dominant language, always maintaining Spanish as the primary language of their interactions. The presence of English was carefully managed by the teacher, who insisted learners would use only Spanish when reporting the results of their activities in front of the class or contributing to whole-class discussions. But she adopted a more relaxed attitude when learners were working in pairs and small groups, dealing with language-related difficulties and engaging in cognitively demanding metalinguistic and knowledge building activities. This is how, in this classroom, English supported, did not substitute for, the Spanish language, and instead of being a problem, code-switching became a valuable pedagogical resource.

# References

Alegría de la Colina, A., & García Mayo, M. P. (2009). Oral interaction in task-based EFL learning: The use of the L1 as a cognitive tool. *IRAL-International Review of Applied Linguistics in Language Teaching*, 47(3–4), 325–345.

Antón, M., & DiCamilla, F. (1998). Socio-cognitive functions of L1 collaborative interaction in the L2 classroom. *Canadian Modern Language Review*, 54(3), 314–342.

Azkarai, A., & Mayo, M. P. (2015). Task-modality and L1 use in EFL oral interaction. *Language Teaching Research*, 19(5), 550–571.

Beaudrie, S. (2011). Spanish heritage language programs: A snapshot of current programs in the southwestern United States. *Foreign Language Annals*, 44(2), 321–337.

Beaudrie, S. (2012). Research on university-based Spanish heritage language programs in the United States: The current state of affairs. In *Beaudrie & Fairclough* (Eds.), pp. 203–221.

Beaudrie, S., & Fairclough, M. (2012). *Spanish as a heritage language in the United States: The state of the field*. Washington, DC: Georgetown University Press.

Benmamoun, E., Montrul, S., & Polinsky, M. (2010). *Prolegomena to heritage linguistics* [white paper]. University of Illinois at Urbana-Champaign and Harvard University.

Bullock, B. E. & Toribio, A. J. (2009). Themes in the study of code-switching. In B. E. Bullock & A. J. Toribio (Eds.), *The Cambridge handbook of linguistic code-switching* (pp. 1–10). New York NY: Cambridge University Press.

Canagarajah, S. (2011). Codemeshing in academic writing: Identifying teachable strategies of translanguaging. *The Modern Language Journal*, 95(3), 401–417.

Carreira, M., & Kagan, O. (2011). The results of the national heritage language survey: Implications for teaching, curriculum design, and professional development. *Foreign Language Annals*, 44(1), 40–64.

Carvalho, A.M. (2012). Code-switching: From theoretical to pedagogical considerations. In *Beaudrie & Fairclough* (Eds.), pp. 139–157.

Cashman, H.R. (2005). Identities at play: Language preference and group membership in bilingual talk in interaction. *Journal of Pragmatics*, 37(3): 301–315.

Colombi, M.C. (1997). Perfil del discurso escrito en textos de hispanohablantes: Teoría y práctica. In M.C. Colombi & F. Alarcón (Eds.), *La enseñanza del español a hispanohablantes: Praxis y teoría* (pp. 175–189). Boston, MA: Houghton Mifflin.

Creese, A., & Blackledge, A. (2010). Translanguaging in the bilingual classroom: A pedagogy for learning and teaching? *The Modern Language Journal* 94(1): 103–115.

Espinosa, C.M., & Herrera, L.Y. (2016). Reclaiming bilingualism: Translanguaging in a science class. In O. García, & T. Kleyn (Eds.), *Translanguaging with multilingual students: Learning from classroom moments* (pp. 160–177). New York, NY: Routledge.

Fairclough, M. (2016). Incorporating additional varieties to the linguistic repertoires of heritage language learners: A multidialect model. In M. Fairclough & S.M. Beaudrie (Eds.), *Innovative strategies for heritage language teaching: A practical guide for the classroom* (pp. 143–165). Washington, DC: Georgetown University Press.

Fishman, J. (2001). 300-plus years of heritage language education in the United States. In J. Peyton, D. Ranard, & S. McGinnis (Eds.), *Heritage languages in America: Preserving a national resource* (pp. 87–97). McHenry, IL: Center for Applied Linguistics and Delta Systems.

Gánem Gutiérrez, A. (2008). Microgenesis, method and object: A study of collaborative activity in a Spanish as a foreign language classroom. *Applied Linguistics*, 29(1), 120–148.

García, O. (2009). *Bilingual education in the 21st century: A global perspective*. Malden, MA: Blackwell.

García, O. (2011). The translanguaging of Latino kindergarteners. In K. Potowski & J. Rothman (Eds.), *Bilingual youth: Spanish in English-speaking societies* (pp. 33–55). Amsterdam: John Benjamins.

García, O., & Kleyn, T. (Eds.). (2016). *Translanguaging with multilingual students: Learning from classroom moments*. New York, NY: Routledge.

García, O., & Wei, L. (2014). *Translanguaging: Language, bilingualism and education*. New York, NY: Palgrave Macmillan.

Gumperz, J. (1982). *Discourse strategies*. Cambridge: Cambridge University press.

He, A.W. (2010). The heart of heritage: Sociocultural dimensions of heritage language learning. *Annual Review of Applied Linguistics*, 30, 66–82.

Lasito, N. Storch. (2013). Comparing pair and small group interactions on oral tasks. *RELC Journal* 44(3), 361–375.

Lowther Pereira, K.A. (2010). *Identity and language ideology in the intermediate Spanish heritage language classroom*. Unpublished PhD dissertation. University of Arizona.

Martin-Beltrán, M. (2010). The two-way language bridge: Co-constructing bilingual language learning opportunities. *The Modern Language Journal*, 94(2), 254–277.

Martin-Beltrán, M. (2014). "What do you want to say?" How adolescents use translanguaging to expand learning opportunities. *International Multilingual Research Journal*, 8(3), 208–230.

Montrul, S. (2012). The grammatical competence of Spanish heritage speakers. In *Beaudrie & Fairclough* (Eds.), pp. 101–120.

Montrul, S. (2016). *The acquisition of heritage languages*. Cambridge: Cambridge University Press.

Otheguy, R., García, O., & Reid, W. (2015). Clarifying translanguaging and deconstructing named languages: A perspective from linguistics. *Applied Linguistics Review*, 6(3), 281–307.

Pascual y Cabo, D. (2016). *Advances in Spanish as a heritage language*. Amsterdam: John Benjamins.

Poplack, S. (1980). Sometimes I'll start a sentence in Spanish y termino en español: Toward a typology of code-switching. *Linguistics*, 18(7–8), 581–618.

Poplack, S. (2004). Code-switching. In U. Ammon, N. Dittmar, K. J. Mattheier, & P. Trudgill (Eds.), *Sociolinguistics/Soziolinguistik: An international handbook of the science of language* (2nd ed., pp. 589–596). Berlin: Walter de Gruyter.

Potowski, K. (2009). Forms and functions of code-switching by dual immersion students: A comparison of heritage speaker and L2 children. In M. Turnbull & J. Dailey-O'Cain (Eds.), *First language use in second and foreign language learning* (pp. 87–114). Bristol: Multilingual Matters.

Potowski, K. (2014). Heritage learners of Spanish. In K. L. Geeslin (Ed.), *The handbook of Spanish second language acquisition* (pp. 404–422). John Wiley & Sons.

Potowski, K., Parada, M., & Morgan-Short, K. (2012). Developing an online placement exam for Spanish heritage speakers and L2 students. *Heritage Language Journal*, 9(1), 51–76.

Reyes, I. (2004). Functions of code switching in schoolchildren's conversations. *Bilingual Research Journal*, 28(1), 77–98.

Sánchez Muñoz, A. (2007). *Register and style variation in speakers of Spanish as a heritage and as a second language*. Unpublished PhD dissertation. University of Southern California.

Silva-Corvalán, C. (1983). Code-shifting patterns in Chicano Spanish. In L. Elías-Olivares (ed.), *Spanish in the US setting: Beyond the southwest* (pp. 69–87). Rosslyn, VA: National Clearinghouse for Bilingual Education.

Silva-Corvalán, C., & Treffers-Daller, J. (2016). *Language dominance in bilinguals: Issues of measurement and operationalization*. Cambridge: Cambridge University Press.

Storch, N., & Aldosari, A. (2010). Learners' use of first language (Arabic) in pair work in an EFL class. *Language Teaching Research*, 14(4), 355–375.

Storch, N., & Wigglesworth, G. (2003). Is there a role for the use of the L1 in an L2 setting? *TESOL Quarterly*, 37(4), 760–769.

Swain, M. (2000). The output hypothesis and beyond. In J. P. Lantolf (Ed.), *Sociocultural theory and second language learning* (pp. 97–114). Oxford: Oxford University Press.

Swain, M. (2006). Languaging, agency and collaboration in advanced language proficiency. In H. Byrnes (Ed.), *Advanced language learning: The contribution of Halliday and Vygotsky* (pp. 95–108). New York, NY: Continuum.

Swain, M., & Lapkin, S. (1998). Interaction and second language learning: Two adolescent French immersion students working together. *The Modern Language Journal*, 82(3), 320–337.

Swain, M., & Lapkin, S. (2000). Task-based second language learning: The uses of the first language. *Language Teaching Research*, 4(3), 251–274.

Toribio, A. J. (2001). On the emergence of bilingual code-switching competence. *Bilingualism: Language and Cognition*, 4(3), 203–231.

Toribio, A. J. (2002). Spanish-English code-switching among US Latinos. *International Journal of the Sociology of Language*, 158, 89–119.

Valdés, G. (2001). Heritage language students: Profiles and possibilities. In J. Peyton, J. Ranard, & S. McGinnis (Eds.), *Heritage languages in America: Preserving a national resource* (pp. 37–80). McHenry, IL: The Center for Applied Linguistics and Delta Systems.

Valdés, G. (1981). Codeswitching as deliberate verbal strategy: A microanalysis of direct and indirect requests among bilingual Chicano speakers. In R. Durán (Ed.), *Latino language and communicative behavior* (pp. 95–108). Norwood, NJ: Ablex.

Valdés, G. (2007). Making connections: Second language acquisition research and heritage language teaching. In R. Salaberry & B. Lafford (Eds.), *The art of teaching Spanish: Second language acquisition from research to praxis* (pp. 193–212). Washington, DC: Georgetown University Press.

Vu, J., Bailey, A., & Howes, C. (2010). Early cases of code-switching in Mexican-heritage children: Linguistic and sociopragmatic considerations. *Bilingual Research Journal*, 33(2), 200–219.

Vygotsky, L. S. (1978). *Mind in society: The development of higher psychological processes*. Cambridge, MA: Harvard University Press.

Zentella, A. C. (1997). *Growing up bilingual: Puerto Rican children in New York*. Oxford: Blackwell.

# CHAPTER 9

# The Mirroring Project
## Improving suprasegmentals and intelligibility in ESL presentations

Elaine Tarone & Colleen Meyers
University of Minnesota

The Mirroring Project (Lindgren et al., 2003; Meyers, 2013, 2014) is a pedagogical option helping those who speak in a second language to improve their intelligibility in a holistic, context-sensitive way. Longitudinal, video-recorded evidence shows how the suprasegmental phonology of one adult English L2 learner, an international teaching assistant in a U.S. university, changes over time, as she "mirrors" the speech of an English speaker she herself has selected as a model. Importantly, it is the learner's suprasegmentals and nonverbal communication movements which were the focus of instruction, and which noticeably improved due to the Mirroring Project. These findings can be accounted for using the Douglas Fir Group's (2016) transdisciplinary framework, and Baktin's constructs of double voicing and semantic language play (Cook, 2000; Tarone, 2000; Broner & Tarone, 2001).

## Introduction

The broad topic of speaking in a second language encompasses a myriad of skills and contexts. This chapter focuses narrowly on a research-based pedagogy to meet the second-language speaking needs of a large, specific group of advanced second-language (L2) learners. In the United States, large numbers of international graduate students must attain a high level of second-language speaking ability for the specific purpose of teaching American undergraduates disciplinary content in an academic field of study. These learners, International Teaching Assistants (ITA's), are given responsibility to teach college courses in disciplinary fields such as mechanical engineering, mathematics, biology, and history. In this chapter "speaking in a second language" for the ITA refers *primarily* to the ability to use the L2 to produce comprehensible *short oral monologues* about disciplinary content, and secondarily, the ability to *respond in interaction to student questions* about that content. This chapter will focus on these adult learners' development

https://doi.org/10.1075/aals.17.09tar

of the ability to produce comprehensible L2 speech in *short rehearsed oral monologues*.

ITAs may take a specialized class providing language, culture, and professional teaching support for their development of this ability. It is widely agreed that the primary learning objective of such ITA classes should not be the ability to speak with a "native speaker accent," but rather the ability to intelligibly convey information via L2 (see, e.g., Murphy, 2014). Oral intelligibility, defined broadly as whether "listeners can understand the speaker's message" (Derwing & Munro, 2015: 1), is central because of the high-stakes nature of the information being conveyed in the ITA-taught class – disciplinary content that a group of university students needs in order to pass an oral proficiency exam to be certified to teach undergraduates. And for purposes of oral intelligibility, it has been clear for decades that the mastery of L2 segments like phonemes is far less important than the effective use of such L2 suprasegmental features as intonation (pitch range and movement) and prominence (emphasis of linguistic units) within thought groups, pausing and rhythm; these occur in synchrony with such nonverbal elements as gesture, eye contact and head movement, and body movement (Hardison, 2018). In other words, ITAs must master L2 suprasegmental phonology coordinated with accompanying nonverbal communication. With the needs of these learners in mind, this chapter will review relevant variationist research on the acquisition of L2 phonology, and more specifically on documented difficulties of ITAs in using suprasegmentals to make the information structure of their monologic discourse understandable to their audience. Based on that research, we reject a decontextualized bottom-up pedagogical approach focused on teaching phonological forms and units, and support the use of a top-down pedagogical approach in which learners develop the ability to monitor their own use of suprasegmentals and nonverbals and to focus holistically on the communication skills of identity models as they create meaning in social context. The chapter concludes with a case study showing how one such pedagogical approach successfully assists an ITA in modifying her monologic oral discourse (both suprasegmentals and nonverbal communication) to make it more engaging and clear to her audience.

## Review of relevant research on L2 pronunciation

Many second language acquisition researchers (e.g. Douglas Fir Group, 2016) are shifting away from a decontextualized cognitivist approach to second-language acquisition (SLA) and towards a more transdisciplinary understanding of second language use and acquisition that takes into account the impact of *community*, *norm*, *choice*, *identity* and *agency* on the development of interlanguage systems. In this framework, speaking in a second-language is seen as "… emergent, dynamic, unpredictable, open-ended, and intersubjectively negotiated" (Douglas Fir Group, 2016: 19). Many SLA researchers no longer see the process of SLA as a sort of decontextualized cognitive linguistic computation, but rather as a very human process that is holistic, multi-modal and embodied, focused on identity work, where learner agency and emotion are critical. In the following paragraphs we review research on the pronunciation of a second language that provides evidence that the acquisition of pronunciation in a second language is a holistic, multi-modal, agentive, and embodied process where social factors such as interlocutor, identity, and contextual meaning integrally influence learning outcomes.

*Phonology in speaking a L2: Impact of empathy, accommodation, identity, and emotion*

Since the inception of SLA research in 1972, variationist studies on interlanguage phonology have assembled convincing evidence that adults' pronunciation of a second language is dynamic and intersubjective. Guiora et al. (1972) proposed that adults have a "language ego" that is related to body ego and closely tied to pronunciation. They argued that the pronunciation of a second language is profoundly influenced by the "permeability of ego boundaries," where a learner's empathy with speakers of L2 creates "a temporary fusion of self-object boundaries" (Guiora et al., 1972: 421). If a language ego is permeable, it allows a learner to empathize with and adopt pronunciations of second language speakers; if it is not permeable, the learner will find it impossible to adopt those pronunciations. The researchers carried out an experiment designed to use alcohol to artificially induce empathy in an experimental group. They showed that the experimental group's pronunciation of Thai as a second language as they conversed with native speakers of Thai steadily became more native-like as they consumed incremental doses of martinis. A control group's pronunciation did not change. Guiora et al. argued that as the experimental group became more and more empathetic, they merged their language ego boundaries with those of their Thai conversation partners. This study unfortunately became more known for its innovative use of alcohol than for its theoretical framework – a framework which, after decades of being dismissed by SLA researchers with a decontextualized linguistics orientation, today seems very congruent with the Douglas Fir Group's construction of SLA.

Subsequently, "variationist" SLA researchers (reviewed in Tarone, 1978) carried out studies showing that adults' L2 phonology was variable, shifting forms in relation to social contextual variables such as interlocutor and task. Beebe (1980) documented the impact of interlocutor on L2 learners' use of Thai vs. English phonological variants; to explain this dynamic, Beebe and Giles (1984) proposed the Accommodation Theory, saying that L2 learners accommodate to and acquire the phonological features of L2 speakers they identify with. Tarone (1988) is an extensive review of SLA research on variation in learner language, including pronunciation, and provides a detailed, extensive listing of research studies supporting the view that social context and interlocutor affect the variants L2 learners use. Tarone and Swain (1995) explored why elementary level immersion students' pronunciation is excellent until pre-adolescence, when it starts to exhibit more native language transfer. They conclude that in preadolescence, immersion students begin to need to identify with the language used by peers. Pre-teens and teens need adolescent L2 role models of teen vernacular, including nonverbal and verbal behavior. Lacking those, language immersion pre-teens will switch to L1 teen vernaculars. Major (2001) shows that learners' interlanguage phonology clearly shifts variables in response to social context and interlocutor; he concludes that in the pronunciation of second-language learners, "... any model, theory, or purported explanation that fails to account for variation is not accounting for the data, period" (2001:69). Tarone (2005) provides a summary of variationist research on speaking in a second language.

A critical element of phonology in speaking in a second language is "voice," communication that uniquely embodies a given speaker's personality and tone. Suprasegmental elements such as intonation, prominence placement, and pausing, tied to nonverbal elements, are primary conveyers of the speaker's emotion, tone, personal stance and identification with a speech community. Learning to use such elements in speaking in a second language is unlikely to be a logical process of linguistic analysis. Cook (2000) and Tarone (2000), referencing the work of Bakhtin (1981), highlight the importance of language play, particularly semantic language play: "play with units of meaning, combining them in ways which create worlds which do not exist: fictions" (Cook, 2000:228), and of "double voicing," in which a speaker uses someone else's discourse for his or her own purposes, "inserting a new semantic intention into a discourse which already has, and which retains, an intention of its own" (Bakhtin 1929/1984:189). Broner and Tarone (2001) provide multiple examples of semantic language play and double voicing by bilingual children in a 5th grade Spanish immersion program, as they "took on different roles and spoke with different voices, both in English and Spanish ... Sometimes the children acted out parts in a drama, taking the part of someone else: A villain, a radio announcer, a rock star" (p. 372). Leonard, for example, spoke with the voice of a fellow student when narrating an event that had occurred earlier in the classroom:

(1)  I was like, 'Brandon?' and he's, '*no es mi culpa que uso mi dedo medio para mi*'. (It's not my fault I use my middle finger for myself).

It is unlikely that Leonard was reporting literally what he and Brandon said to each other; rather, this is an imaginative dramatization – what Tannen (1989) has called "constructed dialogue" – a narrator's created 'performance' of dialogue by a character in a story. Clark and Gerrig (1990) and Mathis and Yule (1994) subsequently documented the use of constructed dialogue in casual oral discourse as a way to dramatically enact the imagined voices of characters in oral narratives.

More recently, Moreno (2016) documents the way "Heriberto," a bilingual Spanish-English speaker, uses English L2 in several instances of constructed dialogue where he 'performs' the voice of his English L1 ex-roommate, "Charlie." Both perceptual and PRAAT analysis of the pitch, prominence placement, and pausing reveal that when Heriberto performs Charlie's "voice," he shifts to more target-like English suprasegmentals that contrast markedly with those he uses in his "normal" English accent. In other words, when he speaks with Charlie's voice in "constructed dialogue", Heriberto's suprasegmentals become more North American (even recognizable as a form of "surfer talk"). He uses a wider pitch range, and a more emphatic stress pattern with longer pauses; it is a "voice" that holistically communicates the identity and emotional stance of Heriberto's American friend. What this example reveals about Heriberto's mastery of the phonology of English varieties is truly striking: while the suprasegmentals of his "everyday" voice retain Hispanic elements, when Heriberto engages in semantic language play and speaks with the "voice" of Charlie, his suprasegmentals temporarily shift and become very Americanized. Guiora might say that Heriberto's language ego has permeable boundaries that enable him, in play, to empathize with, and temporarily adopt the speech patterns of, a L2 speaker.

### Suprasegmental phonology: Intelligibility in spoken L2 discourse

In this chapter, we use the term "intelligibility", broadly defined, to refer to whether "listeners can understand the speaker's message" (Derwing & Munro, 2015: 1); obviously intelligibility relies heavily on the perception of the interlocutor with whom the L2 speaker interacts. Research has clearly established that listener-defined intelligibility is closely tied to the speaker's ability to master the prosody of the L2, particularly the placement of prominence in a sentence, and the use of pitch height and a variety of pitch patterns in intonation (Hahn, 2004; Kang et al., 2010; Pickering, 2001, 2004). Prominence is the degree to which a constituent, such as a syllable, stands out through pitch, length, and loudness (Chun, 2002). For example, Kang et al. found that such prosodic aspects of L2 speech accounted for 50% of the variance in listeners' ratings of comprehensibility. The specific ways in which suprasegmentals impact intelligibility in authentic oral discourse (such as that of international teaching assistants (ITAs)) have recently been documented by research in two areas: the role of intonation in marking the information structure of extended discourse, and the synchronous relationship in oral discourse of prosody and nonverbal elements as gesture, eye gaze, and head movement.

Suprasegmentals make a lecture's information structure clearer. According to Hahn (2004), recall of undergraduate students was significantly better when a TA produced primary stress that was both accurately placed and easy to perceive. Ground-breaking research on intonation in the L2 speech of university lecturers by Pickering (2001, 2004) is based on Brown's framework of discourse analysis (Brown, 1977; Brown & Yule, 1983), and on Brazil's (1997) model of intonation in English discourse, which explicitly relates intonation to the information structure of oral discourse. Brazil proposes a "paragraph" unit of intonation called a pitch sequence, which is a semantically coherent group of tone units. Prominent syllables in each tone unit manifest 3 interacting systems: tone, key, and termination; key choice is realized on onset syllables in the tone unit and termination choice is realized on its nuclear syllable. Barr (1990) builds on this framework, grouping pitch sequences into a sequence chain (or phonologically defined paragraph) to describe the discourse in academic lectures. Pickering (2001) uses that model to compare native speaker (NS) and non-native speaker (NNS) lectures in the English-medium classroom. She finds that a major obstacle to NNS oral communication is tone choice; while NSs systematically exploit tone choice to increase the accessibility of discourse content to students and improve rapport, the NNSs' tonal composition interferes with the information structure of their discourse and also causes students to view them as unsympathetic. Pickering (2004) shows how native speakers use intonation paragraphs defined by phonological criteria to present the information structure of their oral discourse; however, non-native English-speaking lecturers do not, and this affects the degree to which students understand their discourse. Within an intonation paragraph, NSs use an onset with a high pitch and accelerated rate, pitch range and volume, and close with a low pitch and low volume; they also use longer pauses to define intonation paragraph boundaries. Non-native speaker (NNS) lecturers have difficulty producing such clear intonation paragraphs due to a compressed pitch range and a much lower initial pitch at the beginning of each paragraph, as well as shorter pauses at paragraph boundaries. The focusing markers used by NNSs within these paragraphs also are much less prosodically distinct, making it more difficult for listeners to identify key information in the lecture. Pickering's work makes it much clearer why ITAs need to master English prosody to make their lectures more intelligible to their students.

A second recent line of research documents the inter-related nature of English prosody and synchronous nonverbal elements of communication (cf. Key 1980). Decades ago, David Abercrombie, a well-known British phonetician, described that relationship this way: "We speak with our vocal organs, but we converse with our whole body; conversation consists of much more than a simple interchange of spoken words" (Abercrombie, 1968: 55). Pennycook (1985) shows the importance of this fact for improving the intelligibility of second language speakers. According to Pennycook,

> These 'kinesic markers'- head nods, eye blinks, small lip movements, chin thrusts, and other body movements –mark the rhythm of the speech and are produced, according to Dittman (1974), as a by-product of the speaker's ongoing task of casting thoughts into speech. Thus, such body movements provide important clues to the listener in the ongoing task of understanding what the speaker has said. (p. 263)

Hardison (2018) reports research on the link between prosody and gesture in academic lectures, showing how a native speaker lecturer's beat gestures align with prominent units to emphasize the discourse importance of a particular phrase. Hardison's findings also reveal a correspondence between intonation and gesture, with auditory-visual components of the speech event (hand gesture, brow raise, and head position) co-occurring with $F_0$ peaks at the nuclear-accented syllables.

## Pedagogy on pronunciation to improve intelligibility

Traditional approaches to teaching pronunciation tend to segment it into a series of discrete linguistic components with rules that students are encouraged to explicitly internalize, much as when they study the grammar of their L2. A popular teacher education book (Celce-Murcia, Brinton, & Goodwin, 2010) is rich in linguistic information representing to teachers phonemes and suprasegmentals such as intonation; however, these are given as a descriptive list of mechanical segments, levels, processes, and functions. For example, the chapter on intonation consists of a long series of rules describing pitch contours, illustrated through sentences taken out of context, with glosses that describe the emotion that supposedly goes along with each illustrated pitch pattern.

Typically even student pronunciation textbooks take this bottom-up approach, often beginning with segmental phonemes, and then moving up through phonotactic patterns such as "blending" in syllable structure, through stress, and with intonation at the very end – if indeed they even get to intonation at all (Gilbert, 2012; Grant, 2017). This approach focuses on building explicit knowledge about L2 phonemics and phonological patterns by starting with an analysis of the smallest linguistic units and providing explicit rules on how to combine them to create larger linguistic units. This pedagogical approach does not seem to draw at all upon the research we have reviewed in this chapter, on the central influence of social context, interlocutor, empathy, and nonverbal elements on pronunciation of a second language.

There has been recent acknowledgement that this pedagogy designed to improve pronunciation in an L2 needs to be improved (Levis, 2005; Kannellow, 2009; Thomson & Derwing, 2015). While pedagogy on phonology for international teaching assistants (ITAs) has benefited from a primary focus on intelligibility of speaking rather than nativeness of pronunciation (cf. Levis, 2005), it is fair to say that even the pedagogical efforts to improve the intelligibility of ITAs have taken a relatively decontextualized approach; they have not yet fully explored the implications of SLA research findings on the importance of interlocutor, community, norm, choice, identity and agency, findings that might suggest a more "top-down," holistic pedagogy to better harness the agentive energy of such intelligent, motivated, and goal-oriented L2 learners. Even when there have been calls for a less-analytical, form-focused approach to teaching L2 pronunciation (cf. Pennington, 1988), the activities recommended to replace the old ones are still relatively decontextualized and disembodied, with little sense of emotion, personality or "voice." Almost all instruction continues to rely almost exclusively on linguistic analysis and form-focused instruction, even in view of the research we have reviewed.

Foote's dissertation study (2015) argues that the way to facilitate improvements in L2 pronunciation is to help language learners "to better perceive differences between their speech and that of the target language" (p. 2) – again, an analytical, cognitive goal. To that purpose, Foote proposes use of a technique called "shadowing:" "repeating and copying speech nearly simultaneously with a target recording." (p. 3). While her study shows some positive outcomes from use of this technique, it must be pointed out here that the approach still does not take into account many of the relevant research findings just reviewed as important for development of interlanguage phonology: the importance of learner agency in selecting a speaking model, the internalization of the holistic "voice" of this model including emotion and personality, and the ability to use nonverbal and suprasegmental elements to reinforce one another and signal information structure in a presentation or lecture.

It is in this context that we consider the usefulness of a pedagogical approach called the Mirroring Project (Lindgren et al., 2003; Meyers, 2013, 2014) that does take these research findings into account. In the next section, we offer a case study describing how an international teaching assistant used the Mirroring Approach (along with more traditional ITA instruction) to dramatically change both suprasegmental and nonverbal elements of her second-language speech to improve the intelligibility of her presentations.

A pedagogical study

This section describes a longitudinal study of the way speaking in English as a second language changed over time for a Chinese graduate student as she underwent International Teaching Assistant (ITA) training and participated in the Mirroring Project.

*Participant*

During spring semester, 2012, "Mary" (a pseudonym) was an international graduate student in her mid-twenties from mainland China enrolled in an upper-level ITA training class at the University of Minnesota. She was earning her Ph.D. in business through the Carlson School of Management, and she was required to take an English proficiency test to demonstrate she was qualified to teach accounting courses in her department. The result of the proficiency exam indicated that she would need to enroll in an upper-level ITA training class in order to earn a level "1" exemption. She had been living in the US for two years before entering the course, and she had studied English in China for 16 years before coming to the US.

Mary was selected for this study primarily because she was the first student in the program to request a non-native speaking model for her project (described in the next section); she chose to emulate a short segment that was part of Yang Lan's Ted Talk "The generation that's remaking China" (Lan, 2011). In a recent conference presentation (later published as Murphy, 2014), Murphy had argued that clear non-native pronunciation models are very useful due to "their transparency as aspirational models and relevance to learners' pronunciation needs" (2014:258). Thus, Mary's choice of an intelligible, comprehensible non-native model made her a very relevant case study.

Yang Lan, otherwise known as the "Oprah of China," is an excellent model of intelligibility and dynamism. In the video segment from Ted Talks, Yang Lan effectively uses suprasegmentals and body language to highlight the words which she makes prominent. For example, she raises her eyebrows when she stresses the word "final," and she stands tall and bends over, literally acting out the intonation pattern of the phrase "China's got talent show," to highlight her point that the talent show she references is in China (not America).

*Pedagogical treatment*

The 15-week class in which Mary was enrolled during spring semester 2012 was designed as a practicum for international graduate students desiring to teach undergraduate students at the University of Minnesota. The instructor of this course is the second author of this chapter. The course was divided into two components: a weekly lecture, focusing on teaching and culture, and a weekly language lab, focusing on language and simulated teaching practice. In addition to teaching simulations during lab, students practiced various aspects of the English language, including the sound system as related to information structure. As recommended by decades of research (e.g., Anderson-Hsieh, 1992; Anderson-Hsieh et al., 1992; Kang, 2010), language work in labs focused primarily on explicit instruction focused on elements impacting whether listeners can understand them (suprasegmentals such as intonation, pausing and phrase-level stress-placement to assign prominence to linguistic units in thought groups and to highlight information structure in the discourse). This was followed by video-recorded practice in front of small audiences, where transcripts of video-recordings were subsequently evaluated by the learners and the instructor with electronic visual feedback on prosody via PRAAT software and perceptual instructor feedback. That feedback included nonverbal communication, since considerable research, including that of Hardison (2018), reveals that nuclear-accented syllables in intonation phrases co-occur with auditory-visual components such as $F_0$, hand gesture, brow raise, and head position. In electronic feedback to ITAs, priority was accorded to use of suprasegmentals such as intonation, pausing and stress-placement within the thought group to highlight information structure in the discourse. Coursework culminated in a "Mirroring Project" (Lindgren et al., 2003; Meyers, 2013, 2014) during the final weeks of the semester.

The Mirroring Project was designed to help students integrate and apply what they learned in a holistic way that would enable them to internalize the "voice" of a self-selected speech model (cf. Bakhtin, 1981; Broner & Tarone, 2001). (A detailed description of steps to be taken in executing the Mirroring Project is provided in Appendix A.) Briefly, each student was asked to choose a proficient speaker of English as a model whose spoken presentation they wanted to emulate or "mirror," expressing through their intonation, rhythm, and nonverbal communication the same level of emotion or enthusiasm that their speech model expressed. In other words, they were not just to memorize and repeat decontextualized phrases, but to attempt to communicate to an audience the same level of passion that their model speaker did in order to establish rapport, since rapport has been found to be a top predictor of TA success in the U.S. (Gorsuch, 2003).

*Data collection*

For this study, Mary's speech was recorded three times during the 15-week semester; all three data samples were in a rehearsed, presentational mode. Recording 1 was made at the end of Week 3 (Time 1); as part of a simulated, rehearsed but not scripted teaching practice, Mary introduced herself and provided a course overview on the first day of an imagined accounting class to a small audience with minimal knowledge of the field of accounting, consisting of an undergraduate student, another ITA and the instructor (the second author). This audience asked Mary questions during and after her presentation. This was Mary's first oral presentation of the semester, a type of diagnostic to evaluate her strengths and weaknesses in the English language, her teaching skill and cross-cultural accommodation. Recording 2 of Mary's rehearsed and scripted presentation was made in Week 13 of the semester (Time 2); it was Mary's first attempt to mirror the segment of Yang Lan's Ted Talk she had chosen. The instructor operated the camera while Mary spoke; there was no other physical audience. Recording 3, Mary's final version of her project, was made of her rehearsed and scripted presentation 7 days later in Week 14 (Time 3); again, only she and the instructor were present. While Mary's real audience at Times 2 and 3 consisted of one person and a video camera, we would like to argue that she was addressing a virtual audience – the large group in the auditorium that Yang Lan spoke to. While not physically present, this imagined audience had a clear impact on Mary's presentation. We see evidence to support our argument in Mary's scanning of eye movement back and forth across the room to her imagined audience, and her constant shifting in body position from one side of the room to the other.

During the 7 days between Time 2 and Time 3 in the Mirroring Project, Mary viewed her Time 2 video, compared it to Yang Lan's Ted Talk video, and then shared with the instructor what she felt were her strengths and weaknesses in terms of segmentals, volume, suprasegmentals, body language, emotion and tone[1] as compared to the original speaker (these criteria were stipulated in the Mirroring Project grading rubric, provided in Appendix B.) After that, the instructor gave Mary her feedback on the specific areas of overall volume or voice projection, suprasegmentals, and portraying emotion, as well as suggestions for improvement in these areas which both Mary and the instructor had identified as needing the most work. During the ensuing time period, Mary practiced her script in private several times so that she knew it by heart. In this phase, students generally practice with the video, repeating and mirroring the model speaker, and then practice by themselves or with another person outside of class. Thus, 10 weeks elapsed between Times 1 and 2, and 1 week intervened between Times 2 and 3.

Links to these short video-recordings of Mary at Times 1, 2 and 3, and to Yang Lan's original recording, are available at Meyers (2013).

---

1. Here tone refers to something different from intonation. "Intonation" refers to pitch movement in the thought group. "Tone" refers to attitude (such as enthusiasm, irony, or boredom) transmitted by a combination of intonation, pausing, prominence placement, and accompanying nonverbal communication.

## Data analysis

*Acoustic analysis.* Mary's speech samples at Times 1, 2, and 3 were analyzed acoustically using PRAAT (Boersma & Weenink, 2017) pronunciation software designed for speech analysis. For our purposes of analysis, we used the pitch and intensity settings because they are most useful when analyzing speech supraseg-mentals. The first short segment[2] of each recording was analyzed to ensure consistency in terms of pitch variation as related to key choice for intonational paragraphs (Pickering, 2004). This is because, as Pickering points out, it is in the first intonational paragraph of a segment of talk that a speaker sets overall key choice (beginning pitch level) for intonational paragraphs (where an intonational paragraph is defined as "a unit above the level of the tone unit and equivalent to the paragraph in written discourse… the most prominent cues being high pitch onset (as measured by fundamental frequency [Fo]) with an accelerated rate and volume" (p. 20)). A PRAAT recording was made of the introductory speech segment produced at Time 1, 2 and 3, and then converted into a .wav file. The PRAAT analysis consisted of analyzing each of the 3 speech segments for Fo/pitch (Hz) and intensity (dB) using the editor menu.

In this paragraph we offer guidance in how to read PRAAT visuals, using Figure 1 in Results as an example. The length of the speech segment is indicated at the bottom of the visual in time per seconds. For instance, the recording in Figure 1 is a total of 6.01 seconds long. The 2 rows at the top of the visual display the amplitude of the wave form of the utterance over time; we can infer syllable strength and length in this display. In Figure 1, for example, we can see that the first two bursts of amplitude on the top left correspond to the two syllables of "today;" the first burst is much shorter than the second indicating the amount of time it takes the speaker to produce each syllable. We also see that the amount of effort expended for "to" is less than that of "day" as "to" does not deviate much from the center line, while "day" deviates quite a bit. In the bottom row of the visual, a thin line indicates traces of the fundamental frequency (Fo), or pitch, as the speaker says the utterance; pitch or Fo in English is related to listeners' perception of intonation. Again, using "today" as an example, we see that "to" is lower in

---

2. Analysis of the Time 1 segment focused on the first two utterances which Mary produced as part of her teaching content (about 6 secs), and on the first utterance she produced in the Times 2 and 3 segments (about 15 secs). Syllable duration was not measured because as Chun (2002:5) states, "the duration of individual sound segments can be measured on a waveform or spectrogram, but the criteria are not always simple for determining precisely where one sound segment ends and where the next begins. In addition, "the same sound or syllable can vary in length depending on the neighboring sounds, whether the syllable a sound is in is stressed, or whether the syllable occurs immediately before a pause." (p. 6)

pitch than is "day," and that the phrase "today we're going to cover" starts with a higher pitch on the first stressed syllable ("day") and progressively lowers in pitch through the end of the phrase; this kind of declination in pitch over the duration of the thought group (the informational units of speech) is characteristic of the English used by effective speakers (see McGregor et al., 2016).

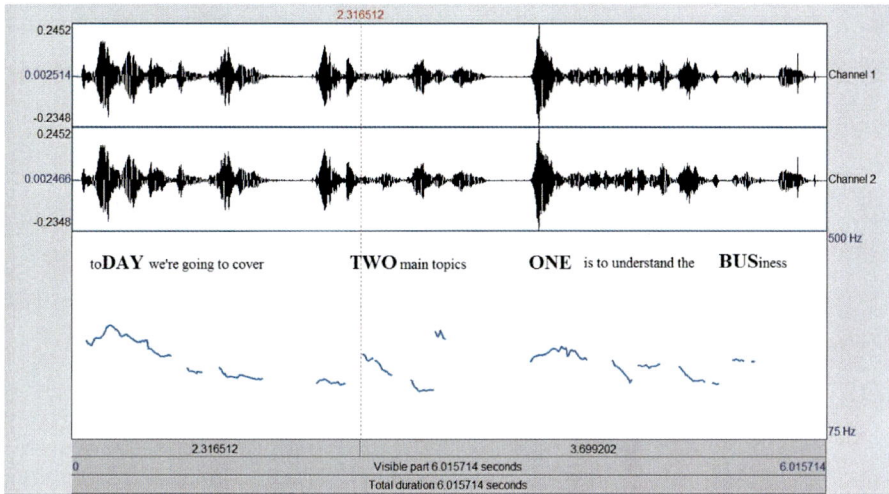

**Figure 1.**   Mary's microteaching sample at time 1, PRAAT analysis

*Perceptual data analysis.* While acoustic analysis can be compelling, it cannot capture all the important differences between Mary's intelligibility and effectiveness at Times 1, 2 and 3. For one thing, only a perceptual analysis can evaluate intelligibility, identify patterns of nonverbal behavior, or evaluate the emotion or tone of a speaker. For another, listeners very rarely, if ever, interpret speech suprasegmentals using pronunciation software, instead relying on their perception of what they see and hear as they engage with a speaker. At the level of suprasegmentals, there is not a one-to-one relationship between physical changes in pitch or intensity, and the change in intonation or stress the human perceives. For example, studies show that factors like syllable length, loudness, and visual cues (head nods, beat gestures) all affect the perception of syllable prominence (Hardison, 2018; Krahmer & Swerts, 2007; Levis, 1999; Levis & Wichmann, 2015).[3]

---

3. In addition, the perception of intonation and stress is based only partially on pitch. According to Chun (2002:5), "When a syllable or word is perceived as 'stressed' or 'emphasized,' it is pitch height or change in pitch, more than length or loudness, that is likely to be mainly responsible (cf. Fry, 1958; Fudge, 1984; Gimson, 1980:222–226; Lehiste, 1976) …. It is generally agreed

To apply a perceptual analysis to the data, we watched and listened to Mary's three speech samples (Times 1, 2, and 3), identifying thought groups, prominent words and syllables, and patterns of intonation in relation to her intelligibility. We also documented Mary's use of gesture, facial expression, eye contact, and changes in body position as these occurred relative to the prosody of her speech (including assigning of prominence, pitch movement on prominent syllables, and pausing), as these are known to contribute to the degree to which listeners can understand speech.

## Results

### Results of acoustic analysis

**Time 1.**  *Micro-teaching*

The first two utterances that Mary produced in her micro-teaching sample at Time 1 appear in Excerpt (2).

(2)  "Today we're going to cover two main topics. One is to understand the business."

Figure 1 above shows the PRAAT analysis of pitch (Hz) and intensity (dB) of this utterance (in Mary's first intonational paragraph), and Table 1 displays the specific pitch (Hz) and intensity (dB) levels Mary used to produce the utterance.

**Table 1.**  Pitch and intensity levels of Mary's microteaching sample at Time 1

|       | Pitch (Hz) | Intensity (dB) |
|-------|-----------|----------------|
| Mean  | 231.15    | 60.10          |
| Max   | 307.68    | 73.53          |
| Min   | 172.46    | 24.94          |
| Range | 135.22    | 48.59          |

**Time 2.**  *Trial mirroring*

At time 2, Mary performed the trial version of her Mirroring Project. As above, the first two utterances that Mary said in this sample at time 2 appear in Excerpt (3).

---

that the three features of pitch, length, and loudness form a scale of importance in bringing syllables into prominence, with pitch being the most significant, duration next, and loudness the least important factor (cf. Cruttenden, 1997:13)."

(3)  "The night before I was heading for Scotland I was invited to host the final of China's got talent show in Shanghai with the 80,000 live audience in the sta-dium."

Figure 2 shows the PRAAT analysis of pitch (Hz) and intensity (dB) of the time 2 utterances, and Table 2 displays the specific pitch (Hz) and intensity (dB) levels Mary used to produce the utterances.

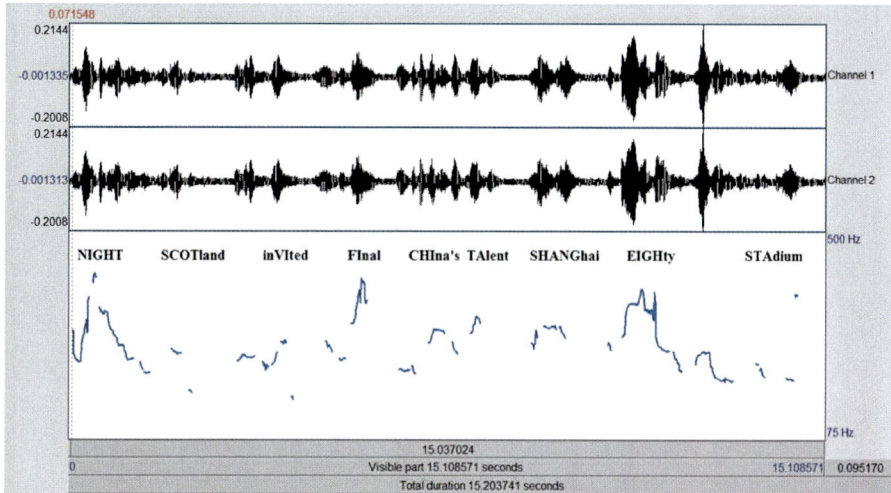

**Figure 2.**  Mary's trial version of mirroring at Time 2, PRAAT analysis

**Table 2.**  Pitch and intensity levels of Mary's trial version of mirroring at Time 2

|       | Pitch (Hz) | Intensity (dB) |
|-------|------------|----------------|
| Mean  | 270.65     | 59.34          |
| Max   | 414.55     | 74.31          |
| Min   | 157.30     | 45.15          |
| Range | 257.25     | 29.16          |

**Time 3.**  *Final mirroring*

At Time 3, Mary performed the final version of her Mirroring Project. The first two utterances that Mary said in this sample at Time 3 appear in Excerpt (4); the words are identical to those in Excerpt (3).

(4)  "The night before I was heading for Scotland I was invited to host the final of China's got talent show in Shanghai with the 80,000 live audience in the sta-dium."

Figure 3 shows the PRAAT analysis of pitch (Hz) and intensity (dB) of the Time 3 utterances. Table 3 displays the pitch (Hz) and intensity (dB) levels Mary used to produce these utterances.

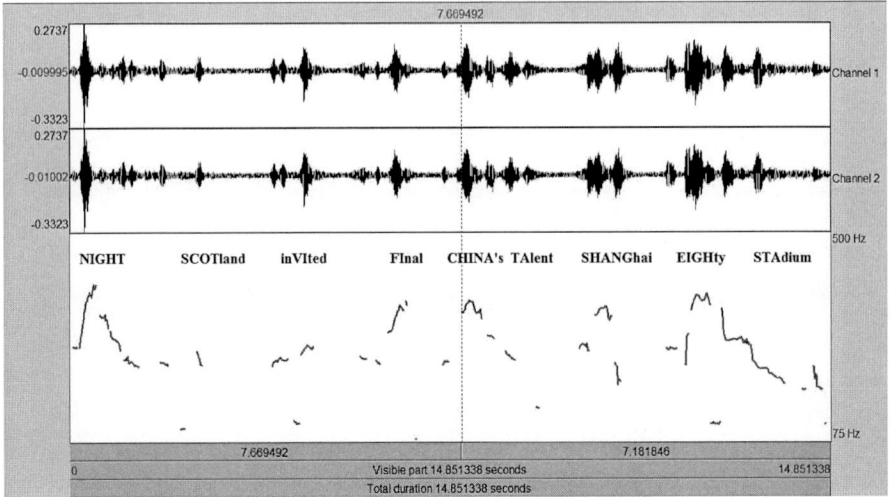

**Figure 3.** Mary's final version of mirroring at Time 3, PRAAT Analysis

**Table 3.** Pitch and intensity of Mary's final version of mirroring at Time 3

|  | Pitch (Hz) | Intensity (dB) |
|---|---|---|
| Mean | 267.71 | 59.57 |
| Max | 396.77 | 75.58 |
| Min | 82.05 | 44.96 |
| Range | 314.72 | 30.62 |

Table 4 displays and compares the pitch and intensity levels of the introductory utterances Mary produced at Times 1, 2 and 3 – before, during and at the end of her mirroring project focused on "channeling" the words, emotions, and indeed, the personality of Yang Lan.

Table 4 shows that Mary's maximum pitch at Time 1 (307.68 Hz) is much lower than that at time 2 (414.55) and 3 (396.77Hz), and her pitch range, (like that of the NNSs in Pickering (2001, 2004)) is very restricted at Time 1; however, her pitch range increases progressively over the course of the study by a total of 180.48 Hz (moving from 135.22 at Time 1 to 257.25 at Time 2 and 314.7 at Time 3). Mary's increase in pitch range makes it more similar to that of the native speaker TAs described in Pickering (2004) and will enable Mary to use intonation in more

**Table 4.**  Comparison of pitch and intensity Mary produced at Times 1, 2 and 3

|                      | Time 1 | Time 2 | Time 3 |
|----------------------|--------|--------|--------|
| Mean pitch (Hz)      | 231.15 | 270.65 | 267.71 |
| Max pitch (Hz)       | 307.68 | 414.55 | 396.77 |
| Min Pitch            | 172.46 | 157.30 | 82.05  |
| Pitch range          | 135.22 | 257.25 | 314.72 |
| Mean intensity (dB)  | 60.10  | 59.34  | 59.57  |
| Max intensity        | 73.53  | 74.31  | 75.58  |
| Min intensity        | 24.94  | 45.15  | 44.96  |
| Intensity range      | 48.59  | 29.16  | 30.62  |

native-like ways to more clearly mark information structure as she mirrors Yang Lan.

In the review of relevant literature, we saw that undergraduate students recalled significantly more information and evaluated the TA more favorably, when the TA's lecture was delivered with correct primary stress (Hahn 2004). At Time 1, although Mary assigns correct primary stress to the key words in her two utterances (*today, two, one,* and *business*), her extremely narrow pitch range makes it difficult to easily discern exactly which words she is making prominent. At Times 2 and 3, however, Mary's use of prominence is much more salient. Making use of the much wider pitch range we noted earlier, she uses a higher Fo/pitch for the prominent words in each thought group (*night, invited, final, talent, eighty*) in the utterance. At Time 3, these words are even more acoustically prominent due to her high pitch and intensity on the syllables of those words, and so are even more likely to be perceived by her audience.

Mary's pattern of intensity is somewhat different than her pitch pattern. For example, her intensity range starts out very wide at Time 1, and gets smaller over time. At Time 1, her intensity range is 48.59 dB, much wider compared to her range of 29.16 dB at Time 2 and 30.62 at Time 3. This wider intensity range at Time 1 occurs because her minimum intensity is extremely low, 24.94 dB, while her maximum intensity remains about the same at Times 1, 2 and 3 (73.53 dB, 74.31 dB, 75.58 dB). Mary's very low minimum intensity at Time 1, while it widens her intensity range, also suggests to us that her utterances are fading out, making her stress placement hard to hear in places. Her more narrow intensity range at Time 2 and 3 reflects an improvement in that she achieves this by increasing her minimum intensity levels at Time 2 (to 45.15 dB) and 3 (44.96 dB); this increased intensity overall is likely to make stress placement across the entire utterance easier for a listener to hear.

## Results of perceptual analysis

At Time 1, her instructor judged Mary as having good control of her English segmentals, but needing to work on intelligibility by using suprasegmentals to more clearly signal thought groups and convey prominence. Mary's Time 1 speech sounds monotonous, and is hard to hear at times. In addition, she appears to lack the confidence required of a teacher in a US academic context; she appears distant and disengaged from her audience, lacking effective nonverbal communication patterns that might not only help signal prominence, but better communicate rapport, such as gestures, facial expressions, and body movement (see Appendix C).

At Time 2, her first attempt to mirror Yang Lan, Mary has clearly benefitted from weeks of ITA instruction. Her speech is much more audible than at Time 1; in addition, she makes use of a wider intonation range. For example, her clause "The night before I was heading for Scotland" has more noticeable variation in intonation levels, with the characteristic "jump up step down" intonation pattern of North American English (Bolinger, 1964). In addition, she pauses more between thought groups than she did at Time 1, and uses body movement to help signal prominence to speech units; for example, when she says, "I was invited to host the final," she moves her hand during "invited" and changes her facial expression, widening her eyes and raising eyebrows when she says "final." There seems to be more volume and energy in her voice, making her appear more confident. On the other hand, at Time 2 Mary mainly looks at the camera whereas in the original recording Yang Lan scans the entire audience. Mary has still not fully memorized the segment, so she falters a bit as she tries to remember it, making her sound disfluent and a bit robotic; as a result, she does not yet totally convey the same level of emotional energy Yang Lan did.

In Time 3, Mary's overall volume or voice projection, pausing, pitch range, and use of prominence have all improved, and the emotion she conveys is more palpable. For instance, when Mary says, "Guess who was the performing guest? Susan Boyle," her pitch range is even more varied than it was at Time 2, and there is clear lengthening on "who", "guest", and "Boyle." An important aspect of Mary's speech in Time 3 that is not captured in the PRAAT acoustic analysis is her nonverbals. She uses gestures that are more expressive and expansive. Her arms move more widely in time with prominent syllables (see Appendix C), also contributing to the perception that she owns the space around her body. We see her move her gaze, looking back and forth at different members of her imagined audience as Yang Lan does in the original video. Mary's presentation at Time 3 makes the viewer sense that she could be Yang Lan's twin sister in terms of speech style and nonverbal communication; she patently speaks with Yang Lan's "voice," embodying her personality and overall communicative style.

Discussion and pedagogical implications

This longitudinal case study provides evidence that the Mirroring Project was an effective component of a curriculum designed to help an international TA increase her intelligibility by improving her production of English intonation, prominence and rhythm tied to nonverbal communication patterns in highlighting information structure. The activity of internalizing the voice of a model Chinese L1 speaker whom the learner herself had selected appeared to improve the ITA's intelligibility and persuasive energy in ways that are consistent with relevant research in second language acquisition; that research includes findings on the impact of semantic language play on the development of new "voices" characterized by more engaging and intelligible patterns of pronunciation, including suprasegmentals. Important elements of the pedagogical approach used by the Mirroring Project are:

- the exercise of learner agency in selecting a speaking model
- the internalization of the holistic "voice" of this model including emotion and tone
- a focus on the use of suprasegmentals to emotionally engage listeners and improve intelligibility
- the synchronous and interlocking use of nonverbal and suprasegmental elements in signaling the information structure in a presentation.

It must be acknowledged that this "top down" pedagogical activity occurred only as a part of, and at the conclusion of, a course that had earlier provided more "bottom-up" analysis of discrete suprasegmental and nonverbal elements of speech including the use of electronic visual feedback. This analysis was provided in a setting that allowed for considerable individualized input and scaffolding by a highly skilled instructor, so that learners' individual disciplinary needs and personal agency could be supported, but we cannot claim that Mary's improvement was solely due to the use of the Mirroring Project.

To what extent are the gains exhibited in this setting generalizable to an actual classroom context? More work remains to be done to explore the degree to which "voices" acquired through a Mirroring Project can be drawn upon for different purposes, such as to deliver disciplinary content in an academic lecture. The next step in this pedagogical approach would be, at the end of the ITA class, to ask Mary to transcribe 30 seconds of her Time 1 lecture, and then present that same material in the embodied "voice" of Yang Lan. In other words, we would ask Mary what it might look like if Yang Lan were to teach accounting! Mary's generalization of suprasegmentals and nonverbal patterns learned in producing Yang Lan's words, to the use of those same patterns in producing her own rehearsed accounting lecture, would entail Mary's use of what Bakhtin (1981) has termed "double voicing." It is instructive to conclude with Bakhtin's account of how double voicing may lead to acquisition:

> Language, for the individual consciousness, lies on the borderline between oneself and the other. The word in language is half someone else's. It becomes 'one's own' only when the speaker populates it with his own intention, his own accent, when he appropriates the word, adapting it to his own semantic and expressive intention.                                          (Bakhtin, 1981:288)

As a pedagogical approach that is congruent with the emerging transdisciplinary understanding of second language use and acquisition (Douglas Fir Group, 2016), the Mirroring Project has potential to enable L2 speakers to cultivate different voices for their own purposes. It harnesses the power of semantic language play and double voicing; it incorporates awareness of the impact of *community*, *norm*, *choice*, *identity* and *agency* on the development of interlanguage systems; and it supports the development of the ability to speak in a second language in a way that is holistic, multi-modal and embodied, in a context where expression of emotion and exercise of learner agency are central.

# References

Abercrombie, D. (1968). Paralanguage. *International Journal of Language and Communication Disorders*, 3, 55–59.

Anderson-Hsieh, J. (1992). Using electronic visual feedback to teach suprasegmentals. *System*, 20(1), 51–62.

Anderson-Hsieh, J., Johnson, R., & Koehler, K. (1992). The relationship between native speaker judgments of nonnative pronunciation and deviance in segmentals, prosody and syllable structure. *Language Learning*, 42, 529–555.

Bakhtin, M. M. (1929/1984). *Problems in Dostoevsky's poetics*. Minneapolis, MN: University of Minnesota Press.

Bakhtin, M. M. (1981). *The dialogic imagination: Four essays by M. M. Bakhtin*, M. Holquist (Ed.), trans. C. Emerson & M. Holquist. Austin, TX: University of Texas Press.

Barr, P. (1990). The role of discourse intonation in lecture comprehension. In M. Hewings (Ed.), *Papers in discourse intonation* (pp. 5–21). Birmingham, UK: University of Birmingham, English Language Research.

Beebe, L. (1980). Sociolinguistic variation and style shifting in second language acquisition. *Language Learning*, 30, 433–447.

Beebe, L., & Giles, H. (1984). Speech-accommodation theories: A discussion in terms of second-language acquisition. *International Journal of the Sociology of Language*, 46, 5–32.

Boersma, P., & Weenink, D.. (2017). PRAAT: Doing phonetics by computer. Retrieved from <http://www.praat.org/> (6 January 2017).

Bolinger, D. (1964). Around the edge of language: Intonation. *Harvard Educational Review*, 34, 282–296.

Brazil, D. (1997). *The communicative value of intonation in English*. Cambridge: Cambridge University Press.

Broner, M., & Tarone, E. (2001). Is it fun? Language play in a fifth grade Spanish immersion classroom, *Modern Language Journal*, 85, 363–379.

Brown, G. (1977). *Listening to spoken English*. London: Longman.

Brown, G., & Yule, G. (1983). *Discourse analysis*. Cambridge: Cambridge University Press.

Celce-Murcia, M., Brinton, D., & Goodwin, J. (2010). *Teaching pronunciation: A course book and reference guide* (2nd ed.). New York, NY: Cambridge University Press.

Chun, D. (2002). *Discourse intonation in L2: From theory & research to practice*. Amsterdam: John Benjamins.

Clark, H., & Gerrig, R. (1990). Quotations as demonstrations. *Language*, 66, 764–805.

Cook, G. (2000). *Language play, language learning*. Oxford: Oxford University Press.

Cruttenden, A. (1997). *Intonation* (2nd ed.). New York, NY: Cambridge University Press.

Derwing, T., & Munro, M. (2015). *Pronunciation fundamentals: Evidence-based perspectives for L2 teaching*. Amsterdam: John Benjamins.

Dittman A. T. (1974). The body movement-speech rhythm relationship as a cue to speech encoding. In S. Weitz (Ed.), *Nonverbal communication* (pp. 169–181). New York: Oxford University Press.

Douglas Fir Group (Dwight Atkinson, Heidi Byrnes, Meredith Doran, Patricia Duff, Joan Kelly Hall, Karen Johnson, James Lantolf, Diane Larsen-Freeman, Bonny Norton, John Schumann, Merrill Swain, & Elaine Tarone). (2016). A transdisciplinary framework for SLA in a multilingual world. *Modern Language Journal*, 100(Supplement 2016), 19–47.

Foote, J. & McDonough, K. (2017). Using shadowing with mobile technology to improve L2 pronunciation. *Journal of Second Language Pronunciation*, 3(1), 34–56.

Fry, D. (1958). Experiments on the perception of stress. *Language and Speech*, 1, 126–152.

Fudge, E. C. (1984). *English word stress*. Sydney: George Allen & Unwin.

Gilbert, J. (2012). *Clear Speech: Pronunciation and listening comprehension in American English* (4th ed.). Cambridge: Cambridge University Press.

Gimson, A. C. (1980). *An introduction to the pronunciation of English* (3rd ed.). London: Edward Arnold.

Gorsuch, G. J. (2003). The educational cultures of international teaching assistants and U.S. universities. *TESL-EJ*, 7(3), 1–17.

Grant, L. (2017). *Well said: Pronunciation for clear communication. Student book* (4th ed.). Belmont, CA: Cengage Learning.

Guiora, A. Beit-Hallami, R., Brannon, R., Dull, C., & Scovel, T. (1972). The effects of experimentally induced changes in ego states on pronunciation ability in a second language: An exploratory study. *Comprehensive Psychiatry*, 13(5), 421ff.

Hahn, L. (2004). Primary stress and intelligibility: Research to motivate the teaching of suprasegmentals. *TESOL Quarterly*, 38, 201–223.

Hardison, D. M. (2018). Visualizing the acoustic and gestural beats of emphasis in multimodal discourse: Theoretical and pedagogical implications. *Journal of Second Language Pronunciation*, 4(2).

Kang, O. (2010). Relative salience of suprasegmental features on judgments of L2 comprehensibility and accentedness. *System*, 38(2), 301–315.

Kang, O., Rubin, D., & Pickering, L. (2010). Suprasegmental measures of accentedness and judgments of language learner proficiency in oral English. *The Modern Language Journal*, 9, 554–566.

Kannellow, V. (2009). The practice of pronunciation teaching in current ELT manuals and handbook: a review. *Speak Out: IATEFL Pronunciation Special Interest Group Newsletter*, 40, 1–5.

Key, M. R. (Ed.). (1980). *The relationship of verbal and nonverbal communication*. The Hague: Mouton.

Krahmer, E., & Swerts, M. (2007). The effects of visual beats on prosodic prominence: Acoustic analyses, auditory perception and visual perception. *Journal of Memory and Language*, 57, 396–414.

Lan, Y. (2011). The generation that's remaking China. *Ted Talks*. Retrieved from <http://www.ted.com/talks/lang/en/yang_lan.html> (5 January, 2017).

Lehiste, I. (1976). Suprasegmentals. In N. J. Lass (Ed.), *Contemporary issues in experimental phonetics* (pp. 225–239). New York, NY: Academic Press.

Levis, J. M. (1999). Intonation in theory and practice, revisited. *TESOL Quarterly*, 33, 37–63.

Levis, J. M. (2005). Changing contexts and shifting paradigms in pronunciation teaching. *TESOL Quarterly*, 39, 369–377.

Levis, J. M., & Wichmann, A. (2015). English intonation –Form and meaning. In M. Reed & J. M Levis (Eds.), *The handbook of English pronunciation* (pp. 139–155). Chichester: John Wiley & Sons.

Lindgren, J., Meyers, C.M., & Monk, M. (2003). Approaches to accent: The Mirroring Project. Paper presented at the annual conference of Teachers of English to Speakers of Other Languages (TESOL), Baltimore, MD.

McGregor, A., Zielinski, B., Meyers, C., & Reed, M. (2016). An exploration of teaching intonation using a TED Talk. In J. Levis, H. Le., I. Lucic, E. Simpson, & S. Vo (Eds.), *Proceedings of the 7th Annual Conference of Pronunciation in Second Language Learning and Teaching (PSLLT)* (pp. 143–159). Ames, IA: Iowa State University.

Major, R. (2001). *Foreign accent: The ontogeny and phylogeny of second language phonology*. Mahwah, NJ: Lawrence Erlbaum Associates.

Mathis, T., & Yule, G. (1994). Zero quotatives. *Discourse Processes*, 18, 63–76.

Meyers, C. (2013). Mirroring project update: Intelligible accented speakers as pronunciation models. *TESOL Video News*. Accessed at <http://newsmanager.commpartners.com/tesolvdmis/issues/2013-07-27/6.html> (9 September, 2016).

Meyers, C. (2014). Intelligible accented speakers as pronunciation models. In J. Levis & S. McCrocklin (Eds.), *Proceedings of the 5th Annual Conference of Pronunciation in Second Language Learning and Teaching (PSLLT)* (pp. 172–176). Ames, IA: Iowa State University.

Moreno, L. (2016). *Channeling Charlie: Suprasegmental pronunciation in a second language learner's performance of others' voices*. Unpublished MA Qualifying Paper. University of Minnesota. Available at the University of Minnesota Digital Conservancy: <http://conservancy.umn.edu/handle/11299/183052>

Murphy, J. M. (2014). Intelligible, comprehensible, non-native models in ESL/EFL pronunciation teaching. *System*, 42, 258–269.

Pennington, M. (1988). Teaching pronunciation from the top down. *University of Hawai'i Working Papers in ESL*, 7(1), 203–227.

Pennycook, A. (1985). Actions speak louder than words: Paralanguage, communication and education. *TESOL Quarterly*, 19, 259–282.

Pickering, L. (2001). The role of tone choice in improving ITA communication in the classroom. *TESOL Quarterly*, 35(2), 233–255.

Pickering, L. (2004). The structure and function of intonation paragraphs in native and nonnative speaker instructional discourse. *English for Specific Purposes*, 23, 19–43.

Tannen, D. (1989). *Talking voices: Repetition, dialogue, and imagery in conversational discourse*. Cambridge: Cambridge University Press.

Tarone, E. (1978). The phonology of interlanguage. In J. C. Richards (Ed.), *Understanding second and foreign language learning* (pp. l5–33). Rowley, MA: Newbury House.

Tarone, E. (1988). *Variation in interlanguage*. London: Edward Arnold.

Tarone, E. (2000). Getting serious about language play: Language play, interlanguage variation and second language acquisition. In B. Swierzbin, F. Morris, M. Anderson, C. Klee, & E. Tarone (Eds.), *Social and cognitive factors in SLA: Proceedings of the 1999 Second Language Research Forum* (pp. 31–54). Somerville, MA: Cascadilla Press.

Tarone, E. (2005). Speaking in a second language. In E. Hinkel (Ed.), *Handbook of research in second language teaching and learning* (pp. 485–502). Hillsdale, NJ: Lawrence Erlbaum Associates.

Tarone, E., & Swain, M. (1995). A sociolinguistic perspective on second-language use in immersion classrooms. *Modern Language Journal*, 79, 166–178.

Thomson, R., & Derwing, T. (2015). The effectiveness of L2 pronunciation instruction: A narrative review. *Applied Linguistics*, 36(3), 326–344.

## Appendix A.    Pedagogical steps in using the mirroring project

The Mirroring Project comprises 9 steps, which can be undertaken over a period of 3 weeks during the semester. The steps are:

1. Identify L2 speaker's pronunciation and body language challenges using rubric
2. Choose appropriate speaker model and short speech sample
3. Analyze model's speech sample for communicative effectiveness using rubric
4. Transcribe speech sample, identifying and marking thought groups, prominence and non-verbal communication
5. Mirror ("channel") model producing original recording–one thought group at a time
6. Practice internalizing speech/nonverbal communication for pronunciation features
7. Video-record a trial version
8. Critique the trial version
9. Video-record a final version

Step 1.   Identify learner's pronunciation and body language challenges

The first stage of this process is analyzing a monologic speech sample the learner has video-recorded in a social context that is as "authentic" as possible, i.e. as close as possible to the target communication situation. For example, "micro-teaching" is a simulated (i.e. not authentic) teaching environment in that the audience consists of the ITA class, and not actual undergraduates learning the content of an introductory college course. Analyze this video-recording for challenges in areas identified in grading rubric (Appendix B): intonation, word stress, volume and voice projection, body language, emotion/tone.

Step 2. Choose appropriate model

The learner finds a speech sample produced by a speaker they consider a model for emulation. Many students choose as models speakers from Ted.com: (1) the speakers are highly articulate and express their ideas succinctly in English; 2) a transcript for each speech is provided–not only in English, but often in other languages; and (3) one can click on the segment of the speech under study to hear a particular sentence (or thought group) repeated over and over again.

Step 3. Analyze model's speech sample for overall communicative effectiveness

Focus on the "big picture:" what meaning is the speaker trying to convey, and how does the speaker want the audience to respond to that message? Ask students to look at specific things the speaker does to create an overall impression, such as how they use their voice and how they use nonverbal communication (eye contact, facial expressions, gestures, and use of space) to get the audience to pay attention to the message and to respond in the way the speaker intends. The following techniques can be useful in getting students to notice these features.

**Focus on nonverbal communication**

Turn off the video's sound and just watch the body language. How much can you tell about the speaker? Do you think this is a formal or informal speech?

**Focus on verbal communication**

Next, view the video with the sound on and continue focusing on the big picture. How would you describe this person's speech? Is it fast or slow? Loud or soft? Does it have a lot of variation or is it monotone? Does the person lengthen his/her vowels or not? Does the person pause a lot or very little? If the speech rate, perceived loudness, intonation, or pausing change during the segment, how and why does it change?

Step 4. Mark a short transcript for pronunciation feature(s) and nonverbal communication

The student transcribes a short segment of the video-recorded speech (if a transcript is not already provided, as with Ted Talks). A segment length of about 30 seconds to 1 minute (roughly speaking, 5–7 sentences or thought groups) is enough but not overwhelming. The student divides the transcript into thought groups, locates the prominent words in each thought group, and then draws in by hand the body movement which corresponded to each prominent word.

Step 5. "Mirror" the short selected segment one thought group at a time

Viewing the selected video segment on a computer, students play each thought group and pause, and then verbally and nonverbally mirror each phrase back to the computer screen. They can do this in two stages: (1) first focusing only on spoken language; and (2) then adding the nonverbal communication to the spoken language.

Step 6. Practice using read, look up, and say technique

Students retype their annotated transcript from *Step 4*, typing the script in large font, one thought group per line. They type in bold the prominent word(s) of each thought group. Finally, they draw in the accompanying nonverbal communication by hand. Using this reworked transcript, they work in pairs, taking turns as each partner speaks. First the speaker looks down and reads the first thought group. Then the speaker looks up, makes eye contact with the listener, and says that thought group to his/her partner the way the model said it. Eye contact serves several purposes; it (1) forces students to incorporate long enough pauses to separate thought groups; (2) reminds students of how important eye contact is in speaking English in order to communicate sincerity and not just "parrot" words; and (3) helps students incorporate this way of speaking into their own speech.

Step 7.  Record trial version

Students video-record themselves standing up and speaking the entire selected segment of the transcript, either during class or at home. During class, other students can be enlisted to help each performer make eye contact with their audience, and not just read from the paper. Students can place their transcripts on a table or ask another student to hold it up so that they can read from it.

Step 8.  Critique trial version

Students annotate their trial recording, identifying places where they are doing well and those which can be improved. The instructor adds comments. For example, at this point, the recording may be good technically, but it may lack the emotion and/or the tone conveyed in the original recording because the student is still memorizing the script and may not be trying to produce the script 'in character' – or, in Bakhtin's terms, using the 'voice' of the original speaker.

Step 9.  Record final version with emotion

A week or so later, students make their final video recording, trying to speak and move in same way their model did. For this final recording, students should ideally have memorized the script; an alternative is to write it in large font and put the paper somewhere they can see it easily. To help them get into the mood of the original recording, students should be encouraged to think about what the person is feeling in the original recording. Is the speaker enthusiastic? Sad? Angry? What is the speaker trying to accomplish? Teach? Inspire? Entertain? All of this makes the final product much richer and more beneficial for students. Students can perform and record the script as many times as they wish, focusing on trying to speak with the same overall emotion and personality as their model, and not worrying if they make a simple segmental mistake. Other students may be present and can serve as 'directors' or audience members.

## Appendix B.    Mirroring Project grading rubric

| Grading criteria | 10 points | 5 points | 3 points |
|---|---|---|---|
| Prominence & Intonation (pausing, prominence, linking & reduction, intonation) | Almost always matches original | Sometimes matches original | Seldom or Never matches original |
| Enunciation/Word Stress (clear articulation of sounds and stress on correct syllable) | Almost always matches original | Sometimes matches original | Seldom or never matches original |
| Overall Volume & Voice Projection | Almost always matches original | Sometimes matches original | Seldom or never matches original |
| Body Language (gestures, facial expressions, eyebrow movements, use of space) | Almost always matches original | Sometimes matches original | Seldom or never matches original |
| Emotion/Attitudinal Tone | Almost always matches original | Sometimes matches original | Seldom or never matches original |

## Appendix C:    Mary's body movements signaling prominence at Times 1, 2 and 3

**Time 1.**  "Today we're going to cover…"

Time 2.  "Guess who was the performing guest?"

Time 3.  "I told her I'm going to Scotland"

# CHAPTER 10

# Speaking in a second language

## Where are we now?

Rosa Alonso Alonso
University of Vigo

This concluding chapter presents an overview of the speaking skill in the history of language teaching from the Grammar Translation Method to current Task-based Approach. It then moves on to the role of speaking in current usage-based perspectives, which view language as a social activity and where the social and the cognitive are no longer considered separate entities. As meaning is at the centre and language is considered to emerge out of usage, spoken interaction is promoted and speaking is considered both a social and a cognitive construct. We will observe how the different chapters in the volume fall within usage-based approaches and some of them provide usage-based inspired pedagogy. Finally, future research directions are proposed.

In today's multilingual, transnational and globalized society, L2 users outnumber monolingual native speakers. Interacting with others in a language which is not the one used from birth has become a daily activity for millions of individuals all over the world. Speaking in a second language lies at the basis of international communication, as language is used for social and interpersonal action. This volume brings together different perspectives on speaking in a second language. In the following pages we will briefly provide an overview of the speaking skill in the history of language teaching. Then, we will describe current approaches to speaking and we will deal with how the main contributions of the different chapters view speaking as a social and cognitive construct and how usage-based-inspired pedagogical approaches are proposed. Finally, we will see future directions and summarize the novel proposals of the different chapters.

https://doi.org/10.1075/aals.17.10alo

## Traditional approaches to L2 speaking

The teaching of speaking has evolved from its invisible presence in the early Grammar-Translation Method to its relevance to current usage-based approaches. This volume brings together recent perspectives on acquisition and teaching which view language as a social activity, which is action-based and language use as the basis of language learning. This implies the need for new pedagogical approaches as a necessary step towards the learning of speaking. As background to the argument that speaking has a central role in current approaches to SLA, I will first give a brief historical account of the different approaches to speaking.

In the heyday of the Grammar Translation Method, which is framed within what Howatt and Smith (2014) call The Classical Period, emphasis was placed on literary aims and therefore grammar, reading and writing were central. However, this method failed to attach speaking the necessary relevance since its main aim was not to communicate but to develop the ability to read texts and translate passages from the first language to the second. This method viewed the learning of languages as an intellectual discipline so that little room was left for listening or speaking skills. It was the need to communicate that led to a growing interest in developing the command of the spoken language, which can be said to have begun with the Reform Movement (Howatt & Smith, 2014). This interest was reinforced by the establishment of the International Phonetics Association and the International Phonetic Alphabet in 1886 which advocated for the study of spoken language. Both the natural and the Berlitz methods turned their attention to teaching conversation and question-and-answer sequences. Sauveur ((1874) and Berlitz (1898) proposed conversation-based activities and designed conversation-based courses. During that period Gouin (1880) developed the basis of the Direct Method, which focused mainly on structured conversation and teaching was entirely conducted in the target language. This new approach recognized speaking proficiency and promoted the active use of the language in the classroom, where the native speaker of the language was the role model. Speaking practice was organized around questions and answers exchanged between the teacher and the students, but the focus was on pronunciation rather than on communication. Some years later, in 1950 Hornby published his ideas on the Situational Approach. This method consisted of creating a classroom situation where structures were presented with the aim of producing accurate responses in speech situations. In fact, one of the method's main objectives was to respond quickly and accurately in speech situations. It was a popular method during the 50's and classroom materials were presented orally before being introduced in writing. The language that was practiced in classroom situations was expected to be used in real-life situations.

At the end of the 1950's the Audiolingual Method, which was highly influenced by the prevalent psychological trend of behaviourism (Skinner, 1957) extended the use of audiolingual visual aids and the focus on pronunciation. As the method insisted on the stimulus-response-reinforcement model, repetition and memorization were frequently-used. Dialogues were presented by the teacher and memorized by the students. Drills were used as reinforcement activities. Attention began to turn to the use of skills in real-life situations and speaking was taught so as to be used for real-world communication purposes; thus, students were exposed first to oral language and then to written language.

Chomsky's criticism of behaviourism and his focus on children being biologically programmed to learn the language and the creativity of language led to a re-visiting of the Audiolingual model as a valid teaching method. Habit formation was abandoned as a learning theory and there was a turn towards mentalism. Within that revolutionary arena, teaching methods such as the Silent Way (Gattegno, 1972) and the Total Physical Response (Asher, 1966) emerged. In these, emphasis was placed on students taking part in the learning process. In the Silent Way, learning was supported by physical aids such as "Cuisenaire rods" which were used to illustrate meaning. Pronunciation was emphasized and students were encouraged to produce speech and become involved in problem-solving activities. The Total Physical Response method stems from the idea that adult second language learning was similar to child first language acquisition. Thus, in the classroom students responded to commands that included physical movement. Listening preceded oral production as it was believed that students need to understand before producing speaking; however, communication was not given any kind of privileged position. The need to provide students with real-life practice in the classroom paved the way for the Communicative Approach. Wilkins (1976) proposed a functional-notional syllabus focused on meaning and communication. From this approach learners are encouraged to create meaning and speaking is key as the main aim is successful communication, rather than acquiring native-like pronunciation. In order to create real life situations in the classroom, learners negotiate and cooperate by means of speaking activities like role-play, simulations or problem-solving tasks.

This notion of communication as a key point in language learning is also developed in the Task-based Approach, which promotes the use of meaningful tasks to use the language being learnt. From this perspective, lessons are based around the completion of a task or series of tasks. This approach meant moving the focus from simply learning to communicate in a second language to actually learning while language and communication are used as a means to complete the task. Therefore, students use communicative experiences to succeed in communicative competence and conversation is a cornerstone. Task-based language teaching involves students in communication to achieve a goal and tasks provide both the input and output needed for second language acquisition provided they are meaningful, such as talking on the phone or buying a ticket in the train station.

## Current approaches to L2 speaking

Both the Communicative Approach and the Task-based Approach are learner-centred and tend to consider speaking and communication as key elements. They also emphasize the role of meaning in the way we use language. Explicit attentional interventions seem to obtain better results (Norris and Ortega, 2000) and the focus is turned to learner needs. Current approaches tend to focus on activities that promote meaning. They include Task-based Language Teaching (Ellis, 2003; Van den Branden, Bygate, & Norris, 2009); Content Integrated Language Learning/ Content-based instruction (Cenoz, Genesee, Gorter, 2014) Focus on Form (Long, 1991; R. Ellis, 2016) and Form-focused Instruction (Collins, 2013). Content and Integrated Language Learning can be defined as " a dual-focused educational approach in which an additional language is used for the learning and teaching of both content and language" (Mehisto, Marsh, & Frigols, 2008: 9). It can include a wide range of educational practices where an additional language is the means of instruction, but also where language and content should be balanced. From this perspective, speaking skills are key. As teachers use the additional language to convey meaning, students are exposed to the additional language and language learning is based on learners' exposure to and meaningful use of the second language.

Meaning is placed at the centre of concept-based approaches to teaching language and hence visual aids are frequently used to help learners understand. For example, (Lantolf & Poehner, 2008) used diagrams to explain the use of the simple and the preterit in Spanish and van Compernolle and Kinginger (2013) used drawings to explain social distance in the difference between tu/vous in French. In concept-based teaching meaning can be constructed through conceptual categories in the process of L2 development (Negueruela, 2003). Learners in the classroom learn by participating in culturally-mediated contexts, where learning activities promote conceptual development. As new language is internalized, second language learning is transformed. In this process it is important that teachers present systematic explanations of relevant concepts and the practice of speaking focuses on how meanings are created in communication. Activities, such as dialogues are used where students are taught how to construct and participate in a dialogue. For this, pragmatic, sociocultural and semantic elements, as well as concepts involved in a dialogue are taught, such as the concept of modality.

By following this approach, students analyse the communicative situation, select the necessary resources for communication, monitor their own learning and thus learn how to construct meaning in the second language.

Content-based approaches are compatible with usage-based linguistics. Usage-based linguistics holds that linguistic knowledge is derived from and shaped by our experience with language. (Beckner et al. 2009; Bybee 2013). Embodiment and multimodality constitute central issues in these approaches. It is considered that multimodal and embodied experiences support language learning. In a study by Lindstromberg and Boers (2005), students were asked to convey the meaning of a motion verb by enacting or miming it. The students who participated in the experimental group showed better retention of the verbs than those in the control group in the gap-fill retention test they conducted shortly after instruction, i.e. enacting or miming a verb resulted in better retention than simply explaining the motion verb. The students in the experimental group who had enacted the literal senses of the motion verbs also outperformed the control group in identifying the motion verbs when they were used metaphorically. From this perspective, speaking activities involving embodiment are promoted, for example, Verspoor (2017) follows a Film Language Integrated Learning approach so as to facilitate for-use-meaning mappings. Students are exposed to repetitive chunks of two minute segments of films. Then, they repeat what they have heard, role-play conversations or create new ones through playful interaction.

Moreover, in usage-based approaches, languages are considered to emerge out of usage, therefore interaction with the real world is fostered. In second language acquisition focus is on the role of input and interaction in developing L2 competence acquisition (Eskildsen 2008; Larsen-Freeman 2011; Ellis 2013), especially in adulthood. Usage-based inspired pedagogy also promotes interaction. Eskildsen and Theodórsdóttir (2015) and Wagner (2015) propose a usage-driven approach which breaks down the barriers between the classroom and the real world, which they call "the wild". In this methodology, speaking is acquired through a combination of instruction in the classroom and practice outside the classroom. In the project "The Icelandic Village" started at the University of Iceland, service places such as cafés or bookshops welcome students of Icelandic as a Second Language to practice the L2 in real-life contexts. First, in the classroom, students work in groups and discuss the language they will need for the interaction in the real world; then the teacher focuses on pronunciation by acting out both sides of the interaction, which the students role-play at the end of the class. Then students leave for "the wild", i.e outside the classroom, carrying preparation material, such as a passport, a map and a list of useful phrases. In the real world they go to for example a café, which is part of the Icelandic village network, where there is a "practice corner" with leaflets and guidelines that they can use in the conversation. Students carry out the interaction and have it recorded. The conversation is uploaded in the cloud space to be shared with the other students and the teacher. Finally, in the classroom learners have a "workshop" to share their experiences and materials and perform role-play. After this, the teacher gives them feedback.

Usage-based linguistics has gone through an upsurge in recent years and varied pedagogical applications of usage-based approaches are gaining ground in SLA. Ortega (2015b) considers that this growth is mainly due to the interdisciplinary nature of the approach and the fact that the social and the cognitive are no longer considered as dichotomous separate entities and that adult L2 learners are considered as successful L2 users rather than simply less able in the second language than native speakers. As can be observed, these pedagogical approaches consider speaking to be central, activities must convey meaning, embodied learning is promoted and language is acquired out of usage.

We will now observe how the different chapters in this book fall within current approaches to speaking. More specifically we will see how they deal with speaking as a social and cognitive construct and how they follow usage-based inspired pedagogy.

## Speaking as a social and cognitive construct

Interacting with others is a social activity. When L2 learners engage in speaking they must not only pay attention to consistency in grammar, accuracy in vocabulary and constructing meaningful messages but also to their own identity and those of the interlocutors, the context and all the sociolinguistic aspects that come into play in human interaction. Chapter 1 elaborates on the relevance of these factors as failures in communication may arise in the misuse of markers of formality, politeness, solidarity, friendship, or group membership. In fact, there are different types of social information that are conveyed in speech, from factors that are related to the speaker to those that change from one interactional context to another for a single speaker. It is in this area that the development of sociolinguistic competence adds to the study of L2 speech. Therefore, on the one hand we find the culturally constructed tools made available in one's environment such as language forms or interactional routines while on the other hand lies their contextualized use.

Moreover, the interactional nature of speaking is an area which in cognitive/usage-based linguistics has been mainly approached from the perspective of Conversation Analysis (CA-SLA or CA-for-SLA, Kasper & Wagner, 2011; Hall, Hellermann, & Pekarek Doehler, 2011) where language is perceived as social action and speaking is used for interactional and communicative purposes and we learn to speak a second language by using the language. In this sense, from a usage-based perspective the L2 speaker needs evidence that is directly observable either in social interaction or in the classroom setting. Here frequency has a fundamental role since frequency-biased phenomena are open to analysis and learning. As the acquisition of language is derived from usage, so is the acquisition of speaking. Both usage-based approaches and conversation analysis share the idea that language learning is interactional and usage-driven and that language is learnt by exposure to meaningful linguistic constructions and the observation of culture and interaction in the target discourse community (cf. Eskildsen & Cadierno, 2015). This view of speaking as social accomplishment can be found in Chapter 4, Eskildsen and Markeee analyse data from inside and outside the classroom using a usage-based approach from the perspective of ethnomethodological conversation analysis where pedagogy is focused on action-construction relationships. The notion of "doing", that is, where language is seen as social action and "doing learning" that is, the interactional nature of learning are intertwined in this chapter. Language is viewed as action in which form-meaning mappings are designed and learnt as actions in situ. It is also occasioned, i.e. afforded by the environment. Moreover, language is socially distributed and co-constructed. Individuals alone cannot build reciprocal linguistic utterances. From this perspective language learning is also a socially displayed activity and as such it is observable. Besides, language and cognition are socially distributed as they rely on the actions of other people. This chapter does not focus on form-meaning relationships but on action-construction relationships, social agency, and as the authors highlight on letting L2 students have opportunities to use the appropriate semiotic resources for the appropriate actions at the appropriate moments in time.

Sociocultural aspects, which are represented in the main by Vygotskian sociocultural psychology (Vygotsky 1978, 1986) are characterized by a focus on the development of interactional competencies, specifically the notion of mediated action (Wertsch, 1994) Speaking abilities are considered as a product and a driver of L2 development. In the mediated action perspective on IC (van Compernolle, 2015) we find on the one hand the culturally constructed tools made available in one's environment, such as language forms and interactional routines and their contextualized use on the other. Instead of considering IC as exclusively spoken interaction, van Compernolle in Chapter 2 proposes an expanded evidential basis for IC development which includes extra communicative tasks such as private speech and writing during verbalized reflections, problem-solving and awareness-raising tasks. The tension between what IC resources are made available through the environment (i.e., pedagogy) and what learners actually do in interaction with others pervades the whole study. This IC perspective facilitates the debate on reconceptualizing the acquisition of speaking and instruction as the development of speaking abilities in the classroom in terms of IC and mediated action.

The sociocultural view of knowledge as socially constructed and language as a semiotic tool mediating language learning (Vygotsky, 1978; Swain, 2000, 2006) can also be observed in classroom interaction. In Chapter 8, Dobao analyzes peer interaction from a sociocultural perspective, showing that heritage speakers resort to code switching both as a strategy to establish intergroup solidarity and membership and as a cognitive tool to mediate their language learning.

This is connected with the dynamic systems theory approach to language development (de Bot, Lowie, & Verspoor, 2007; Lowie, 2013). Speaking is seen as an emergent process where development is not predetermined and it constitutes an individual process, as linguistic, cognitive factors or context interact. As this theory tends to focus on the process of development, Chapter 5 gives a through account of speaking and its development over time and how teaching can be applied in that process.

The chapter by Gilquin is closely linked to this approach, exploring the constructions that can be found in learner speech. The identification of these constructions relies on the LINDSEI corpus that has been tagged for part-of-speech. Applying the framework of constructional analysis to SLA allows us to obtain an approximation of the spoken constructions that are part of learners' linguistic repertoire. Constructions fully describe lexicon and grammar and usage-based approaches are construction-based approaches but constructional analysis is only one of the available usage-based approaches to analyse speaking in SLA. Usage-based linguistics in the area of SLA has a wider scope. It analyses the role of input and interaction in the development of L2 competence trying to put accounts of L1 and L2 acquisition under a wider cognitive theory of language learning.

Sociolinguistic and sociocultural factors are complemented by the study of gesture as it is an integral part of language and interaction, the imagistic aspect of language. In Chapter 3 Stam emphasizes that overlooking this would mean taking a static idea of language, whereas speaking is action. This provides the whole picture of speaking as a social construct where the sociolinguistic aspects of interaction co-exist with sociocultural aspects in the shape of the development of interactional competencies and with speaking as an action-based activity. Gesture analysis which views speaking and teaching as action-based is closely linked with Conversation Analysis where language is perceived as social action and also to the "thinking" aspect in that the gestures learners make are not only indicators of their proficiency but also of their thinking in the L2 or as McNeill (2012:xi) puts it as a "language-as-action-and-being" phenomenon, which we believe characterizes the new view of language as action.

## Usage-based inspired pedagogy on speaking

Usage-based instruction has proved to be useful in teaching students to communicate orally in a second language (Gettys, 2017) This author proves that students following this type of instruction show better pronunciation and grammatical accuracy. Usage-based approaches are distinguished from traditional approaches as in the classroom students are taught constructions as units of learning and meaningful communicative activities are used . From a usage-based perspective, structure emerges from use and instruction should relate form and meaning, thus Nattinger and DeCarrico (1992) and Nattinger (1980) consider the "lexical phrase" the pedagogically applicable unit of pre-fabricated language" (Nattinger, 1980: 341) on the basis that teaching should be focused on the patterns, how they can be put together, their variation and the context where they occur. Lewis (1993) following the lexical approach considers that the idioms and fixed expressions to be taught should be those which are more frequently occurring in spoken language, as learning is promoted by frequency of exposure. In this sense, corpora can become an essential element in teaching (Cobb, 2007; Sinclair, 1996). Acquiring a second language means acquiring the form, function and frequency of constructions. Also from a cognitive perspective, the Cognition Hypothesis (Robinson, 2005, 2007) states that tasks should be sequenced to increase the cognitive complexity that the situation requires in the conceptual domain where it takes place. Therefore learners' attention should be focused on the linguistic aspects needed to understand cognitive/conceptual distinctions, as Ellis and Cadierno (2009) assert, in other words, as learners rethink for speaking. Task-based approaches to SLA help in understanding these distinctions as they differ from traditional approaches in that the teaching is not organized around grammatical structures or functions but around tasks which aim at using language as if it was a real life situation. From this perspective, in Chapter 7, Martin Bygate suggests two particular ways in which tasks can be made to contribute. Students need to be exposed to different types of tasks so as to practice different kinds of oral discourse and from the teacher's viewpoint tasks can be used to structure and motivate class talk through and across lessons. In fact task-based learning can be made compatible with current understandings of language and of language learning.

When we think of speaking in the L2 classroom, L2 speakers are the main aim, yet heritage speakers constitute an interesting group of study. These speakers have usually acquired the language in naturalistic contexts; therefore they tend to be stronger in spoken than in written skills but as they have not been schooled in the language, these speakers usually use a colloquial variety. Dobao, in Chapter 8 focuses on the development of this oral academic register of the language. As code-switching serves a variety of interactional and social functions, Dobao raises the interesting issue of how code-switching using English in the Spanish heritage language classroom can serve both social and cognitive functions and help in the development of academic oral Spanish.

A key element in the teaching of speaking is pronunciation. This hallmark in learning how to speak a L2 has been analysed among others by Kanellow (2009) and Munro & Derwing (2011). Teachers tend to be familiar with traditional bottom-up approaches which have had mixed results. A recent alternative top-down approach which is being used at the University of Minnesota seems to be producing more positive results. The "Mirroring" approach, as it is called, is consistent not only with the principles of sociocultural and other usage-based theories of second language acquisition but also with gestures. Students select an intelligible model whose speech and nonverbals they learn how to analyze, imitate, and internalize holistically (Meyers, 2014). Selecting the model by themselves may also help students to increase their motivation and develop their L2 identities. Choosing intelligible accented speakers as pronunciation models has been highlighted in recent research (Murphy, 2014) and it is also consistent with the multicompetence framework which Cook (2012) and Ortega (2013, 2014, 2015) have defined as the knowledge of two or more languages in the same mind. In this framework, native speakers of an L2 are not considered to be the norm (Ortega 2013, 2014, 2015). Instead, L2 users are independent speakers. These researchers (Ortega, 2013, 2014, 2015a; Cook, 1999, 2003, 2016) also claim that attention should be paid to late bi/multilingualism so as to understand the development of the human capacity of using multiple languages. This integration continuum approach needs a new teaching perspective. In the field of pronunciation comprehensible/intelligible speakers can be used as a model as they are perceived to be attainable by learners. In fact, cognitive linguistics states that such models are particularly helpful for improvement in pausing, use of prominence, and use of nonverbal communication to portray confidence in speaking a second language

Future directions

Throughout the different chapters, authors have proposed future research directions. These can be grouped into five main groups.

1.  Analysis of multiple languages: Future studies should go beyond the analysis of a single second language and focus on the acquisition of more than one language. From a sociolinguistic perspective it has been indicated that research could observe typological differences in varied language pairs so as to observe whether acquiring sociolinguistic competences is connected with cultural or

with typological differences across languages, and also consider the difference between perception and production in varied learning contexts. It has also been suggested that the analysis of interactional competences could look into how different languages use tasks, such as written discourse completion tasks. Gesture analyses also need be done in further studies comparing the context where various languages produce beats or head movements and the relevance that they may have for second language learners.

2. Focus on L2 users: A great deal of research has focused on the native speaker as a role model. However, L2 users are becoming the norm rather than the exception in a global, transnational society. Research directions such as the multicompetence framework (Cook 1999, 2003, 2016; Ortega, 2013, 2014, 2015a) and the studies on multilingualism conducted by the Douglas Fir Group (2016) constitute good examples of the new path applied linguists are treading. The Mirroring Project in Chapter 9 suggests using L2 users rather than native speakers as role models for presentations by second language learners. Researchers should also consider opening the door to different pedagogical instruments in the classroom, such as code-switching, which seems to be a psychological tool that makes the development of the L2 easier.

3. Research contexts: Most studies on speaking have focused on data from classroom practice. New research directions could deal with L2 learners acting in situated contexts and observe their way of adapting to their co-participants in line with the research conducted by Eskildsen and Theodórsdóttir (2015) and Wagner (2015) Their studies show that students would benefit from participating in situated and locally calibrated contexts as they can be useful in helping them develop spoken-interactive abilities.

4. The role of frequency: Usage-based linguistics give relevance to frequency. From a sociolinguistic viewpoint, it is also important to practise different aspects of the L2, such as the frequency of a structure, which can lead to fruitful results. In gesture analysis it could also be interesting to observe how frequently L1 and L2 speakers resort to beats or head movements in expressing aspects such as deixis or negation and teach them to use these gestures in other contexts. Corpora can also be used to determine the frequency of a construction and its relevance in teaching. In corpora analyses further studies could also consider if the frequency of a construction in a corpus can be a reliable indicator of the degree of entrenchment of the construction in mental representations.

5. New pedagogical instruments and assessment: New ways of communicating, such as on-line and video spoken exchanges and the pervading influence of new technologies in our lives call for new teaching tools. Holistic, multimodal and embodied activites need to be explored further. Mirroring, for

example can be further analysed to look into the degree to which voices acquired through this technique can be used for varied purposes, such as academic lectures. Video data can be used for microanalytic research which views second language as socially distributed and can lead to creating new teaching material, like situated audio and videorecording which can then be reviewed with students in the classroom. The same instrument can be used for the teaching of gestures. Corpora, such as LINDSEI can be used to compare speech and writing and look at the specificities of each construction to further pedagogical applications. Effective tasks also need to be explored so as to create spaces for speaking in the classroom and also tasks that enable group talk and can extend this to plenary discourse. The role of individual coaching versus language teaching in groups should also be explored, which also means reflecting on the type of speaking assessment learners are exposed to. A dynamic systems perspective points to on-going assessment, rather than final evaluation as the latter only looks at the learners' performance at one point in time. On the other hand, the difficulties of assessing speaking in large groups of students favour final assessment or even no assessment of this skill at all, not only at some High Schools and Universities but also in University entrance examinations or in studies such as the First European Survey on Language Competence (European Commission, 2011). Research on individual and continuous assessment techniques for larger groups is needed.

## Conclusion

The different chapters in this volume have been included with the aim of providing novel approaches to the study of speaking in a second language. They consider its sociolinguistic aspects, usage-based perspectives and current teaching issues. They offer a wide perspective on the current state-of-affairs of L2 speaking so as to improve its acquisition and teaching. The novel points that each chapter has included can be summarized in nine elements: (a) provide an overview of sociolinguistic aspects of L2 competence with a dedicated focus on research conducted using oral production data, (b) offer an expanded perspective on speaking development that includes extra communicative data/tasks, integrating interactional competence and Vygotskian sociocultural psychology with a focus on pedagogy, (c) focus on the dynamic nature of speaking where gestures are indicators of learners' proficiency and their thinking when looking at speaking in a second language, (d) view speaking as social accomplishment and analyse data from inside and outside the classroom using a usage-based approach from the perspective of interactional competence where pedagogy is focused on action-construction relationships, (e) work out a new view on speaking development, which moves from a focus on results to a focus on the process of acquisition, focusing on how speaking develops over time has not been dealt with this depth of analysis, and although the approach is compatible with emergentist and usage-based perspectives, the process-based focus on change over time is unique, (f) conduct an exploratory study that offers a broad overview of the constructions that one is likely to find in learner speech using a large database of EFL speech that has been tagged for part-of-speech, providing a useful starting point for future research on the acquisition of speech from a constructionist perspective, (g) relate our understanding of oral second language skills to task-based pedagogy, explaining how task-based learning might be compatible with current understandings of language and of language learning, explaining two ways in which tasks can contribute to classroom pedagogy, firstly in terms of the different types of discourse they lead students to engage with, and secondly as a tool for structuring whole class talk through the lesson, (h) analyse code switching in a Spanish heritage language classroom, where the main linguistic goal is to develop Spanish literacy skills and academic speaking skills, revealing that code switching can also have a cognitive function and serve as a cognitive tool to mediate language learning, an finally (i) describe a unique, new approach, the "Mirroring Project," a top-down holistic method teaching students how to adopt the "voice" (Bakhtin, 1981) of another as a single coherent package in which suprasegmental and nonverbal elements can be successfully analyzed, imitated, and internalized.

There is still a bulk of research to be conducted in the acquisition and teaching of speaking. The future research directions that have been proposed here hope to indicate ways of expanding and opening areas of study that will add to the understanding and development of how L2 speakers/users acquire this skill.

# References

Asher, J. J. (1966). The learning strategy of the Total Physical Response: A review. *Modern Language Journal*, 50, 79–84.

Bakhtin, M. M. (1981). *The dialogic imagination*: Four essays by M.M. Bakhtin, M. Holquist (Ed.), transl. by C. Emerson & M. Holquist. Austin, TX: University of Texas Press.

Beckner, C., Ellis, N. C., Blythe, R., Holland, J., Bybee, J., Ke, J., Christiansen, M.H. Larsen-Freeman, D. Croft, W. Schoenemann, T. (2009) Language is a complex adaptative system. *Language Learning*, 59, 12: 1–26.

Berlitz, M. D. (1898) *The Berlitz Method for Teaching Modern Languages, English Part*. 1st book (10th ed. revised). Berlin: Cronbach.

Bybee, J.L. (2013). Usage-based theory and exemplar representations of constructions. In T. Hoffmann & G. Trousdale (Eds.), *The Oxford handbook of construction grammar* (pp. 49–69). Oxford: Oxford University Press

Cenoz, J., Genesee, F., & Gorter, D. (2014). Critical analysis of CLIL: Taking stock and looking forward. *Applied Linguistics*, 35, 243–262.

Cobb, T. (2007). Computing the vocabulary demands of L2 reading. *Language Learning and Technology*, 11(3), 38–63.

Collins, L. (2013). Form-focused instruction. In C. Chapelle (Ed.), *The Encyclopedia of Applied Linguistics*. Oxford: Wiley-Blackwell

Cook, V.. (1999) Going beyond the native speaker in language teaching. *Tesol Quarterly* 33(2), 185–209

Cook, V. (2003). *Effects of the second language on the first*. Clevedon: Multilingual Matters

Cook, V. (2012) Multi-competence and nativeness and language pedagogy. In C. Chapelle (Ed.), *The encyclopedia of applied linguistics*. Oxford: Wiley-Blackwell.

Cook, V. (2016) Transfer and the relationship between the languages of multi-competence. In R. Alonso Alonso (ed.), *Crosslinguistic influence in second language acquisition* (pp. 24–37). Clevedon: Multilingual Matters.

de Bot, K., Lowie, W., & Verspoor, M. (2007). A dynamic systems theory approach to second language acquisition. *Bilingualism: Language and Cognition*, 10(1), 7–21.

Ellis, N., & Cadierno, T. (2009). Constructing a second language: Introduction to the special edition. *Annual Review of Cognitive Linguistics*, 9, 111–139

Ellis, N.C. (2013). Second language acquisition. In G. Trousdale & T. Hoffmann (Eds.), *Oxford handbook of construction grammar* (pp. 365–378), Oxford: Oxford University Press

Ellis, R. (2003). *Task-based language learning and teaching*. Oxford. Oxford University Press

Ellis, R. (2016). Focus on form: A critical review. *Language Teaching Research*, first published on February 11 2016. doi: https://doi.org/10.1177/1362168816628627.

Eskildsen, S.W. (2008). *Constructing a second language inventory-the accumulation of linguistic resources in L2 English*. Unpublished PhD dissertation. University of Southern Denmark.

Eskildsen, S.W. & Cadierno, T. (2015). *Usage-based perspectives on second language learning*. Berlin: De Gruyter Mouton.

Eskildsen, S.W. & Theodórsdóttir, G. (2015). Constructing L2 learning spaces: Ways to achieve learning inside and outside the classroom. *Applied Linguistics*, 38(2),1–23.

European Commission. (2011). First European Survey on Language Competences. Available from <https://ec.europa.eu/dgs/education_culture/repository/.../language-survey-final-report_en.pdf>

Gattegno, C. (1972). *Teaching foreign languages in schools: The silent way*. New York, NY: Educational Solutions

Gettys, S. (2017). *Teaching students to talk a foreign language: Usage-based instruction*. Wilmington, DE: Vernon Press.

Gouin, F. (1880). *Essai sur une réforme des méthodes d'enseignement. Exposé d'une nouvelle méthode linguistique. L'art d'enseigner et d'étudier les langues*. Paris: Fischbacher

Hall, J.K., Hellermann, J., & Pekarek Doehler, S. (2011). *L2 interactional competence and development*. Clevedon: Multilingual Matters.

Hornby, A.S. (1950). The situational approach in language teaching. *ELT Journal, 4–6*: 4(4): 98–103; 4(5): 121–28; 4(6): 150–156.

Howatt, A.P.R., & Smith, R. (2014).The history of Teaching English as a Foreign Language, from a British and European perspective. *Language and History*, 57(2), 75–95.

Kannellow, V. (2009). The practice of pronunciation teaching in current ELT manuals and handbook: A review. *Speak Out: IATEFL Pronunciation Special Interest Group Newsletter*, 40, 1–5.

Kasper, G., & Wagner, J. (2011). A conversation-analytic approach to second language acquisition. In D. Atkinson (Ed.), *Alternative approaches to second language acquisition* (pp. 117–142) New York, NY: Taylor and Francis.

Lantolf, J. P., & Poehner, M. E. (Eds.). (2008). *Sociocultural theory and the teaching of second languages*. London: Equinox.

Larsen-Freeman, D. (2011). A complexity approach to second language development/acquisition. In D. Atkinson (ed.), *Alternative approaches to second language acquisition* (pp. 48–72). London: Routledge

Lewis, M. (1993). *The lexical approach*. Hove: Language Teaching Publications.

Lindstromberg, S., & Boers, F. (2005). From movement to metaphor with manner-of-movement verbs. *Applied Linguistics*, 26(2), 241–261.

Long, M. H. (1991). Focus on form: A design feature in language teaching methodology. In K. de Bot, R. Ginsberg, & C. Kramsch (Eds.), *Foreign language research in cross-cultural perspective* (pp. 39–52) Amsterdam: John Benjamins.

Lowie, W. (2013). Dynamic systems theory approaches to second language acquisition. In C. Chapelle (Ed.), *The encyclopedia of applied linguistics* (pp. 1806–1813). Oxford: Wiley-Blackwell.

Mehisto, P., Marsh, D., & Frigols, M.J. (2008). *Uncovering CLIL*. London: Macmillan.

McNeill, D. (2012). *How language began: Gesture and speech in human evolution*. New York, NY: Cambridge University Press.

Meyers, C. (2014). Intelligible accented speakers as pronunciation models. In J. Levis & S. McCrocklin (Eds), *Proceedings of the 5th Annual Conference of Pronunciation in Second Language Learning and Teaching (PSLLT)*, (pp. 172–176). Ames, IA: Iowa State University

Munro, M. J., & Derwing, T. M. (2011). Research timeline: Accent and intelligibility in pronunciation research. *Language Teaching*, 43(3), 316–327

Murphy, J. M. (2014). Intelligible, comprehensible, non-native models in ESL/EFL pronunciation teaching. *System*, 42, 258–269.

Nation, P. (1990) *Teaching and learning vocabulary*. Boston, MA: Heinle & Heinle.

Nattinger, J. (1980). A lexical phrase grammar for ESL. *Tesol Quarterly*, 14, 337–344.

Nattinger, J. R., & DeCarrico, J. S. (1992) *Lexical phrases and language teaching*. Oxford: Oxford University Press.

Negueruela E. (2003). *A sociocultural approach to teaching and researching second languages: Systemic-theoretical instruction and second language development*. Unpublished PhD dissertation. The Pennsylvania State University, University Park, PA.

Norris, J. M., & Ortega, L. (2000). Effectiveness of L2 instruction: A research synthesis and quantitative meta-analysis. *Language Learning*, 50(3), 417–528.

Ortega, L. (2013). SLA for the 21st century: Disciplinary progress, transdisciplinary relevance, and thebi/multilingual turn. *Currents in Language Learning*, 63(Supplement 1) .

Ortega, L. (2014). Ways forward for a bi/multilingual turn in SLA. In S. May, *The multilingual turn. Implications for SLA, TESOL and bilingual education* (pp. 32–53). London: Routledge

Ortega, L. (2015a) Inroads of multicompetence into the mainstream of SLA. In V. Cook & L. Wei (Eds.), *The Cambridge handbook of linguistic multicompetence*. Cambridge: Cambridge University Press

Ortega, L. (2015b) Usage-based SLA: A research habitus whose time has come. In T. Cadierno & S. W. Eskildsen (Eds.), *Usage-Based perspectives on second language learning* (pp. 353–374). Berlin: Mouton de Gruyter

Robinson, P. (2005). Cognitive complexity and task sequencing: A review studies in a componential framework for second language task design. *International Review of Applied Linguistics in Language Teaching*, 43(1), 1–33.

Robinson, P. (2007). Task complexity, theory of mind, and intentional reasoning: Effects on L2 speech production, interaction, uptake and perceptions of task difficulty. *International Review of Applied Linguistics in Language Teaching*, 45(3),193–213.

Sauveur, L. (1874). *Causeries avec mes élèves*. Boston, MA: Schönhof and Möller.

Sinclair, J. McH.. (1996). *Preliminary recommendations on corpus typology*. EAGLES Document TCWG-CTYP/P <http://www.ilc.cnr.it/EAGLES/corpustyp/corpustyp.html>.

Skinner, B. F. (1957). *Verbal behavior*. Englewood Cliffs, NJ: Prentice-Hall.

Swain, M. (2000). The output hypothesis and beyond. In J. P. Lantolf (Ed.), *Sociocultural theory and second language learning* (pp. 97–114). Oxford: Oxford University Press.

Swain, M. (2006). Languaging, agency and collaboration in advanced language proficiency. In H. Byrnes (Ed.), *Advanced language learning: The contribution of Halliday and Vygotsky* (pp. 95–108). London: Continuum.

The Douglas Fir Group. (2016). A transdisciplinary framework for SLA in a multilingual world. *The Modern Language Journal*, 100(4), 19–47

van Compernolle, R. A. (2015). *Interaction and second language development: A Vygotskian perspective*. Amsterdam: John Benjamins.

van Compernolle, R. A., & Kinginger, C. (2013). Promoting metapragmatic development through assessment in the zone of proximal development. *Language Teaching Research*, 17, 282–302.

Van den Branden, K., Bygate, M., & Norris, J. (Eds.). (2009). *Task-based language teaching. A reader*. Amsterdam: John Benjamins

Verspoor, M. (2017). Complex Dynamic Systems theory and L2 pedagogy: Lessons to be learned. In A. E., Tyler, L., Ortega, & M. Uno (Eds.), *Usage-inspired L2 instruction: Researched pedagogy*. (pp. 143–162) Amsterdam: John Benjamins.

Vygotsky, L. S. (1978). *Mind in society: The development of higher psychological processes*. Cambridge, MA: Harvard University Press.

Vygotsky, L. S. (1986). *Thought and language*. Cambridge, MA: The MIT Press.

Wagner, J. (2015), Designing for language learning in the wild: Creating social infrastructures for second language learning. In T. Cadierno & S. W. Eskildsen (Eds.) *Usage-Based perspectives on second language learning* (pp. 75–104) Berlin: Mouton de Gruyter.

Wertsch, J. V. (1994). The primacy of mediated action in sociocultural studies. *Mind, Culture, and Activity*, 1, 202–208.

Wilkins, D. (1976). *Notional Syllabuses:A Taxonomy and its Relevance to Foreign Language Curriculum Development*. London: Oxford University Press

# Index